UNCOMMON
VALOUR

'The Cross shall only be awarded to those who have served Us in the presence of the Enemy.'
Victoria R

'The only enemy is yourself.'
John Smyth VC

UNCOMMON VALOUR

THE STORY OF THE VICTORIA CROSS

GRANVILLE ALLEN MAWER

Pen & Sword
MILITARY

AN IMPRINT OF PEN & SWORD BOOKS LTD.
YORKSHIRE - PHILADELPHIA

First published in Great Britain in 2019 by
PEN AND SWORD MILITARY
An imprint of
Pen & Sword Books Ltd
Yorkshire – Philadelphia

ISBN 978 1 52675 538 4

Printed and bound in England by TJ International, Padstow, Cornwall, PL28 8RW
Typeset in Times New Roman 11.5/14 by
Aura Technology and Software Services, India

Pen & Sword Books Limited incorporates the imprints of Atlas, Archaeology,
Aviation, Discovery, Family History, Fiction, History, Maritime, Military, Military
Classics, Politics, Select, Transport, True Crime, Air World, Frontline Publishing,
Leo Cooper, Remember When, Seaforth Publishing, The Praetorian Press,
Wharncliffe Local History, Wharncliffe Transport, Wharncliffe True Crime and
White Owl.

For a complete list of Pen & Sword titles please contact
PEN & SWORD BOOKS LIMITED
47 Church Street, Barnsley, South Yorkshire, S70 2AS, England
E-mail: enquiries@pen-and-sword.co.uk
Website: www.pen-and-sword.co.uk

Or
PEN AND SWORD BOOKS
1950 Lawrence Rd, Havertown, PA 19083, USA
E-mail: Uspen-and-sword@casematepublishers.com
Website: www.penandswordbooks.com

In memory of Alec Hill and John Ward
who inspired

Contents

CONTENTS

Acknowledgements

This book has had more false starts than I care to remember but for the last decade it has been informally coached by Professor Peter Stanley of the Australian Defence Force Academy. It is not going too far to say that without his enthusiasm for the project and his encouragement it might never have left the blocks cleanly.

I had the privilege of being able to access the collections of the National Library of Australia through its Petherick Room. The assistance of Andrew Sergeant, the Petherick Librarian, and the other staff members made the research an adventure rather than a chore. I am grateful to them all, and likewise to a number of Petherick colleagues who have humoured me over the years. Foremost is Dr Penny Olsen, who has always been kind enough to listen and act as a sounding board. Thanks are also due to Dr Ann Moyal, who suggested that the work might benefit from early exposure to a chapter of the University of the Third Age. She was right.

In these interesting times for writers and publishers of non-fiction I was fortunate that Rupert Harding, commissioning editor for Pen & Sword, could see possibilities in an unconventional treatment of the Victoria Cross.

List of Illustrations

Illustrations are courtesy of Wikimedia Commons unless otherwise attributed

1. Queen Victoria distributing the first Victoria Crosses in Hyde Park, 26 June 1857. (George Housman Thomas) p13
2. The Plain Cross of Valour (*Punch*) p14
3. Guy Penrose Gibson (Ministry of Information) p25
4. Incidents in Kavanagh's Perilous Journey (*Heroes of Britain in Peace and War*) p27
5. Private Mariner bombing the enemy … (William Spencer Bagdatopulos) p30
6. Billy Bishop and his Nieuport Scout. p32
7. Death of Lieutenant Anstruther (C. R.) p35
8. Roberts winning the Victoria Cross (Sidney Paget) p36
9. Spurred for the river … hotly pursued by the enemy (Stanley Llewellyn Wood) p37
10. Lieutenant the Hon F.H.S. Roberts, falling wounded while saving the guns at Colenso. (Frank Algernon Stewart) p38
11. Major Wheeler riding to his death at the North Mound. (William Spencer Bagdatopulos) p41
12. The Russian took to his heels and fled, and Bell, seizing the bridle of one of the horses, was leading him … (*Heroes of Britain in Peace and War*) p43
13. Lieutenant W.N.W. Hewett refusing to spike the gun in the Lancaster Battery. (*The Victoria Cross, By Whom it was Won*) p44
14. The last stage of Lieutenant Smyth's heroic journey. (Margaret Dovaston) p46
15. Heroes of Manchester Hill. (*Daily Sketch*) p48
16. P.A. Porteous (O'Connell) p51

LIST OF ILLUSTRATIONS

Figures

Introduction

The motto inscrolled on every Victoria Cross proclaims that it is awarded 'For Valour', but it must have been uncommon valour for so few to have been issued since 1854. Many of the citations refer to acts of duty, but they must have been valiant acts above and beyond anything that could reasonably have been expected of the recipient. The initiators of the Cross took it for granted that valour was the pre-eminent military virtue. For this they had the authority of writers going back to ancient times, but they chose to overlook hints in those authorities that virtue could be the handmaiden of vice. They soon found that it was not the only contradiction that the Cross harboured.

The Victoria Cross was a remarkable innovation for its time. Open to all ranks and with only one grade, it sat uneasily with military hierarchy and aristocratic monopoly of honours. Prince Albert, concerned to protect the royal prerogative against encroachment by politicians, in honours as in other matters, saw in the Cross a means of harnessing democratic sentiment in support of the monarchy. He was responsible for the most radical features of the new decoration: self-nomination and election by peers. By associating the Queen with a levelling initiative he was joining her to the people in a common cause that transcended politics. Albert died only six years after the Cross was instituted, but by then it had more than fulfilled his political expectations for it. The first investiture, at a review in Hyde Park, had demonstrated beyond doubt that a new bond had been forged between the sovereign and her common soldiers and sailors, and beyond them with the lower classes from which they came.

The statistics suggest that in the infancy of the Cross standards were more relaxed than they have been since. Nearly one in four of the total had been awarded before the decoration itself was four years old, and for wars that involved comparatively limited numbers of troops. Thereafter the administering authorities became more selective, conscious that

1

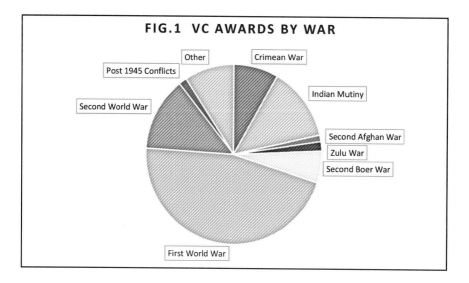

FIG.1 VC AWARDS BY WAR

the rarer the distinction, the greater the honour. The world wars of the early twentieth century, when the British Empire fielded armies of a size inconceivable in the nineteenth, accounted for nearly sixty per cent of all Crosses awarded. Those awards, however, were far fewer in proportion to troops engaged than was the case in the Crimean War and Indian Mutiny. It is a singular fact that as many Crosses were won in the Mutiny, when there were only thousands eligible, as in the Second World War when there were millions.

The awards lend themselves to some statistical analysis. This book sets out not only to examine individual deeds with a view to understanding them, but also to align them collectively with the expectations of those who instituted the decoration and those who administered it thereafter. It will become apparent that the fit is not perfect. The citations published in the *London Gazette* since 1856 are taken to be the authoritative explanation of the reason that each Cross was awarded – i.e. one of their functions is to demonstrate that the deed conforms to the conditions of award. That too will be seen to be a debatable proposition in some cases. Where possible the citations have been supplemented from other sources, of which the most colourful are the reminiscences of recipients. The most authoritative supplementary source is unfortunately incomplete: the files that held the recommendations for most First World War VCs were 'weeded' in a fit of post-war tidiness. The cull destroyed nearly half of all the successful recommendations made to that date.

INTRODUCTION

Each award has been assessed, necessarily subjectively, against the purposes of the Cross as originally conceived. In the interests of transparency the assessments are summarized in Appendix 2, which also provides basic information on each recipient. Many of the awards – one in seven – are given fuller treatment in the text, where they are used to illustrate various facets of the Cross. Although the sample is large it is not necessarily representative. The images used to illustrate examples are usually uncritical and in some cases involved neither observation nor first-hand report. They cannot be regarded as impartial or accurate records.

It needs to be emphasized that although the VC is the ultimate bravery award, there is no objectively drawn line that marks it off from lesser ones. Bravery, courage and valour are best thought of as a spectrum. Where one colour ends and another begins is in the eye of the beholder. Much is subjective. How does the act in question compare to other awarded acts? How experienced, informed, unbiased, and free from external pressure are the people making the comparison? Without fixed gradation, it must be the case that what strikes one man as a VC-worthy act might only qualify for a Mention in Dispatches to another. It follows that analysis of the VC in isolation, conveniently manageable though it is, is an artificial construct. That itself is an argument in favour of a single, classless award for bravery, as was originally intended. One consequence of the proliferation of subordinate awards has been unedifying debates about why the deeds of their recipients were judged to be unworthy of a Victoria Cross.

It is hoped that the questioning spirit that animates these pages will not be thought to disrespect men who have been singled out for the greatest honour that their countrymen can bestow. None of their deeds is less than brave, including those prompted by desperation; the more extreme seem beyond the capabilities of mortals. The ancients would have ascribed them to demigods.

Chapter 1

What Price Glory?

In 2009 the Victoria Cross and Bar won by Captain Noel Chavasse, one of only three double awards ever made, was reported to have changed hands for nearly £1.5 million.[1] Chavasse was a medical officer in the First World War, as was one of the other double awardees. Their medals were not for heroic action against the enemy, but for saving wounded men in the face of the enemy, a form of humanitarianism. As he pinned the medal on Chavasse George V might have told him, as he had told others, that the intrinsic value of the Cross was one penny. That had been literally true of the metal in 1856, but even in 1915 the materials of the complete package – medal, ribbon and cardboard box – could be purchased for fourpence halfpenny, next to nothing. That had been a matter of policy, a form of inverted snobbery to emphasize that the honour and esteem that went with the decoration were priceless. It was a prize worth having and it cost the state very little, even allowing for the £10 annual pension that went with it. Napoleon, cynical and unsentimental as always, had noted a century earlier that soldiers would do almost anything for the distinction of a bit of ribbon. Decorations, however, are not immune to the laws of economics; inflate supply and you undermine value, whence Talleyrand's greeting to an unadorned Castlereagh at the Congress of Vienna. *Pas decoré? Ma foi, c'est bien distingué*! The rarer an award, the greater the value placed on it. The VC is esteemed both for its distinguished history and for the fact that in 2018 there are only nine recipients living.

Chavasse died of wounds two days after the action for which he was awarded his second Cross. Severely wounded while carrying in an officer, he had continued to tend the wounded under fire and bring in men who would otherwise have died. When stretcher-bearers were sent out for him he told them to take another wounded man. Knowing that he was dying, he sent a message to his fiancée: 'Give her my love. Tell her duty called and called me to obey'. It was Chavasse's duty to tend the wounded; what marked his performance for the second distinction was the element of self-sacrifice. Many years later his twin brother, a clergyman, reflected that those last words might be thought 'heroic enough, and yet rather terrible and inhuman'. Rather, Christopher Chavasse explained, 'what he termed duty was simply the call of humanity'.[2]

It was Queen Victoria's personal decision that her Cross should be for valour rather than for bravery or gallantry. The Army already had at its disposal the Distinguished Conduct Medal (DCM, 1854) and the Royal Navy had a Conspicuous Gallantry Medal (CGM, 1855); despite the former's name both were individual gallantry awards for those below officer rank. More elevated language would indicate the superiority of the new Cross over these lesser decorations, as would its place in the Order of Precedence: holders of the Victoria Cross would defer to no one who was not at least a peer of the realm. The annuity that went with the DCM and CGM was larger than that for the VC and, because of Treasury concern, a limiting factor in the number of awards. Victoria's Cross was subject to no such limitation; there could be as many as there were acts of valour. Furthermore, from highest officer down to redcoat and bluejacket all ranks were eligible, although officers were denied the annuity. To the Treasury's chagrin the decoration's first four years of existence saw 296 VCs awarded, amounting to nearly a quarter of the 1,363 issued down to the present day. Neither the profligacy, nor the cut-rate pension, did anything to diminish the prestige that went with precedence in the honours system and receipt of Her Majesty's own medal from Her Majesty's own hands. Such was the enthusiasm for the new decoration that the Admiralty asked if the CGM could be exchanged for a VC. The answer was yes, but only with the smaller annuity.[3]

Public honours and awards are, on the face of it, an indication of the values that the state wishes to encourage in its citizens. When the pre-eminent decoration is for valour, one could be forgiven for thinking that this must be a martial nation in which, of all professions, that of arms is the most highly esteemed. And yet the nations of the 'old Commonwealth' – Britain and the white settler states of its former empire, in which the Victoria Cross takes precedence over all other honours – are ambivalent about the military. Enthusiasm for this necessary instrument of external security is tempered by realization that its monopoly of armed force also makes it a potential threat to civilian rule. The self-conscious elitism, strict hierarchy and internal discipline of the military are rightly held to be uneasy bedfellows for political liberty and social equality, but even though the old Commonwealth states have supposedly equal civilian awards for bravery (e.g. the George Cross) the Order of Wearing still privileges the Victoria Cross. When a person is entitled to wear both decorations, the VC takes the place of honour, on the far right of the medal bar. To the casual observer it would seem that martial valour is more highly valued than common or garden bravery, even though the cause may be as disinterested and the risks as great should a passerby go to the assistance of a stranger being attacked in the street.

In reality, the distinction being made is between bravery in the interests of the state and bravery in the interests of society, although in a democracy state and society should be indivisible. It is the use of the word valour that introduces a military flavour, reinforced by its adjutant 'gallantry'. Both are exalted words, connoting nobility and chivalry. Truth to tell, valour, bravery, courage and gallantry inhabit a semantic thicket that entangles authorities whenever they try to rationalize awards. In the 1990s Australia, Canada and New Zealand decided to award Victoria Crosses independently of the British system. Australia would have continued to use the qualification set out in the British warrant ('most conspicuous bravery'), but found the wording incompatible with that used for its own post-1975 military awards. So the Australian VC is now for 'most conspicuous gallantry', ranking above 'conspicuous gallantry' for the Star of Gallantry, which in turn is superior to plain 'gallantry' as stipulated for the Medal of Gallantry. But the Australian VC, like the British, remains inscribed 'for valour'. Even more confusingly, Australia's George Cross equivalent, available to the military but primarily for civilians, is called the Cross of Valour and is inscribed 'for gallantry'. As if valour was not sufficiently problematic, the Canadians had to satisfy the requirements of bilingualism. Ingeniously, they rejected English and French in favour of a language that was ancestral to both: the Canadian VC inscription is in Latin, '*pro valore*'. New Zealand introduced a further complication by reviving the New Zealand Cross, a local decoration that mimicked the VC in appearance, introduced during the Maori wars because it was mistakenly thought that militia were not eligible for the real thing. Although the new version is a replacement for the George Cross, its shape is still that of the VC. Sensibly, the New Zealand Cross bears no motto.

The Victoria Cross for New Zealand, however, is still inscribed 'for valour' but declared to be awarded for gallantry.

In one respect the motto is misleading because an act of valour is not, nor ever has been, the only way to qualify for a VC. An act of devotion to country was similarly recognized, but this concept was so vague that it was later amended to devotion to duty, thereby allowing extreme examples such as Chavasse's to be eligible for consideration. Chavasse's last message to his fiancée spoke of duty but did not specify whether that duty was to his country, his Hippocratic oath or his comrades. He would no doubt be astounded to know that a century later his ninepence worth of glory has appreciated forty million-fold. The medal's creators had intended that it should be 'highly prized and eagerly sought after', but by recipients, not collectors. Ever-rising auction prices at least demonstrate that the Cross has never lost its hold on the public imagination. Indeed, the public at large views the Cross as a public good that on the death of a recipient should revert to a semblance of public ownership, such as being lent to a museum. Thanks to the philanthropy of men like the Conservative politician Lord Ashcroft in Britain and media proprietor Kerry Stokes in Australia, that is often the outcome when they come on the market. It is ironic that a 'bit of ribbon' and a small piece of bronze are now a substantial store of value that recipients can use as a retirement fund or to secure the financial future of their families.

Such thinking was anathema to Havildar (Sergeant) Umrao Singh, who in Burma in 1944 had set about the Japanese with the gun-bearer rod of his 25-pounder when there was nothing else to hand. In 1995 he successfully lobbied for an increase in the VC pension, which had last been set in 1959. He was not well off, but had nonetheless rejected several substantial offers to buy his medal because it would 'stain the honour of those who fell in battle'. Here lurks the idea that for every VC awarded, many brave men have gone to their graves with equally meritorious deeds unhonoured. After his death the medal was sold.[4] One suspects that his family would have been more reluctant to part with the bronze if that had entailed surrendering the post-nominal initials that went with it. The letters VC, intangible but imperishable, are more durable than any metal.

Chapter 2

Set in Bronze

It was during the Crimean War, the British Army's first outing in a major European conflict since the defeat of Napoleon, that anomalies in the system of honours began to attract attention. After the battle of Inkerman Lord Raglan's dispatch named generals and staff officers, but not the men who had done the fighting. Apart from being mentioned by name in the dispatch, the rewards that would usually follow were the Order of the Bath or brevet promotion, both confined to officers and in the former case not below the appointment of battalion commander. *The Times* fumed, having been reliably informed by its correspondent William Howard Russell that Inkerman was entirely fought and won by subordinate officers and soldiers, and was referred to in camp as the Soldiers' Victory. Where was the acknowledgement for line officers or 'the most prominent soldiers'?[1] The Secretary of State for War, the Duke of Newcastle, that same day wrote to the Queen on the subject, observing that 'some who have done little to deserve such reward will receive them whilst many who have borne the burden and heat of the day will feel slighted'.[2]

When Newcastle proceeded to raise the matter with Commander-in-Chief Lord Hardinge, the representation fell on deaf ears, partly because on 4 December a royal warrant had instituted the Distinguished Conduct Medal for 'distinguished, gallant and good conduct in the field' by ranks other than officers. Some observers were still dissatisfied. A fortnight later, former naval captain George Scobell moved in the House of Commons for an address to the Queen praying that she would institute an Order of Merit for distinguished and prominent personal gallantry. It should be open to all Army and Navy personnel in the present war irrespective of rank. Newcastle quickly took up the matter with Albert, the Prince Consort, having already noted in correspondence with him that 'the alliance in which we have engaged' seemed to make change desirable.[3] This was a reference to the French, whose Legion of Honour was open to common soldiers.

Newcastle proposed the creation of a new order. With the Queen as its sovereign it would be styled the Military Order of Victoria and have only one grade of membership with no limitation on numbers. Possible mottos might be *Pro patria mori, Mors aut Victoria* or *God Defend the Right*.[4] The insignia, a cross of steel or bronze suspended by a red ribbon for the army and a blue one for the navy, should be of little intrinsic value but highly prized and eagerly sought after. To qualify, a person would have to display conspicuous bravery in the performance of 'some signal act of valour or devotion to his country' in the presence of the enemy. The qualifying act would have to be performed under the eye of the officer commanding, subject to confirmation by the sovereign. In cases falling outside the rules, or well-founded claims not established on the spot, the Queen would confer the decoration, being graciously pleased to bind herself to abstain in the absence of conclusive proof of the claimed act.

Albert was supportive, seeing the need for a mode of reward 'neither reserved for the few nor bestowed upon all' to distinguish individual merit in junior officers and the lower ranks, but he foresaw a difficulty.

> How is a distinction to be made, for instance, between the individual services of the 200 survivors of Lord Cardigan's Charge [of the Light Brigade]? If you reward them all it becomes merely a Medal for Balaclava, to which the Heavy Brigade and the 93rd [Highland Regiment] have equal claims.[5]

The solution that he suggested to Newcastle was that the Cross should be claimable by an individual, such claim to be established before a jury of peers and subject to confirmation by higher authority. The same procedure could be followed for general actions, after which the officers, sergeants and privates of a formation would each empanel a jury to allocate a set number of awards for that rank. Enforced selection would 'diminish the pain to those who cannot be included'. He also counselled against any mention of the 'entirely arbitrary' Legion of Honour, which he characterized as a tool of corruption that French governments had expanded to 40,000 members.[6]

On 29 January 1855 Newcastle rose to speak in the House of Lords on the question of a Balaclava clasp for the Crimean Medal. He also announced that Her Majesty had been advised to create a new Cross of Military Merit with elective rules like those in force for similar awards in Spain, Prussia and Austria. On the following day the Balaclava debacle claimed its last casualty: the government resigned rather than face a motion for enquiry into the condition of the army and the conduct of the departments charged with supporting it. Newcastle left office and with his departure there could have been a loss of impetus, but matters were now sufficiently advanced that his successor, Lord Panmure, understood that the Cross was not a matter that would go away if ignored. It was nonetheless almost a year before a draft warrant was submitted to the Queen for preliminary approval. Albert returned it to Panmure, assuring him that he and the Queen had carefully gone through it together and 'marked in pencil upon it all that occurred to us'.[7] That, as the marginalia indicated, was quite a lot.

The royal couple had struck out Military Order of Victoria and suggested, with a query, 'Victoria Cross'. They rejected the mottoes put forward in favour of one that 'should explain the decoration and exclude the possibility of its object being misunderstood', proposing *The Reward of Valour*, *The Reward of Bravery* or *For Bravery*. Michael Crook, the historian who painstakingly traced the evolution of the Cross, pointed out that this was a radical departure. The mottoes of all British orders to that time had been exhortatory, as had been Newcastle's offerings. Even the idea that merit should be recognized by a decoration rather than an order had only a solitary precedent, the Peninsular Gold Cross of Wellington's Iberian campaign. The thinking behind making the Cross a decoration was that, unlike an order of knighthood, it would not be a fraternity of which the sovereign was a member. In a profoundly egalitarian gesture, the Queen herself would be excluded from wearing the Cross unless she had won it according to the rules. This was not a question of requiring her explicitly to 'bind herself', to use Newcastle's words, because as Victoria and Albert pointed out 'the Queen must be *supposed* to adhere to the rules which She Herself promulgates'. Albert took the opportunity to insert his idea of having claimants and unit representatives judged by peers. Representative awards would proclaim that the unit had 'performed a deed of valour superior to any an individual could perform', influencing the fate of a battle or even a campaign. He went as far as to hope that this might be the most common form of award. The defence of the Sandbag Battery, the charge of the Light Brigade and the storming of the Sebastopol Quarries were, he wrote, deeds more valuable than the throwing of a shell out of a battery or carrying a wounded officer from the field.[8]

The Sandbag Battery at Inkerman, held by the British, had been attacked by 15,000 Russians. A British counterattack from within the battery had dislocated their advance. Another attack saw 2,000 British defending it against 7,000 Russians. The battery changed hands several times, but eventually the British secured the position. Albert was lauding a successful defence against odds that affected the outcome of the battle. Interestingly, the individual VC awarded to Major Sir Charles Russell of the Grenadier Guards was for offering to dislodge a party of Russians from the battery if anyone would follow him. Sergeant Norman and privates Palmer and Bailey (who was killed) volunteered.[9] Of the three volunteers Palmer also received the Cross for saving Russell in the same action, but Albert would have said that Russell could not have won his medal if there had been no volunteers. This was clearly a case in which election by the participants would have been appropriate.

At Balaclava a brigade of five regiments comprising 670 light cavalry had been mistakenly directed against Russian artillery in a frontal assault. Nearly half of the number were killed, wounded or taken prisoner. The Charge of the Light Brigade was a military disaster, but Albert was drawing attention to the men's devotion to duty ('theirs but to do or die') in an enterprise that must have seemed to any participant little short of suicide. Had the VC rules been then in place, there were sufficient survivors of the Brigade to have elected four troopers, two non-commissioned officers and two officers. Instead, there were three individual awards, and all were for saving comrades or officers.

At Sebastopol on 7 June 1855 the 7th Foot had captured the Quarries and held them tenaciously. Five individual VCs were awarded, but Albert would have argued that a regimental ballot would have produced a similar number with a greater sense of regimental ownership. Raglan, no enthusiast for recognizing rankers, wrote in his dispatch that '… nothing could be more spirited than the attack of the Quarries or more creditable to every officer and man engaged in the operation …'.[10] Many of the individual awards in all three actions were for exploits like throwing shells from batteries and saving wounded officers. Albert was not disrespecting those feats, but querying their value in forwarding the campaign. The valour he was looking to reward was valour useful to the state.

Responding to the royal couple, Panmure submitted two drawings of possible designs for the decoration. One of them was modelled on the Peninsular Cross, which conformed to no recognized heraldic standard but was close to a Maltese cross in form.[11] Both designs had *For The Brave* inscrolled upon them. Victoria altered the motto to *For Valour*, on grounds that otherwise it could be inferred that only those who wore the Cross were brave. She could have simply reverted to *For Bravery*, as earlier suggested, but this later and apparently personal decision was perhaps influenced by the chivalric connotations of the word valour. Victoria was critical of other aspects of the design when a proof was submitted. She told Panmure that

> The Cross looks very well in form, but the metal is ugly; it is copper and not bronze and will look very heavy on a red coat with the Crimean Ribbon. Bronze is, properly speaking, gun-metal; this has a rich colour and is very hard; copper would wear very ill and would soon look like an old penny. Lord Panmure should have one prepared in real bronze, and the Queen is inclined to think that it ought to have a green varnish to protect it; the raised parts would then burnish up bright and show the design and inscription.[12]

She also seems to have been critical of the plain suspender and link that held the Cross to its ribbon. The Secretary of State hastened to obey. Bronze gun-metal was substituted, sourced from captured cannon. Victoria was right about its durability; it was so hard that it broke the dies when struck more deeply than usual, which was another of the Queen's requests. The maker, Hancock of Bruton Street, had to resort to casting. Having fixed the design to her satisfaction, including a V-shaped suspender, the Queen asked that the approved sample be kept at the War Office 'as the Tradesmen invariably alter the original pattern agreed upon if they are not watched'.[13] In its final form the Victoria Cross stood apart, and no more so than when in company. Most modern decorations shine in faux silver or gold, suspended from multicoloured ribbons that the military cheerfully refer to as fruit salad, but when the wearer has

Queen Victoria (centre) pinning the navy VCs in Hyde Park on 26 June 1857. The much larger army contingent is lined out on the right.

also won the VC it takes pride of place on the right of the medal bar, overlapping all the others, and it hangs from a monochrome red ribbon.[14]

None of this was accidental. Even before medal bars were invented, the design of the Cross distinguished it from whatever else the recipient might be entitled to wear scattered across his breast or around his neck. Observers felt that it was ugly and unworthy of the eminence it was meant to convey. *The Times* reported that the spectators who attended the first awards, made at a review in Hyde Park on 26 June 1857, were all more or less critical.

> Than the Cross of Valour nothing could be more plain and homely, not to say coarse-looking. It is a very small Maltese Cross, formed from the gun-metal of ordnance captured at Sebastopol.[15] In the centre is a small crown and lion, with which latter's natural proportions of mane and tail the cutting of the cross much interferes. Below these, is a small scroll (which shortens three arms of the cross and is utterly out of keeping with the upper portions) bearing the words For Valour ... the whole cross is, after all, poor looking and mean in the extreme.[16]

THE PLAIN CROSS OF VALOUR.

HERE's Valour's Cross, my men; 'twill serve,
   Though rather ugly—take it.
JOHN BULL a medal can deserve,
   But can't contrive to make it.

Like the *Times*, *Punch* was not taken with the look of the Cross and blamed Panmure.

The reporter might have had his expectations raised by references to the Cross as an Order, associated in the public mind with showy stars and assorted paraphernalia. If so, his disappointment was entirely in keeping with what the creators intended, an honour of no intrinsic worth but of great esteem, which in no small part arose from the Queen's decision to make the first awards in person. *Punch* read it as a personal gesture that set the decoration high in the firmament of honours, although it too was critical of the design.

Marking her sense of something, still,
A central nobleness that lies
Deeper than rank which royal will,
Or birth, or chance, or wealth supplies.
Knighthood that girds all valiant hearts,
Knighthood that crowns each fearless brow,
The knighthood this bronze cross imparts –
Let Fleece and Bath and Garter bow![17]

So potent was the direct royal connection that after the review some recipients were reluctant to surrender their medals to be engraved, for fear that they would not get back the one they had received from Her hands. Citations published in the *London Gazette* documented their heroism. Many had been wounded in action and the ceremony itself had not been without hazard for Lieutenant Henry Raby, whose Cross was literally pinned to his chest when the Queen, from horseback, misjudged the thickness of his uniform coat.

Raby was one of four members of the Naval Brigade who, after an attack on the fort known as the Redan during the siege of Sebastopol, ran across 70 yards of open ground under heavy fire to reach a soldier of the 57th Foot who had been shot in both legs. Three of the rescue party received the Victoria Cross. The fourth, Lieutenant D'Aeth, died shortly afterwards. Although there was nothing in the Warrant to preclude the posthumous award of what was clearly stated to be a decoration, Lord Panmure insisted that the Cross was an Order, and Orders were reserved for the living. It might have been hoped that things would become clearer once the Warrant was tabled in Parliament. Not so: it was printed under the heading 'Order of Victoria' and although the Queen was clear in her own mind that it was a decoration, when recording the inaugural parade in her journal she referred to it as 'the new and honourable order of valour'.[18]

As members of Britain's senior service, Raby and his fellow seamen were first in line for pinning, but there were far more army recipients. It has been a complaint of the Royal Navy ever since that it is hard to get individual heroism recognized when service at sea is essentially a collective endeavour. To a lesser extent the same problem has bedevilled the Royal Air Force since warfare took to the clouds. And it was an article of faith among colonial forces that they had never received their due.

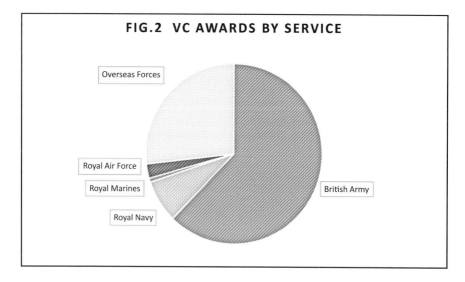

FIG.2 VC AWARDS BY SERVICE

The statistics seem to give credence to the grievances of the navy and air force, but they undermine those of the colonials. The army's experience, however, is not uniform across all arms. Statistically, you are more likely to win a VC if you accept another cross – that of the infantryman. They make up the bulk of armies and their contact with the enemy is usually more direct and intimate than that experienced by soldiers in other arms. They have more opportunity to shine and to die. Approximately two-thirds of all Victoria Crosses have been won by the 'poor bloody infantry'.[19]

At about the time of the parade, and therefore months after the Warrant had been signed, the Queen had a supplementary thought; although the Cross was not properly an Order, as it was without a constitution, recipients should nonetheless be allowed to bear 'some distinctive mark' after their names. VC might be obvious but 'would not do'. The first letter in most post-nominal initials was titular, as in KG, Knight of the Garter. 'No one could be called a Victoria Cross', the Queen said, and anyway VC already stood for Vice-Chancellor. She suggested DVC (Decorated with the Victoria Cross) or BVC (Bearer) and favoured the latter. Given Panmure's solicitude in meeting the Queen's wishes about the form of the Cross, it is remarkable that in this matter not only were her suggestions disregarded, but the designation fixed upon was also one that she had expressly rejected.[20]

Chapter 3

The Virtue of Valour

The Romans believed that what set them apart from their neighbours and enemies was civic discipline. The bedrock on which it rested was self-discipline. As their proverb put it, he conquered who conquered himself. In the military context, the part of self that had to be subjugated was fear of injury and death. Valour, the denial of fear, is meritorious in proportion to the quantum of fear that it overcomes. In his treatise on human nature the philosopher Thomas Hobbes classified fear and hope as emotions, irrational perturbations of the mind prompted by the apprehension of adverse circumstances. In the struggle against those circumstances imagination could excite the emotions in one of two directions: when it suggested that adversity could be overcome the result would be hope; when it suggested the contrary, fear. Hope would manifest itself as righteous anger, a desire to requite evil. Revenge was also a form of anger, but served only after it had cooled, the object being to make the evil-doer repent. Such was the wrath that Achilles directed against the Greeks for the insult of Agamemnon. Fear, on the other hand, would simply vacate the field.

> As hope brings out anger, so fear controls it, that is, just as through imagination the animal spirits are poured into the nerves to make them stronger against attacking evil, so through imagination of greater evil they are withdrawn to the heart for its defence, or for flight.[1]

Putting seventeenth-century biology to one side, Hobbes is here allowing that the same man might be valiant on one occasion but fearful on another, depending on the magnitude of the evil being faced and his degree of confidence in dealing with it. It would, however, seem to require the sort of rational assessment that emotion was said to deny.

Revenge – anger after the event – likewise could only be actioned on a timescale that allowed for rational second thoughts.

Viscount Gort, whose misfortune it was be in command of the British Expeditionary Force in France in 1940, there bore up against a disaster that would have crushed a lesser man. At the same time he again displayed the personal bravery that had won him a VC in 1918 while commanding the 1st Battalion, Grenadier Guards.[2] Then, while personally leading two platoons in the attack across the Canal du Nord, a shell-burst had wounded him over the eye. Bandaged by his soldier-servant Ransome, he crossed open ground to seek support from a tank, during which another shell-burst severed an artery in his left arm. Ransome applied a tourniquet and Gort continued the advance. Collapsing from loss of blood, he then led from a stretcher until the enemy trenches were reached, when he rose and with the foremost companies carried the first and second lines. After organizing defence of the captured position he collapsed again and the medical officer insisted that Ransome take him to the rear. A shell tore off Ransome's arm and Gort went on alone, weak and dazed, to get assistance. He found a doctor and they returned to bandage the soldier, but Ransome died as they withdrew him, still under heavy fire.

In the second war Lord Moran, Churchill's physician, was writing a book on courage. He set Gort down as one of only five men he knew that had minds alert to danger and its possible consequences, but who nevertheless appeared to be beyond fear. Gort denied that it was possible. All animals feel fear, he said.

> When I used to go back to the trenches after some time in the line I had to adjust myself, and even now when I return to Malta after a few days [in Cairo] without [experiencing] any bombing it will be different for a while.[3]

Adjustment required self-discipline, and Gort's was so intense that it quickly overcame any nervousness. He was right to think that human beings are no more indifferent to danger than any other species, having in common with them the survival instinct that prompts a fight-or-flight response. In other species the response is unconscious and sometimes incorrect; in humans the impulse can be resisted and choice take its place. The difficulty is that conscious decision takes time, however little, and by the time it is taken the moment might be irrevocably and disastrously gone. A quality decision taken too late is worse than an unthinking reflex. Drawing on his experience as a battalion medical officer in the first war, Moran concluded that even thinking individuals who could adjust to fear did not have unlimited capacity to do so. He contended that everyone had a bank of courage.

> Courage is will-power, whereof no man has an unlimited stock; and when in war it is used up, he is finished. A man's courage is his capital and he is always spending. The call on the bank may be only the daily drain of the front line or it may be a sudden draft which threatens to close the account.[4]

In the Western tradition Thucydides was one of the earliest writers to analyze bravery. The words of the funeral oration that he put into the mouth of Pericles claim bravery as a uniquely Athenian virtue, but they have the ring of universality.

> We are capable at the same time of taking risks and of estimating them beforehand. Others are brave out of ignorance; and, when they stop to think, they begin to fear. But the man who can most truly be accounted brave is he who best knows the meaning of what is sweet in life and of what is terrible, and then goes out undeterred to meet what is to come.[5]

To do a brave deed one needed an imagination that recognized opportunities for approbation while appreciating but disregarding attendant hazards. Implicitly, the more disregard, the braver the deed. Conversely, to be disarmed by fear was cowardice. Aristotle, as ever looking for a mean between extremes, begged to differ. For him, the path of virtue lay between excess and deficiency. Courage was not an extreme, but the desirable, moderate attribute between cowardice and rashness. Wherever possible, Aristotle wrote, the coward avoids danger in the interest of self-preservation (where the danger is unavoidable, a coward's confrontation of it is desperation, not courage). At the other extreme, the rash or reckless person, ignorant of danger or irrational

19

about it, is oblivious to threat, so the question of courage does not arise. The courageous person, however, is aware of danger and confronts it by choice in pursuit of an end beyond self-interest.[6] Courage is one of the greatest and most honoured of virtues because it is among those most useful to other people in time of war.[7] Rashness likewise can be useful in war and so is a less erroneous extreme than cowardice. Aristotle was not alone in valuing moderation: it is also a desideratum found in other philosophical traditions, such as the Middle Way of Buddhism and *zhong yong* (the doctrine of the mean) of Confucianism.

The word valour is defined by the *Oxford English Dictionary* as the quality of mind that enables a person to face danger in warfare or conflict; unlike courage or bravery it has a specifically military connotation. It derives from the Latin *valeo*, to be strong, so the quality referred to is strength of mind, otherwise fortitude or endurance. Cicero equated fortitude with courage, which he defined as spirit of exultation that raised its possessor above the vicissitudes of life. If employed to further selfish ends, however, fortitude was a vice and unworthy to be called courage. Citing Plato, Cicero labelled such selfish fortitude, the kind not inspired by public spirit, as effrontery.[8] In his view it was the citizen's duty '… to be more ready to endanger our own than the public welfare and to hazard [take risks for] honour and glory more readily than other advantages'.[9]

To adapt the vernacular, intestinal fortitude ('guts') becomes valour only when devoted to unselfish ends, and there is a further caveat: Aristotle insisted that to qualify as valorous a deed serving an unselfish end also had to be noble: that is, morally correct. The acts closest to true courage were those of the citizen soldier, enduring danger to avoid civic shame and desirous of gaining something noble, namely honour.[10] The uncertain element in Aristotle's formula is the nature of those noble, unselfish ends. He takes as his starting point the proposition that to secure the state in war is always a good, and he makes no distinction between just wars (e.g. defensive) and unjust ones (e.g. aggressive). This leaves open the possibility that a person could be considered valiant even while performing an unjust act, provided only that the act was in furtherance of the national welfare. The Waffen SS comes to mind. If the welfare of the nation was served by such acts, it followed that they should be acknowledged in ways that encouraged emulation. A Greek hero might find himself dined at public expense for the rest of his days, as were their sporting champions, but the purpose of such recognition was as much publicity as reward. The valorous act should be exemplary in both senses of the word: setting an example and deserving of imitation. The state has need as well as use for heroes.

The ideal of putting city before self in warfare was common to both ancient cultures, but while the Greeks idolized individual heroism, the Romans placed more value on cohesion and common purpose. In Roman civic life the bundle of rods (*fasces*) carried before a magistrate symbolized the strength of unity. In the military sphere a legion's eagle standard, emblazoned with the initials of the Senate and People of Rome (SPQR), was more than a command locus and rallying point. It too symbolized united purpose and when an eagle was lost its taking disempowered and dishonoured those who had been serving under it. In the nineteenth century a British public school education aimed to instill both Greek heroics and Roman fortitude in the future officers of the world imperium. Young Churchill understood that valour could be seen in endurance as well as in daring:[11] he held that in combination they were sublime, instancing Lieutenant Thomas Watson's action at Bilot on the North West Frontier.

Late on 16 September 1897 Watson and his detachment had been cut off from camp. They entrenched, but with ammunition almost gone Watson resolved that they had to counterattack. He led a handful of volunteers into Bilot village, but they were too few to clear it. Several were killed or wounded, Watson among the latter. After recovering the casualties he led a second assault and was wounded again. With wounds to leg and arm, a shattered thumb and a severed artery, he was carried fainting from the field. Without his actions, and those of Lieutenant James Colvin of the Bengal Sappers, who mounted two further attacks, it was unlikely that the detachment could have held out until relief came the following morning. Both men were awarded the Victoria Cross. Churchill approved:

> After a long day of marching, and fighting, in the dark, without food and with small numbers, the man who will go on, unshaken and unflinching after he has received a severe and painful wound, has in respect of personal courage few equals and no superior in the world.[12]

In the conditions of the Western Front during the First World War endurance was an everyday necessity, but it could be ground away, leading to the condition known as shell-shock or war neurosis. Some called it cowardice; the more perceptive, including Private Fred Dixon, recognized it as nervous collapse.

> A natural reaction to fear is action, either in flight or aggression. Now, the man in the trench, he can't run away and he can't indulge in a one-man offensive against the enemy. I'm inclined to think that many cases of shell-shock were caused by the infantryman having to sit down and take everything which came his way without being able to do anything about it. I also think that a stretcher-bearer was better off, he could busy himself actively with the wounded, and a signal linesman could become actively engaged with mending telephone lines…. Bravery in that case is shown when a man is fearful yet continues to carry out his obligations.[13]

Churchill, and Gort a generation later, viewed military life through the eyes of the imperial officer corps. They believed that for men of their class only self-discipline was needed; for the rankers, Gort believed in the efficacy of external discipline and drill, by which the men were taught to control their fears. The sufferer from shell-shock 'was probably a Yahoo before he was taken into the army and he could not get his nerves under restraint'.[14] Sir Ian Hamilton, soldier, scholar and poet, was also a member of that officer caste, but he could see that modern warfare would make new demands on the common soldier. In the coming democratic age military discipline would have to be built on the everyday virtues of the average citizen. It could no longer be based on unthinking parade-ground obedience. It had to be built upon a sense of public duty, force of example, *esprit de corps* and 'the fear a soldier has of his own conscience (fear that he may be afraid)'. It should be little more than a continuation class in the patriotism taught at home and in the schools.[15] A plain-spoken soldier of the new century considered that after fear of fear had been mastered other factors came into play. Field Marshal Viscount Slim divided highly courageous soldiers into two categories:

… those with quick intelligence and vivid imagination or those without imagination and with minds fixed on the practical business of living. You might almost say, I suppose, those who live on their nerves and those who have not got any nerves. The one suddenly sees the crisis, his imagination flashes the opportunity and he acts. The other meets the situation without finding it so very unusual and deals with it in a very matter of fact way.[16]

These contrasting temperaments are much like those classically attributed to Greeks and Romans. Slim preferred the Ciceronian emphasis on fortitude, citing a Victoria Cross awarded during the Burma campaign. He did not name the recipient, but the details he provided point unambiguously to Rifleman Ganju Lama. On 12 June 1944 Japanese medium tanks had broken through the perimeter of a Gurkha position near Ningthoukhong. In the counterattack, Ganju's company came under point-blank fire from three tanks. He was armed with a PIAT (Projector, Infantry, Anti-Tank), a shoulder-fired weapon with an effective range of 110 metres. On his own initiative and under withering cross-fire that broke his wrist and wounded him in the hand and leg, he moved forward to engage the tanks single-handed. At a range of 30 yards (27 metres) he destroyed two, the third falling to an anti-tank gun. Ganju then moved forward to attack the crews with grenades. He killed or wounded all of the Japanese crewmen before allowing himself to be taken to the Regimental Aid Post. While he was recovering in hospital, Slim asked him why he had walked forward in the open. The Gurkha replied: 'I had been trained not to fire the PIAT until I was certain of hitting. I knew I could hit at thirty yards, so I went to thirty yards'. To Slim this was nerveless fixity of purpose: 'he had only one thought in his head – to get to thirty yards. Quite simple if you are not bothered by imagination'. Ganju's success was a triumph of concentration; his survival was a matter of luck. The citation spoke of an inspiring example that single-handedly retrieved a most critical situation.

Slim had less confidence in the durability of courage shown by the imaginative soldier. 'Anyone can be brave for five minutes', he wrote, perhaps indicating that an imagination might, after perceiving an opportunity, quickly turn to magnifying hazards. Slim likened that five minutes' worth of bravery to spending from Moran's bank of courage. The first sign that one's fund was exhausted was impatience and irritability, followed, as the deficit deepened, by recklessness, foolhardiness and, if one had survived thus far, by depression. Respite from action or leave could top up the balance.

One VC winner who might have been on the edge of overdrawing was Lance Corporal John Kenneally of the Irish Guards. On 28 April 1943 his company had been holding a point on Bou ridge, the key to Tunis. When a company of German panzer-grenadiers prepared to attack Kenneally pre-empted them by launching a single-man assault downhill across bare ground with his Bren gun. The attack broke up in disorder. It gave Kenneally's much-reduced unit a lift and he was personally elated at having closed with the enemy. When the Germans re-formed, Kenneally again ran forward and sprayed them with automatic fire, nullifying the attack. Two days later he employed the same tactic with the same result. Although wounded he refused to give up his Bren gun – explaining that only he understood that particular weapon – and fought through the day. The VC citation spoke of his considerable part in holding the position, which influenced the whole course of the battle.[17] He later sought to explain his behaviour.

> There was no time for fear; a strange 'don't-give-a-damn' feeling takes a grip. This is something every infantryman feels when he is constantly exposed to death in brutal and violent forms.[18]

Kenneally did not sink into depression. Intervals out of action seemed to recharge him and he served until again wounded at Anzio in 1944. To apply Slim's yardstick, while the first charge down Bou ridge might be discounted as impulsive five-minute courage, that there was a second and a third argues deliberation. For Kenneally, constant exposure to death seems to have disarmed apprehension about it. He was not so much devoid of imagination as anaesthetized against its operation.

Moran defined apprehension, the imagination's anticipation of danger, as fear in its infancy. Guy Gibson, who won his VC leading the Dambuster raid on the Ruhr in 1943, relied on the physical and

After dropping his own bomb, Guy Gibson drew enemy fire away from the other Lancasters as they made their runs.

mental tasks of operational flying to suppress apprehension. By keeping busy he restricted his imagination's freedom to roam, but he would rather have been able to close the door on it altogether. 'You must leave your imagination behind', he wrote, 'or it will do you harm'.[19]

Chapter 4

The Vanity of Distinction

To be virtuous, valour must be devoted to noble and unselfish ends. To be unselfish, a deed must be performed without thought of reward. The Victoria Cross therefore harbours a paradox. It seeks to motivate by offering a reward: that is, public distinction in the form of a decoration. The coveting of distinction, a selfish motivation, is incompatible with true valour, which is selfless. That said, any reading of citations for the Victoria Cross reveals that in the vast majority of cases the possibility of receiving a 'reward for valour' was the last thing on the recipient's mind at the time. Many of the men, conscious of brave deeds being performed all around them, were afterwards puzzled that they had been singled out. The answer was simple: they had been noticed and their comrades had not.

Fortitude (valour) is one the four cardinal virtues; the pursuit of distinction is not. It was condemned by Pope Gregory the Great as vainglory, one of the seven capital vices rooted in pride. Gregory's teaching has persisted to the present, with most dictionaries defining vainglory as ostentatious pride. In the Pope's opinion, valour was not a virtue when pursued by the pusillanimous: 'weak minds when they hear good things of others, sometimes kindle themselves to right practice not by the love of virtue, but the delightfulness of applause'.[1]

The custodians of the Cross have usually been wary of glory-hunting, but only to the extent of demanding good evidence of a valiant exploit. Motivation was not their business, particularly in the early days. In the desperate circumstances of the Indian Mutiny civilians voluntarily attached themselves to military units. George Chicken, serving with the field force along the Grand Trunk Road, declared on joining that he would 'win his medal'. Belying his name, at Suhejee he pursued twenty armed rebels, killed five, was wounded and had to be rescued from the remainder. 'Nobly has he won it' wrote his commanding officer, recommending him for the Victoria Cross.[2] Another civilian, however, declared loudly that the Cross was a poor reward for someone as valiant as he.

Thomas Kavanagh of the Bengal Civil Service was the author of a work entitled *How I Won the Victoria Cross*. It was not, as one might think, a collection of various first-hand accounts compiled by an admirer. No, the Victoria Cross Kavanagh held up for public admiration was his own. While besieged in Lucknow with General Outram this self-confessed glory-hunter had volunteered to take a message to General Colin Campbell and guide the relief column to the Residency. He proposed attaching himself to Kanauji Lal, a native spy already tasked with carrying letters to Campbell. Kavanagh, over six feet tall with red hair and blue eyes, whose Hindustani was spoken with a strong Irish brogue, was a poor candidate for clandestine messenger. Outram listened to the offer in disbelief, but agreed to see if the Irishman could disguise himself. Kavanagh blacked up and put on native dress. His Hindustani was convincing enough to deceive some European officers and Outram gave his approval.

INCIDENTS IN KAVANAGH'S PERILOUS JOURNEY.

1, Kavanagh and his guide before the native officer (p. 307); 2, Challenged by the watchman (p. 308); 3, Before the Sepoy picket (p. 308); 4, In the grove of mango trees (p. 308); 5, Kavanagh and the Sikh Officer (p. 310).

Thomas Kavanagh's adventures while escaping from Lucknow.

Kanauji was understandably nervous about being able to maintain his own cover alongside such a striking companion. They were challenged several times. The Indian did most of the talking and in the darkness Kavanagh's disguise held. Kanauji also had to ask the way several times and their wanderings exhausted them. Although the night was slipping away, Kavanagh insisted, against the Indian's fears that the Irishman's disguise would not bear scrutiny in daylight, on sleeping for an hour. In the event, they reached the British lines at four in the morning. Kavanagh's chances of getting through without Kanauji would have been negligible, which at least he had the grace to acknowledge, but he was much more impressed with himself.

> The most delicious visions of the future lingered in my mind as I thought of the success of the enterprize. For less than this, names have descended from age to age as if never to be obliterated from the heroic pages of history.[3]

Campbell hailed it as one of the most daring feats ever attempted, but the directors of the East India Company did not share Kavanagh's opinion of himself. They declined to support the Governor-General's recommendation for the Victoria Cross, suggesting that Kavanagh should be satisfied with the Indian Mutiny medal that would be forthcoming. Despite their opposition, Kavanagh got his Cross, a £2,000 reward and promotion to Assistant Commissioner of Oudh. It was not enough. He saw his exploit as superior to that of Horatius at the bridge, whose devotion and courage had been excited by the heat of battle. By implication, Kavanagh was claiming the Thucydidean high ground of cool, deliberate courage. Had he not earned rewards on a par with those of Horatius?

> Should I be remembered when the records of centuries are condensed for the instruction of youth? Should I be honoured with a statue, and would every Englishman subscribe the cost of a day's food to reward me?[4]

It was only to be expected that Kavanagh would not leave it to reviewers to judge his book. He apologized for leaving out the deeds of others 'as only likely to please the parties themselves', pleading the necessity of keeping the work free of details and thus making it

> … a very simple book, remarkable principally for the extraordinary adventures of the author. It is a strange story, written by a plain man, who, moved by the spirit of his noble companions, endeavoured to do his duty at a time when courage and devotion were needed to preserve the empire of the East.[5]

In Western literature the boastful hero is generally an unattractive figure. We prefer that those whose deeds we admire have the good taste to be modest about them. Kavanagh's wish for a monument was nonetheless granted in 1975 by George MacDonald Fraser. In one of the Flashman novels Fraser conscripts his hero to take Lal's place because the Indian thinks that the risk is too great. Flashman's judgement of Kavanagh is that anyone 'who's as big a bloody fool as that, and goes gallivanting about seeking sorrow, must be called courageous'.[6] This is bravery made possible by a lack of imagination, which reflects more credit on Kavanagh's real companion because he was acutely aware of the risks. If any one person earned a Cross that night it was Kanauji Lal, not Thomas Kavanagh.

Kavanagh was not the only person to pen a work entitled *How I Won the Victoria Cross*. 'Crosscut', an Australian infantryman whose tongue was firmly in his cheek, warned his countrymen to prepare for a barrage of soldiers' tales when the First World War was over; exaggeration would be the norm, garnished with false modesty.[7] It was a happy conceit but wide of the mark: when they got home it was difficult to get veterans to talk about their experiences at all except among themselves. At least three First World War memoirs penned by VC recipients fail to mention the decoration at all. For some, however, it did have its uses. Private William Wignall, 2nd Battalion, King's Royal Rifle Corps, had a pre-war criminal conviction for breaking and entering and had been serving under the alias Mariner when he appeared in court for overstaying his leave. He was wearing the Cross that he had been awarded for bombing a German gun emplacement at Cambrin in May 1915. The magistrate dismissed the charge but sternly warned him 'not to bring that Cross

William Mariner, who won his VC for bombing a German strongpoint at night during a thunderstorm, was told that it was not a leave pass.

into court again in such circumstances'. Mariner had little opportunity to reoffend: he was killed a few months later in the first day of the Battle of the Somme. He was one of 283 medal-winners, and the only VC, listed on the criminals' Roll of Honour issued by the Metropolitan Police Commissioner in 1921.[8]

The First World War was also the setting for a case that posed a much more serious threat to the reputation of the Cross. In 1915 William Bishop, a Canadian, was being trained as an aircraft observer. Even then he was recorded as being confident that he could win a VC given the opportunity.[9] After qualifying as a pilot he set about making up for lost time and quickly posted a tally. He was aggressive and began planning a two-aircraft surprise raid on an enemy airfield, but could not persuade anyone to accompany him. Solo, then. On his own initiative, at first light on 2 June 1917 he crossed the trench lines near Cambrai intending to attack the German airfield at Neuville-St Remy. Disoriented in the dark he found an airfield, but it was deserted so he flew further into enemy territory. Twelve miles behind the lines, at an airfield that he subsequently suggested might have been Awoignt or Esnes, he surprised a dawn patrol on the ground as it prepared for take-off. He destroyed three of the Albatros fighters, following which, ammunition expended, he flew his Nieuport Scout westwards. Ground fire damaged the machine as he re-crossed the lines.

The only evidence for this exploit was Bishop's own combat report. His squadron commander, Major Alan Scott, quickly spread the word, eliciting from Major General Hugh Trenchard, Officer Commanding the Royal Flying Corps, congratulations for 'the greatest single show of the war'.[10] Scott recommended Bishop for the VC and according to Bishop it was not for the first time. On the day before the raid Bishop had written to his fiancée that the DSO he had received for shooting down two aircraft on 2 May had been downgraded from a VC. How he could have known – as such matters were supposed to be confidential until decided – or even whether it was true, because there is no reference to a downgrade on his DSO file, is beside the point.[11] Bishop was VC-hunting, but how could he get one solely on the strength of an open-ended accumulation of victories, however large? While the VC Warrant no longer required a single act of valour or, in Trenchard's words, a single great show, it was still the surest way to display conspicuous bravery, the fundamental qualification. Bishop's raid appeared to qualify, but there was still a procedural hurdle: the act had not been witnessed by Scott or performed in the sight of Trenchard, who was required to 'call for such description and attestation of the act as he may think requisite' before making a recommendation. Wing headquarters sought more information from Bishop's squadron. In reply, the acting commander confirmed that time and distance put the raid within the Nieuport's operational range and endurance. The aircraft had returned damaged. As to attestation, there was only 'personal evidence'.

Lack of corroboration should have precluded further consideration, but the process was allowed to drag on. As weeks went by the story of the raid found its way into Canadian newspapers. The lack of a decision was becoming an embarrassment. Bishop's VC was gazetted on 11 August. Instead of being credited with acting on his own initiative, he was said to have been 'sent out to work independently'. Whatever doubts might have been harboured privately in Whitehall, the citation was the officially sanctioned account of his feat until peace made it possible to start looking for corroborative evidence on the other side of the line. Intensive research by several generations of Canadian scholars, enthusiasts and sceptics alike, has failed to find documentation in German records or

Billy Bishop and a Nieuport Scout, with shrapnel bursting in the distance.

credible witnesses. It is not possible to prove that something did not happen, but that is not what the Warrant demands: it requires the claimant or the recommending authority to prove that something *did* happen. On those grounds alone Bishop should have been refused the VC. Whether his account was true or not was beside the point.

Offstage a small imperious voice can be heard protesting that occasional injustice to individuals was less important than the integrity of dear Albert's cross. For Victoria, every recipient had to be a Bayard, the chevalier without fear and beyond reproach. No one ever queried Bishop's nerveless courage, but there were many who had doubts about his character. Fortunately, the awkward precedent set by the award was regarded as an exception that reinforced the rule. The controversy that the Bishop award ignited smoulders to this day, generating heat but no light. Another such might do irreparable damage to the brand or, worse, engage the authorities in endless correspondence justifying their unwillingness to break the rules for yet another 'special case'. After a century, Bishop's remains the only VC awarded solely on the statement of the claimant.

The most bizarre attempt to appropriate the glory associated with the Cross was surely that of Idi Amin Dada, the erratic and bloodthirsty dictator of Uganda during the 1970s. He promoted himself to field marshal and awarded himself a Victorious Cross (*sic*), with his own portrait in place of crown and lion, and wore it whenever in uniform. Britain diplomatically ignored the violation, but the secretary of the Victoria Cross & George Cross Association did not. Didy Grahame's late husband had been Amin's company commander in the King's African Rifles before Uganda became independent. When she visited the country in 1976 Amin allowed her total freedom of movement if she would spend twenty minutes a day listening to his military reminiscences. During one of these sessions she pointed to the Cross ('For Supreme Valour') among his many medals and told him that he should take it off because he didn't deserve it. Amin protested that he did, to which the formidable Mrs Grahame replied: 'Quite frankly, I know you don't. You're making yourself a laughing stock by wearing it'. The chastened tyrant, a man who had no compunction about eliminating anyone who crossed him, removed the decoration.[12] Or so it was said, but later photographs still show a bronze cross in second place on his medal bar, now partly obscured by a flashy star.

Chapter 5

Trophies of Honour

During medieval times valour was one of the attributes of chivalry, along with gallant behavior and honourable conduct. By then, the legion's eagle had been replaced by the lord's crest and coat of arms and his follower's obligation was personal, rooted in feudal obligation, but honour was no less bound up in the defence of the insignia and continued to be so when they eventually morphed into regimental colours.

Alma was the first land action of the Crimean War and the first for which the Victoria Cross was awarded to soldiers. There were seven in total, three of which were for upholding the colours of the Scots Fusilier Guards. Captain Robert Lindsay was carrying the Queen's colour when the Light Division, ahead, began falling back in response to a false recall. Russian fire and the retiring units disordered the Fusilier line, but Lindsay stood his ground, assisted by Sergeant James McKechnie and Private William Reynolds. Soon the line of infantrymen had been bent back into an angle of which the flag, on a broken pole and with twenty bullet holes in it, was the apex. 'By the centre, Scots, by the centre; look to the colours and march by them', bellowed McKechnie. As it would have on parade, the line re-dressed on the colour and advanced beside it. The citation said of Lindsay that his example and energy tended greatly to restore order, whereas those for McKechnie ('behaved gallantly') and Reynolds ('behaved in a conspicuous manner') were less enthusiastic. It seemed that more honour attached to carrying the flag than rallying men to it. In another VC incident at Alma, Sergeant Luke O'Connor was with the colour party of the 23rd Foot when the officer carrying the flag fell wounded, spattering it with his blood. O'Connor was hit at the same time but picked up the colour and bore it for the remainder of the day although urged to relinquish it and have his wound seen to. After the action the colour was found to have been holed twenty-six times.[1]

Luke O'Connor took the colour from the dead hand of Lieutenant Anstruther.

On the other side of the coin, capturing enemy colours was a symbolic feat of arms. During the Indian Mutiny Lieutenant Frederick Sleigh Roberts of the Bengal Artillery took part in the charge of Younghusband's Squadron at Khudaganj.

> We overtook a batch of the mutineers, who faced about and fired into the squadron at close quarters. I saw Younghusband fall, but I could not go to his assistance, as at that moment one of his sowars (native cavalrymen) was in dire peril from a sepoy who was attacking him with fixed bayonet, and had I not helped the man and disposed of his opponent, he must have been killed. The next moment I descried in the distance two sepoys making off with [their] standard which I determined must be captured, so I rode off after the rebels and overtook them, and while wrenching the staff out of the hands of one of them, whom I cut down, the other fired his musket close to my body; fortunately for me it missed fire, and I carried off the standard … For these two acts I was awarded the Victoria Cross.[2]

Roberts wins the VC.

Some months earlier he had confided to his mother that the Cross was a reward that he sought above all ('how jolly I should be'). His motivation was not fame or honour as such, welcome though they would be, but career advancement ('a good appointment').[3]

Heroic failure while trying to prevent a colour becoming a trophy was no less honourable. At Isandhlwana during the Zulu War lieutenants Teignmouth Melvill and Neville Coghill were killed in a futile attempt to save the Queen's colour of the 24th Foot. That the Zulus attached no importance to such symbolic gestures became apparent when the colour was found downstream from the bodies some days later. It was policy not to make posthumous awards, but in lieu thereof it was publicly announced that both officers would have been awarded the Cross had they lived.[4]

Melvill and Coghill attempted to save the regimental colour at Isandhlwana.

Two years later, in 1881, it was decided that British regiments would no longer carry their colours into battle. No matter: there had long been other trophies available on the battlefield. Since the invention of gunpowder artillerymen and their commanding officers had made the winning and losing of guns a matter of honour, one with rather more operational implications than the fate of colours. Again a Roberts was in the thick of it.

By the time of the Second Boer War Frederick Roberts was 'Bobs' – Field Marshal Baron Roberts of Khandahar VC – the Empire's most famous soldier and Victoria's favourite. On 23 December 1899 he succeeded Sir Redvers Buller VC as commander-in-chief, South Africa. Eight days earlier Buller had suffered a sharp reverse at the hands of the Boers. At Colenso the guns of the 14th and 66th Batteries Royal Field

Artillery (RFA) had been advanced too far. Intense Boer fire drove the gunners to take shelter in a donga, leaving the guns exposed to capture. Roberts's only son, Lieutenant Frederick H.S. Roberts, was among the men who volunteered to rescue them. Two guns were saved and Roberts was badly wounded. Ten of the guns were lost to the Boers, but several Crosses were awarded for the effort, conforming to the cynic's rule that the greater the setback the better chance of recognition for any brave deed that might deflect criticism. Young Roberts died two days after the action, but the decoration was awarded posthumously and the Queen sent for it so that she could personally present it to his father. For young Roberts to be deemed eligible, a recommendation would have had to have been made in the two days between the action and his death. The papers that would confirm the timing are not in the archives. The citation referred to him as 'since deceased' and was light on heroics: 'Lieutenant Roberts assisted Captain Congreve. He was wounded in three places'.[5] As each of the other rescuers received a Cross for redeeming the honour of the RFA, Roberts alive would have been among their number. As it was, allowing recommendations to be made between deed and death clearly disadvantaged anyone who too quickly succumbed to wounds. Soon afterwards the practice of restricting awards to the living was abolished.

Frederick Sherston Roberts (right) was mortally wounded at Colenso.

That opened the door to retrospective awards, which were granted to Melvill, Coghill and others who in their time had been gazetted as 'would-have-been-had-he-lived'.

The Colenso VCs were awarded on the recommendation of Buller, and Roberts was not the only man who nearly missed out. Captain Harry Schofield of the RFA had been prominent in the recovery, but because they were his regiment's guns Buller held that he had been acting under orders. In Buller's understanding of the Warrant a recommendation for the VC required proof of initiative. He was told that it did not, and moreover that he was being inconsistent because 'acting under orders' could equally be said of Captain Walter Congreve and Lieutenant Roberts, both of whom he had recommended. Buller continued to resist but his objections were overruled.

Having to save guns was an all-too-common experience in the early months of the war. At Korn Spruit on 31 March 1900 two batteries of Royal Horse Artillery (RHA) were ambushed during the retirement from Tabanshu. The leading battery had most of its guns captured, but Major Edmund Phipps-Hornby wheeled his Q Battery about. Although one gun was lost when the wheel horse was shot, those remaining were brought into action. When a further retirement was ordered Phipps-Hornby and Captain Gardiner Humphreys, the only remaining officers, directed the removal of the guns and limbers by hand to where uninjured horses were waiting. Exhaustion took its toll on the men, so horses had to be sent forward with volunteer drivers to retrieve the last gun. All the horses were killed and a number of drivers wounded before the attempt was abandoned. Field Marshal Roberts invoked rule 13 of the VC Warrant for Q Battery to elect an officer, a non-commissioned officer, a gunner and a driver in what was the first ballot conducted since the Indian Mutiny. A flaw in the arrangement was exposed when each of the officers nominated the other. Rather than toss a coin, the army fell back on seniority. Phipps-Hornsby got the Cross; Humphreys got nothing. The DSO he was awarded eighteen months later was for 'service in the operations in South Africa', with no mention of Korn Spruit.

This injustice was a consequence of rules arbitrarily applied, but Roberts also separately nominated three officers who, as a 'self-imposed duty', had come to the assistance of Q Battery. They were rejected by Horse Guards on grounds that 'the affair at Korn Spruit taken as a whole was not of a nature to reflect credit on our Army'.[6] Korn Spruit had been a four-Cross embarrassment, but not a seven-Cross humiliation like Colenso. One of the three volunteers, however, had a sister with a friend at court. Lieutenant Francis Maxwell of the 18th Bengal Lancers had been nominated five years earlier for recovering the body of an officer while under fire during the Chitral campaign but had received no reward. His sister wrote to her friend, Mrs South, and so it was that the War Office received a letter from Windsor Castle.

> The Queen is greatly interested in the family of Maxwell's splendid record of six sons in the Army and five fighting at the front. Miss Maxwell's letter was read to Her Majesty [by Mrs South] who is much struck at the fact that one brother Frank has been twice recommended for the VC and HM cannot help thinking that if this really is the case his claim to the coveted honour is a strong one. Of course Her Majesty does not wish to issue any special orders on the subject but if the Commander in Chief was subsequently able to recommend this officer for the VC she would gladly approve.[7]

And of course he did, but it fell to her son Edward VII to approve. This had been the old queen's last intervention in the administration of Albert's cross; she died two months later. The other two volunteers, Lieutenant William Ainsworth of the 2nd Durham Light Infantry and Lieutenant George Stirling, 2nd Essex, were overlooked. For Humphreys and Stirling it must have been particularly galling to be mentioned in the citation for Maxwell's Cross, which incidentally revealed that their contribution had been no less than his. The episode is best seen as nostalgic respect for Victoria's last wish about something dear to her. The rules nevertheless retained their formal integrity, remaining silent about the notion that two nominations might add up to one Cross, or that the size of a military family was somehow relevant.

So notorious was the artilleryman's aversion to losing or even risking his guns that on one occasion acceptance of the risk had a profound moral effect. On 10 April 1917 Captain Eric Dougal of the RFA was engaging advancing Germans over open sights from an exposed ridge near Messines. The infantry had been forced back to his gun line. He gave the disorganized men some Lewis light machine guns and

George Wheeler lost his life in a vain attempt to capture Turkish flags at Shaiba.

said: 'so long as you stick to your trenches, I will keep my guns here'. The guarantee succeeded in holding up the Germans for twelve hours. Ammunition expended, the guns were manhandled to the rear over half a mile of shell-cratered ground under heavy machine-gun fire. Dougal's VC citation spoke of leadership, inspirational calm and fearlessness. He was killed directing his battery four days later.

Anachronistically, the honour attached to capturing colours persisted into the First World War. At Shaiba in Mesopotamia in 1915 Major George Wheeler of the Hariana Lancers was given permission to attempt the capture of a flag from around which the enemy were firing on British pickets. Wheeler believed that loss of the flag would demoralize the Turks. Charging with the lance, his squadron killed many but had to retire when more emerged from hidden ground. On the following day Wheeler led his men in another charge, this time against a feature called the North Mound. He was last seen far in advance, charging directly for enemy standards on the mound. It was, as the VC citation said, most conspicuous gallantry; that it was of dubious military value and involved unnecessary loss of life went unmentioned.

Chapter 6

Duty and Disobedience

The fifth rule of the original Warrant stipulated that awards were only to be for signal acts of valour or devotion to country. At the time, critics concentrated on the former. Speaking in the House of Commons, Sir William Fraser pointed out that a signal act of valour was inimical to the discipline that fighting in formation demanded. He claimed that while the recently deceased Duke of Wellington's dispatches made much of duty, there was nary a mention of glory.[1] What was required of a soldier was attention to duty and rigid obedience to orders. There was no place for initiative. Stepping out of line or breaking ranks in pursuit of individual distinction was to be decried, not encouraged. Rudyard Kipling, in exhorting Boy Scouts and Girl Guides after the First World War, was firm that the only acceptable form of individual initiative was to volunteer when called upon by superiors to do so. It was cowardly, childish and cheating to neglect duty 'for the sake of stepping aside to snatch at what to an outsider may resemble fame or distinction'. Moreover, they would be judged harshly by their peers, whose opinion was the only one worth having.[2]

Insistence on subordination, however, looked hollow when initiative produced a successful outcome, and the more successful the outcome the more out of date the Wellingtonian prescription looked. At Alma, when the Victoria Cross was not yet a thought in the minds of the great and good, Captain Edward Bell of the 23rd Foot had, without orders, captured a Russian gun that was being removed from a redoubt. He returned with it to his regiment only to be reprimanded for leaving his post, but higher command had observed the incident and decided that it deserved reward rather than censure. When the Victoria Cross came into being, he was one of the first recipients.

A month after Bell's exploit Lieutenant William Hewett of the Naval Brigade was in command of a siege battery at Sebastopol. With the

When Edward Bell captured a Russian gun at Alma he was reprimanded for leaving his post.

Russians advancing, word was passed ordering him to spike the gun and retire before the position was taken. He is alleged to have replied that 'such order did not come from Captain Lushington (his commanding officer), and he would not do it until he did'. So said his citation, but if reported correctly his precise words were 'Retire? Retire be damned!',

LIEUTENANT W. N. W. HEWITT REFUSING TO SPIKE THE GUN IN THE LANCASTER BATTERY.

'Retire be damned', said Lieutenant Hewett.

whereupon he pulled down the parapet and trained the gun on the advancing Russians to good effect. Lushington nominated Hewett for the Cross, so one can infer that success justified disobedience, although it would not do to say so. It was on just such successful defiance of orders that Horatio Nelson had built his reputation.

The more junior the officer, the more risk that a superior might take exception to initiative. During the siege of Delhi during the Indian Mutiny Lieutenant Arthur Jones of the 9th Lancers saw that an enemy gun team had detached from the cloud of dust that his squadron was pursuing. On his own he galloped off in pursuit. Coming alongside the team's horses, he sabred one of the riders, which caused the man to fall between the wheelers and brought the team to a halt. Reinforcements came up to support Jones and the gun was taken. His colonel had no hesitation in recommending him for 'a well-conceived act, gallantly executed', but Jones later reflected that his superior could have taken a different view: 'It is questionable if the VC does not interfere with discipline, which might have demanded a trial by court-martial if I had been riding a slower horse, and so had failed to reach my prey.'[3]

Private Albert Shepherd of the King's Royal Rifle Corps ran a similar risk at Villiers Plouich in France on 20 November 1917 when, having been refused permission to rush a machine-gun post holding up the company advance, he did it anyway. Having removed the obstacle, but with all the officers and NCOs dead or wounded, he then led the company forward and took the objective. Exercising the prerogatives of a *de facto* company commander, he did not report himself for disobeying the order. Bombardier Ernest Horlock of the RFA had been less fortunate. At Vendress in 1914 he was wounded in the thigh and the medical officer at the dressing station ordered him to hospital. Instead he returned to his hard-pressed battery. Wounded again, he was told for a second time to report to hospital, but again went back to the guns. When he received a third wound he would not even report to the MO for fear of being asked to explain why he was not in hospital. For the action he received a Victoria Cross *and* a reprimand for disobeying orders.

In respect of the second qualification for the Cross – a signal act of devotion to country – there was a definitional problem. How could such devotion be identified and weighed? All the Crimean citations that had used the word 'devotion' had been written before the Warrant was issued, and all had been about saving wounded comrades. When in 1897 John Mayo was writing his authoritative work on British medals and decorations he was firmly against rewarding the practice with a Cross.

> That an act of devotion to the country would be an act of valour may be taken for granted, but it by no means follows that an act of valour must necessarily be one of devotion to the country. And, no specific conditions having been prescribed, it has happened that men who led charges against the enemy, and men who carried wounded comrades out of danger, have been held to be equally eligible.... It appears however to be desirable that as much discrimination as possible should be exercised in awarding the Cross, and that it should be regarded in the light of a special reward for acts of valour done *against the enemy*.[4]

If devotion to country meant furthering its military objectives, the extremity would be to sacrifice oneself for the cause. This notion appears to have been in the mind of Prince Albert when he nominated the Charge of the Light Brigade, a suicidal endeavour if ever there was one, as a deed worthy of the Cross. The outcome was irrelevant: if, as in that case, all were performing a signal act of valour together under extremely hazardous orders, valour and devotion were in tandem. It was a reconciliation that Lieutenant John Smyth of the 15th Ludhiana Sikhs would have avoided if he could. At Festubert in France on 18 May 1915 two companies attempting to hold a captured trench 300 metres in front of the British line were running short of ammunition, particularly grenades. An entire resupply party was shot down before it got halfway. Two parties sent back by the companies met the same fate. Smyth's commanding officer asked him, as the battalion's bombing officer, if it was possible to get a supply of grenades across. 'No', replied Smyth, but he would make the attempt if required. The CO consulted the brigadier and rang back, sounding almost in tears, to say that he was sorry but the attempt should be made. Smyth's company commander had been listening and implored his subordinate to refuse what he regarded as a

John Smyth and Mangal Singh, the last of eleven men who started out, delivered the grenades at Festubert as ordered.

suicidal order. Smyth described his own feelings as 'an absolutely blue funk', but said it disappeared when every one of the Sikhs in his trench volunteered. He selected ten. Only one made it across – with Smyth and a box of bombs – but the trench was held. 'I had been very, very lucky as I had bullets through my tunic and cap, and my walking stick had been hit no less than four times'. Smyth certainly earned his VC, but his 'suicidal' act was one of duty. How much more estimable were the men who volunteered to accompany him and who, as Smyth wrote, 'were under no illusions about what it meant?'[5] All of the Sikhs were awarded Indian decorations.

Smyth had been ordered to do his duty, although all concerned understood that it was likely to end in his death. It could and should have been different for Lieutenant Charles Pope of the 11th Battalion, Australian Imperial Force, at Louveral on 15 April 1917. Holding one of several posts that had been bypassed by advancing Germans, Pope sent to the support line for more ammunition but the relief failed. The citation for his Victoria Cross says that he was ordered to hold the post 'to the last'. Whether to the last round or the last man was not specified. The difference is important because surrender when without the means to continue fighting has been generally accepted as an honourable option in the West.[6] At one of the other posts the officer decided that the order did not require him to die. He ordered his pickets to fight to the last round and then to destroy their Lewis guns. When Pope's ammunition was almost gone he led a charge into superior numbers of the enemy and was killed, as were his men. Their bodies were found with eighty German dead nearby. The witness to this deed was his corporal, who was wounded. Pope's last order to his men had been to 'hang on'.[7] His charge had no effect on the outcome and contradicted his own last order. Pope's Cross recognized his feat of arms, but even more heroic was the devotion to duty of those who had followed him to their deaths. The men in the other posts were taken prisoners of war.

Necessity was more in evidence the following year when the German spring offensive threatened to overwhelm the British lines and break through to the Channel ports. When the first blow fell, temporary Lieutenant Colonel Wilfrith Elstob was commanding a battalion of the Manchester Regiment as it held a redoubt near St Quentin. Surrounded, Elstob told his brigade commander that he would defend the position to the last, drawing attention to the fact that the feature being held was

HEROES OF MANCHESTER HILL.

Some of the officers, with Col. Wilfrith Elstob, D.S.O., M.C. (also inset), of the Manchester Battalion, whose heroic last stand on Manchester Hill, near St. Quentin, on the opening day of the German offensive, is one of the epics of the great battle. On left (sitting), Lieut. J. T. Ball, wounded, and Major R. K. Roberts, killed.

Wilfrith Elstob was killed holding Manchester Hill 'to the last'.

called Manchester Hill. The implication of that undertaking became clear when he told his men that 'here we fight and here we die'. He was killed as the Germans stormed the hill.[8]

Elstob had taken the responsibility on himself, but three weeks later Douglas Haig made it the duty of all when he issued what became known as the 'backs-to-the-wall order': 'Every position must be held to the last man. There must be no retirement … each one of us must fight to the end'. Second Lieutenant Bernard Cassidy of the Lancashire Fusiliers honoured it to the letter. His company was in support on the left of the division when a German attack threatened to turn its flank. Ordered to hold to the last, Cassidy repeatedly counterattacked and the post only fell after it had been surrounded and he had been killed. By then the line had been stabilized and the left flank saved. The citation spoke of exceptional devotion to duty.[9]

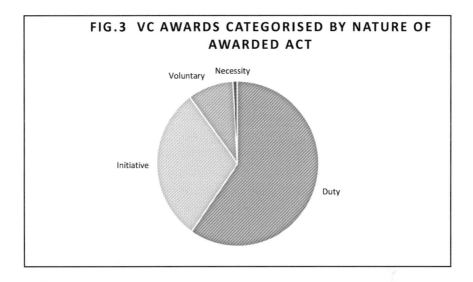

FIG.3 VC AWARDS CATEGORISED BY NATURE OF AWARDED ACT

There is, however, a form of valour even higher than that of obeying an order to sacrifice oneself. When commanders are uncertain that an order involving extreme risk will be obeyed, even though refusal will entail severe disciplinary consequences, there is always the Smyth option: call for volunteers. It is said that old soldiers know better than to step forward ('never volunteer', they allegedly tell recruits), but Smyth's Sikhs must not have been listening. Indeed, as far as the Victoria Cross is concerned the advice has often fallen on deaf ears. Since inception, about one-third of the awards have been for acts of initiative and another one in eleven for voluntary acts.[10]

When Victoria was considering the first recommendations she was pleased that none of them cited mere performance of duty to the satisfaction of superiors. In her reading of the submissions, these awards for devotion to country were in recognition of voluntary acts. She seems to have assumed that they were done with the approval of superiors, which in the case of Bell was patently untrue. That some of them might have been voluntary *initiatives* and therefore unsanctioned, if not insubordinate, does not appear to have troubled her, although others could see the contradiction, as will become apparent. The Queen queried only one recommendation on the list and it was an instance of initiative.

Private Patrick M'Gwire of the 33rd Foot had been on advanced sentry duty before Sebastopol when he was surprised and captured by two Russian soldiers. As he was being taken to the Russian lines he noticed that his captors were being casual with their arms. He knocked one captor down and recovered his own weapon, with which he shot the other. The first man then rose and fired without effect at M'Gwire, who dispatched him with his gun butt, subsequently returning to the British lines with the arms and accoutrements of his erstwhile captors. The Russians had made the mistake of assuming that someone who had surrendered would consider himself bound to take no further part in hostilities. Lord Raglan praised his 'gallantry' and gave him a gratuity of £5. The French awarded him their *Médaille Militaire*.

Victoria characterized the episode as being of very doubtful morality and pointed out that if such behaviour was sanctioned, much less rewarded, the only safe course for a soldier capturing an enemy would be to kill him immediately for fear of being later attacked. M'Gwire's name was removed from the list. The Queen's logic was validated in the worst possible way in Italy in January 1944, when Private George Mitchell, 1st Battalion, London Scottish, displayed what his VC citation characterized as courage and devotion to duty of the highest order. He was operating a 2-inch mortar during an advance on Damiano Ridge when machine-gun fire killed or wounded most of the officers and NCOs in his company. He took up a rifle and charged a machine-gun, shooting one enemy and bayonetting the second. The advance being again held up by small arms fire, he charged forward and, supported by his section, captured the position, killing six Germans and taking twelve prisoners. Under fire from another machine-gun he rushed forward and bayonetted its crew. Now out of ammunition, he charged the final enemy position on the crest, was first into it and largely responsible for its surrender. A few minutes later one of the Germans who had surrendered picked up a rifle and shot him dead.

A similar case to M'Gwire's arose during the First World War. Temporary Captain Robert Gee of the Royal Fusiliers was captured near Masnières on 30 November 1917 when his brigade headquarters was attacked. The Germans neglected to take his officer's stick, which was shod with a lance point. With it he attacked his captor, escaped and organized a scratch counterattack during which, although wounded, he attacked a machine-gun post and killed eight of its crew. The citation for his Victoria Cross mentioned both incidents, incorrectly claiming that he had killed his captor. It used the formula 'taken prisoner', the implication being that Gee had not surrendered his 'arms' and was therefore entitled to use them when opportunity presented. Given that the personal heroism displayed in the counterattack would itself have been sufficient grounds for the award, one can only assume that those then in authority had no qualms about advertising a practice that the late Queen had judged to be of dubious morality. Modern military ethicists have endorsed the principle behind Victoria's reservation. Michael Walzer has hypothesized the killing of a prison guard by a prisoner of war; such an act is murder, for by surrendering the prisoner has given up fighting and resumed some of the civilian obligations that are suspended for soldiers in the face of the enemy.[11]

That individual duty might have to be neglected in pursuit of a unit objective was neatly exposed by Captain Patrick Porteous, serving with 4 Commando at Dieppe on 19 August 1942. Detailed to liaise between two detachments attacking coastal defence guns, he was shot in the hand but disarmed his assailant and killed him with his own bayonet. Seeing that the second detachment was leaderless he ran across to it and led a successful attack on the guns, during which he was severely wounded. After the guns had been destroyed he collapsed from loss of blood. His VC citation included the slightest hint of criticism, referring

Patrick Porteous supplementing his duty.

to 'tenacious devotion to a duty which was supplementary to the role originally assigned to him'.[12] Porteous later revealed how far from his assigned duty, or any other, had been his thoughts that day.

> I was very lucky, I think, extremely lucky to get the award of the VC .... I felt as though it was rather like being in a rugger scrum: you got kicked about a bit and the object was to get over the line, which was all that we did do, in fact. One was scared stiff but there was nothing you could do about it, you had to press on regardless. I was scared from the moment we started getting shot at; or before that, as soon as we realized we were going on an operation, which was all rather frightening. It has to be. I don't think there's any man on earth who's not frightened if he's going into an operation unless he's bone-headed.[13]

Chapter 7

Highly Prized and Eagerly Sought After

Her Majesty's review in Hyde Park had been commanded by Sir Colin Campbell, a senior Crimean general and favourite of the Queen. Shortly thereafter he was sent as commander-in-chief to India to suppress a mutiny of sepoys that had broken out a few months earlier. As a detached General Officer Commanding he had authority under rule 7 of the Warrant to confer Crosses on the spot subject to subsequent confirmation by the Queen. He suggested that a supply of the medals be sent to him so that he could confer and pin at the same time. This was altogether too loose a proceeding for Whitehall, but if the authorities' main concern was about over-enthusiastic issue they need not have been concerned,

During the Indian Mutiny the Victoria Cross was dogged by ambition, scepticism and nepotism.

SIR JAMES OUTRAM.   SIR COLIN CAMPBELL.   SIR HENRY HAVELOCK.

because Campbell was not enamoured of the Cross. His experience of leading British troops had been that they needed to be restrained from pursuit of glory rather than encouraged in it. On arrival in India he found that not even generals were immune.

Major General James Outram had been appointed civil commissioner for Oudh and tasked with relieving the British residency in Lucknow, which was under siege by the rebels. Brigadier General Henry Havelock was already advancing to the relief and when their columns joined Outram did not supersede the lower-ranked Havelock – as was his right and some said his duty – instead accompanying the joint force as a volunteer cavalryman. At Mangalwar on the road to Lucknow he participated in a vigorous charge that took two guns and a sepoy regimental colour, with the general wielding a cudgel in place of a sabre. At the gates of Lucknow he was wounded in the arm but refused to be taken to the rear. Later he made a grandiose claim.

> I state but the truth, to which the whole army will testify, declaring it in self-defence against the imputation of needlessly exposing myself … that had I gone to the rear … the column would not have penetrated into the city, nor without my guidance could it have reached the Residency.[1]

The incompatibility of this claim to leadership after abdication of command was apparent to one of Outram's most valued subordinates, Captain Francis Maude, himself recommended for a VC on that memorable day. He characterized the relief as a gloriously conducted muddle.

> The officers led their men right well; but of generalship, *proprement dit*, that day there was little if any at all. … [Outram] had his wits about him, and was cool and collected enough; but having voluntarily subordinated his rank, he could not take any independent steps without involving a great breach of discipline, while the general who was nominally in command [Havelock] took no initiative action whatever.[2]

In almost his last act before returning command to Outram, Havelock ordered that the officers and men of each corps of the relief force should elect one of their number for the Victoria Cross. The cavalry selected Outram and the corps commander so informed Campbell. The commander-in-chief ruled that as Outram held field officer rank he was ineligible, despite there being no such restriction in the Warrant. Many years later, when the corps commander asked Outram why he had surrendered command, Outram was frank: 'I had the chance of obtaining the highest object of my ambition, the Victoria Cross'.[3] That is what Albert and Victoria had hoped for, but it is doubtful that they foresaw the heavy discount that now seemed to apply to other honours, for Outram had been made a Knight Grand Cross of the Order of the Bath during the Persian War of 1856–7. In Outram's defence, it should be noted that at the relief of Lucknow he could not have known that Campbell would restrict eligibility. On the other hand, as a volunteer cavalryman he would have more opportunity to display personal valour than would a general officer discharging his command responsibilities. Outram was not the only victim of Campbell's interdict. Lieutenant Colonel Hagart was similarly denied, and the precedents so set were honoured until 1917.

Maude was elected by his gunners and Outram did the paperwork. The general had the highest professional regard for Maude, who had lost one-third of his men in advancing two guns to engage the rebel artillery, and he knew his Thucydides.

> … this attack appeared to [me] to indicate no reckless or foolhardy daring, but the calm heroism of a true soldier who fully appreciates the difficulties and dangers of the task he has undertaken; and that, but for Captain Maude's nerve and coolness on this trying occasion the army could not have advanced.[4]

Maude himself doubted that he had done anything to deserve the Cross that day and his election exposed an embarrassing situation. He had previously been elected for the battle of Cawnpore in July, but the only Cross awarded for that action was to General Havelock's son and aide-de-camp, Lieutenant Henry Marshman Havelock. It was contentious in that young Havelock had taken himself across to an apparently leaderless 64th Foot, which was suffering under heavy artillery fire and seemed reluctant to advance. On horseback he accompanied the infantry at foot pace under fire towards the offending gun, which was taken. On his award being gazetted the officers of the 64th protested to Campbell that they not been leaderless. Their commanding officer, Major Stirling, since deceased, had been dismounted and was leading his men on foot, so no assistance needed thank you. Campbell forwarded the protest to London with some views of his own.

> This instance is one of many, in which, since the institution of the Victoria Cross, advantage has been taken by young aides-de-camp and other staff officers to place themselves in prominent situations for the purpose of attracting attention. To them life is of little value, as compared with the gain of public honour, but they do not reflect, and the generals to whom they belong do not reflect, on the cruel injustice thus done to gallant officers, who, beside the excitement of the moment of action, have all the responsibility attendant on this situation.[5]

Sir Colin did not spare Havelock senior, since deceased and now enshrined as a national hero, accusing him of injustice to other officers by giving 'a public preference to those attached to [him]'. Campbell's indignation was reinforced by the knowledge that both of the Havelocks had compounded their respective errors by repeating them. At Lucknow, again without command responsibility, the lieutenant-on-horseback had 'led' the Madras Fusiliers and their dismounted officers in a charge across the Char Bagh bridge. Outram, who had witnessed it, said that he could not conceive a more daring act and hoped that 'a morbidly sensitive delicacy' would not inhibit Havelock from awarding his son a second Cross. Havelock welcomed the absolution.

> On this spontaneous declaration of the Major General, the Brigadier General consents to award the Cross to this officer; which act, if originating with himself, might, from the near relationship Lieutenant Havelock bears to him, assume the appearance of undue partiality.[6]

On this Maude drily commented: 'Well, yes! It might.'[7]

Whitehall deferred to Campbell, who adroitly finessed the issue: General Havelock could not have known when he made the second award that the first had been confirmed in Britain (the implication being that if he had known, he would not have so acted, although the Warrant clearly permitted it); the bar should not be awarded. Edward Pennington, the War Office clerk who administered the awards, related the rejection to Campbell's opinion about the Cawnpore award. 'It seems like saying you were not entitled to it for the first act, but you got it, and you must consider that as your reward for the second act.'[8] One suspects that had it been up to Campbell young Havelock would not have had the first Cross either.

After the second relief of Lucknow, which was made under Campbell's personal command, he ordered a further round of elections for the Cross. All regiments in the force were included. The 9th Lancers declined to nominate on the cogent grounds that they had not been in action that day. That was disobedience and Campbell would have none of it. He demanded a name and the lancers put forward that of their native water-carrier.[9] Campbell's one-in-all-in approach can be interpreted as an attempt to downgrade the Cross to a 'representative participant' award and thereby reduce the glory-hunting of which he was so critical. The 9th Lancers had chosen to express disdain for the procedure by offering up as an insult one of their own who, as Maude wryly pointed out, might as well have deserved the distinction as any other man if the award was for simply doing one's duty. The *bheestie* did not get a medal, but at least he had been nominated. His fellow countrymen, including those serving at the sharp end, were denied even that.

At Delhi on 19 June 1857 Brigadier Grant, commanding the Field Force cavalry, had his horse shot from under him. Two privates of the aforesaid 9th Lancers, Thomas Hancock and John Purcell, stayed with him, as did a sowar of the 4th Irregular Cavalry, Roopur Khan. Hancock was severely wounded and Purcell had his horse killed before Grant was dragged out by Khan's horse. The Englishmen received the Cross; the Indian did not, although Grant praised his 'excellent conduct'. Not until 1867 did members of local forces like irregular cavalry become eligible for the Victoria Cross, and that change to the Warrant was made specifically to provide for white units serving alongside British troops in New Zealand. At the outset of the Mutiny the loyal troops of the East India Company, brown and white, had also been ineligible for the Cross. The Warrant was amended to remedy the deficiency on 29 October 1857 and many deeds prior to that date thereby qualified. In all, seventeen crosses were awarded to men serving in EIC native infantry units. All were officers; none were natives. Many of the citations acknowledged that at the relevant times the white officers had been closely and bravely supported by native troops.

There was no such discrimination, at least in respect of the Cross, against non-whites serving in European units during the Mutiny. Able Seaman William Hall of the Naval Brigade volunteered to assist his ship's gunnery officer, Lieutenant Thomas Young, to breach the walls of a mosque at Lucknow on 16 November 1857. The two guns employed were advanced so close to the wall that every time they fired the crews had to take cover from falling masonry. Enemy fire and grenades took their toll until only Hall and the badly wounded Young were left. Hall kept his 24-pounder in action almost single-handed, which meant totally exposing himself to fire at every laborious reload. When the breach was effected, infantry poured into the mosque. For once Campbell forgot himself, describing the feat as 'almost unexampled in war'. Hall was the Canadian son of refugee American slaves. He was the first black man to win the Cross, which was also awarded to Young.

There is a small sub-set of Cross winners who, far from eagerly seeking the decoration, have found it an embarrassment. John Kenneally, when told that he had been awarded the Cross for his actions in Tunisia, thought that it was the worst thing that could have happened to him. Born Leslie Robinson and serving under that name in the Territorial Army at the beginning of war, he had deserted. When he re-enlisted it was in the name of an Irishman whose identity documents he had acquired. His first reaction to the award was 'now I'm bound to be rumbled'.[10]

Chapter 8

In the Absence of an Enemy

During the Indian Mutiny regiments were hastily dispatched from Britain as reinforcements, among them a contingent of the 54th Foot. Its troopship, the *Sarah Sands*, caught fire 800 miles off Mauritius. Gunpowder in the hold compounded the danger; most of the crew took to the boats, and for eighteen hours it was left to the troops to throw powder overboard and fight the fire. Several men risked asphyxiation to rescue the regimental colours. The ship limped to Mauritius, three of the four masts down, and arrived with the entire stern burnt out.

The burnt-out stern of the *Sarah Sands*.

The senior regimental officer, Major Brett, recommended twenty-five officers and men for the Victoria Cross. Colin Campbell was unsure that the Warrant admitted the case, as there was no enemy present, but remarked that no men in conflict were more deserving of being 'conspicuously marked out' than these of the 54th. Whitehall appeared to concur and a Warrant extending the Cross to cases of 'conspicuous courage and bravery displayed under circumstances of danger but not before the enemy' was approved by the Queen on 10 August 1858. The way appeared to be clear, but when Brett returned to England nearly two years later the new Warrant had yet to be gazetted. He enquired of army headquarters at Horse Guards whether a Cross was to be conferred on the regiment, which indicates that by then he was thinking in terms of a representative decoration.

The delay had been engineered by Pennington of the War Office, perhaps alarmed at the prospect of inflating the number of recipients to that time by 8½ per cent without a shot having been fired. He had outwaited his more enthusiastic superiors and now argued that as the *Sarah Sands* incident pre-dated the Warrant, which made no provision for retrospectivity, there was no clause under which the Cross could be awarded. And in any event, had not the moment passed? This was masterly: it was he who had drafted the Warrant, which was expressly authorized to provide for the *Sarah Sands* case. The army chose to press on. Brett was told to submit a name. He recommended Private Andrew Walsh as 'most conspicuous for daring and valour', having volunteered to clear the powder magazine, helped extinguish the fire at the main topsail yard and conducted himself well, setting an example throughout the time it took to reach Mauritius.[1] As both the magazine clearance and the work aloft were shared endeavours, it was clear that Brett was arguing for a representative award. If it was to be representative it should have been put to an election, but by now so much time had passed that those eligible to vote were long scattered. Time had again been on the side of the bureaucrat.

When sixty years later Rudyard Kipling revisited the story of the *Sarah Sands*, the only mention he made of recognition was to quote the general order that the Commander-in-Chief had caused to be read to every regiment in the army. It was to the effect that the behaviour of the 54th was most praiseworthy, and that the outcome made manifest 'the advantage of subordination and strict obedience to orders under the most alarming and dangerous circumstances'. This, opined Kipling, seemed to be the moral of the tale. And yet he had been moved to retell it as an example of 'long-drawn-out and undefeatable courage and cool-headedness', which are surely the attributes of individual soldiers rather than of regiments.[2]

Pennington's 'no-retrospectivity' argument had successfully denied Walsh the Cross, but the Warrant was still in force and the army tried again in 1866. Private Timothy O'Hea was serving in Canada when a railway car containing ammunition caught fire at the Danville station. He opened the car and called for water and a ladder. By exertion and example he caused the fire to be extinguished. Pennington marshalled the counter-arguments: there was no specific recommendation, just a commendation of conduct; the £10 annuity was a lot of money for a private; the Admiralty had never been told of the existence of this Warrant; O'Hea's feat could be seen as no more than an act of duty; and an award after so many years of dormancy might create an inconvenient precedent. His superiors were unconvinced and, to Pennington's way of thinking, compounded the error when gazetting the award by mentioning the Warrant, eight years after it had been signed.[3] He managed to prevent it being mentioned again when five Crosses were awarded for rescuing comrades cut off by surf and in danger of drowning in the Andaman Islands. Better still, he persuaded his superiors to fob off all subsequent requests for a copy of the Warrant on grounds that it had never been printed or gazetted and therefore it was not expedient to circulate it. The army was not to be thwarted. It brought forward a recommendation for Captain Andrew Scott.

On 26 July 1877 Scott was serving with the 4th Sikh Infantry, then on garrison duty at Quetta in Baluchistan. While on duty at the parade ground that evening he heard an alarm that British officers were being attacked. On reaching the location he found one officer had been cut down. Another, Lieutenant Kunhardt, was hard pressed and wounded, in retreat, and assisted only by a Sikh sepoy. Scott fell on the assailants, who were Pathan coolies. He bayonetted two and grappled with a third, both men falling to the ground. This third Pathan was killed by other sepoys who arrived on the scene. Scott was credited with saving Kunhardt's life. Now, Britain was not at war in Baluchistan and the Pathans were most likely locally engaged labourers. In the absence of any background documentation it can only be assumed that the army saw the Scott case as a *Sarah Sands* type of incident. Pennington might try to hide the Warrant, but he could hardly deny its existence and the War Office allowed the claim, in the citation describing the act as one of courage and devotion. Pennington could have suggested to Horse Guards, and perhaps did, that an Albert Medal for the saving of life would have been more appropriate. There the sleeping dog lay until the Warrants were reviewed in 1881, at which time the 'enemy present' requirement was restated. There was then general agreement that the Albert Medal, created to recognize the saving of life at sea and in 1877 extended to land rescues like O'Hea's, had made the 1858 Warrant redundant.

The issue resurfaced early in the Second World War. During the Blitz, a large number of the German bombs dropped on British cities did not explode on impact. Many were defective, but others had been timed to explode hours after dropping and some were booby-trapped. The ordnance teams tasked with defusing them were not technically 'in the presence of the enemy', although he was most assuredly there in intent: the booby-trapped devices were as precisely targeted as if bullets had been aimed at the defusers. For hours, sometimes days, they had to suppress fear on a sustained basis to secure life and property. Some were killed. Instead of being brought within the ambit of the VC Warrant, bomb-disposal personnel were deemed to be eligible for the George Cross, instituted in May 1940. It was created as the non-combatant's equivalent of the VC, open to military and civilian alike, and similarly awarded for most conspicuous courage, recognizing that in total war the front was everywhere and heroism could be found in unlikely quarters. In place of the absent enemy, 'extreme danger' was the contingent circumstance. The new dispensation, unlike the VC, had two classes, with the Cross reserved for VC-standard heroism and a George Medal 'for wider distribution'. Merchant seamen, clandestine operatives and emergency services personnel, among others, achieved recognition, but still there were anomalies.

When Major Hugh Seagrim was left behind in Burma to organize Karen irregulars he was performing military duties, although of an unconventional nature. He surrendered to the Japanese to save Karen non-combatants and was executed. As the act was deemed sufficiently gallant to be worthy of the George Cross, and performed in the presence of the enemy, why not the VC? The answer probably lies in military distaste for unconventional warfare, a prejudice that also denied the

VC to members of the Special Operations Executive, a clandestine organization that operated in enemy territory. Many of its men and women were military personnel. The fact that they were usually out of their own uniforms and sometimes in those of the enemy meant that their activities, which were beyond the protection of the Geneva conventions, were far more hazardous on a sustained basis than those of their conventional counterparts. Insistence that the VC and GC were equivalent awards convinced few. After the war there was a determined effort by Conservative MP Irene Ward to have some of the SOE women awarded the VC, but that became out of the question once Wing Commander Forest Yeo-Thomas received the George Cross in 1946.

The citation for Yeo-Thomas reads like a lurid spy novel without the adjectives. Three times he had been parachuted into France to gather intelligence and support underground networks. On the third occasion he was betrayed, captured, tortured and imprisoned. He became a serial escaper and organized resistance behind the wire at the risk of his life. After eight attempts to escape from different camps, including Buchenwald where nearly half of his prisoner group were executed, he successfully led a group of ten French POWs through German patrols to American lines. If these were not 'active operations', which Churchill had told the Commons was the line that marked off the VC from the GC, it is difficult to imagine what could be.[4] Equally, it is difficult to see how a woman performing a valiant act on active operations in the presence of the enemy could hope to win the Victoria Cross other than in uniform.[5]

Chapter 9

Stretching the Statutes

Inertia being the prime mover of bureaucracy, it was only when contentious cases arose that there would be debate about whether the rules were inconsistent, restrictive or imprecise. Until 1881 the shades of Wellington and the Prince Consort had frowned down any suggestion that the Cross might be awarded for an act of duty. It took someone as senior and well-connected as the Duke of Cambridge, commander-in-chief of the army and cousin to the Queen, to challenge that view. He did so by forwarding to the War Office a recommendation that he conceded did not come within the terms of the Warrant. At Shahjui during the Second Afghan War (1878–80) Captain Euston Sartorius of the 59th Foot had led a small party to attack an unknown number of enemy on an almost inaccessible hilltop. The precipitous nature of the ground prevented deployment and dictated the use of a pathway. As Sartorius was in the lead the attention of the seven defenders fell first on him. He received sword cuts to both hands, but the hilltop was taken. All the defenders were killed for the loss of one attacker. The Duke suggested that the Warrant be amended to make specific provision for such marked gallantry in the performance of an act of duty. The Secretary of State for War, Colonel Stanley, was cautious. He wanted to know from the Queen's secretary, Ponsonby, how Her Majesty would receive such a recommendation. He was told that the Queen approved in principle, subject to seeing details before a formal submission was made. The civil servant charged with formulating the proposal, Colonel Deedes, considered making the Duke's suggestion the only criterion, doing away entirely with acts of valour and devotion to country. That, he said, would prevent men 'going out of their way' to win the Cross, but it would also exclude a truly gallant act done at great personal risk 'such as Kavanagh did at Lucknow', which was well beyond the requirements of duty. Deedes therefore preferred an incremental approach: the Duke's formula could simply be added to the existing criteria. The Queen approved and interdepartmental consultation on the wording began. It opened a floodgate. Inertia, hitherto friend to the status quo, now carried matters downstream. Those consulted pointed to out-of-date references in the original Warrant and, in Deedes's words, to interpretations where 'the Statutes have been stretched more than once'. What began as a half-line amendment became a root-and-branch revision of the entire document.[1]

This was not what the Queen had approved and when it reached her desk she was not amused. She was perplexed at having to consider, in Ponsonby's words, 'regulations for the purpose of rewarding those who break regulations' (i.e. acting without orders, and thereby beyond the requirements of duty). He went on:

> The original statutes were drawn up under the supervision of the Prince Consort and The Queen's [wish] is that these should remain as they are with all their imperfections – for under them every sort of person has been rewarded and plenty of loopholes existed through which doubtful cases were lugged in.[2]

On the face of it, Victoria (or Ponsonby) was complaining that the redraft highlighted rather than relieved the tension between initiative and duty that had existed since the Cross was first instituted.

Apart from her sensitivity about trifling with Albert's statutes, Victoria's chief concern was that the proposed changes would greatly expand the number of awards. Logic was on her side; if military discipline counted for anything, it was to be expected that far more gallant acts would be performed under orders than by the exercise of individual initiative. The number of awards, she told Ponsonby, was already too large. She was probably thinking of Rorke's Drift. On the morning of 22 January 1879 Zulus had obliterated the British camp at Isandhlwana in Natal while General Chelmsford's column was absent. Ten miles away at Rorke's Drift, a field hospital and depot containing 137 men, mainly from D Company, 2nd Battalion, 24th Foot, received word of the disaster only half an hour before a force of 4,000 Zulus arrived to complete the annihilation. In a desperate twelve-hour defence the garrison, which included many sick and wounded, saw off the attack. Some of the combat was at close quarters, bayonet against assegai.

James Dalton (centre right) distributing ammunition at Rorke's Drift.

The VC Warrant provided that in actions involving not less than fifty personnel, the men themselves could select recipients. If the unit was of company strength, officers would choose one of their number, the NCOs one of theirs, and the privates another two. For D Company that would have produced four VCs. Instead it received seven, all awarded for individual acts. A further four were awarded to men attached from other units or corps, the result being that 8 per cent of the whole garrison and 11 per cent of the effectives received the decoration, by far the highest proportion of participants in any fifty-plus unit action before or since.

Political considerations were a factor. The heroic defence deflected some of the criticism directed against the government for an ill-considered and under-prepared imperial venture; apologies to Her Majesty, but the more medals the better. The Rorke's Drift defenders were disproportionately recognized partly because so few of their regimental comrades had survived. There is no hint in the records that the individual awards for Rorke's Drift aroused the resentment of comrades who were also there, most of whom would have been called on to make similar heroic efforts. The desperation of self-preservation was common that day, as none could have been in the slightest doubt that the consequence of defeat was death. What set most of the recipients apart was their selflessness in assisting others at additional personal risk. Six of those cited were involved with removing patients from the hospital while under close attack. In the circumstances, election by the soldiers might well have produced the same names, but for fewer awards. Election, as Albert seemed to recognize, was a means of limiting the number of medals awarded under rules that otherwise allowed for recognition of an unlimited number of courageous acts.

A belated VC was awarded to Acting Assistant Commissary James Dalton. He received it several months after gazettal of those for officers John Chard and Gonville Bromhead and the redcoats of the 24th. It would not have been awarded at all without a public campaign that was drawn to the attention of Parliament.[3] A comparison of Dalton's citation with the earlier one for Chard and Bromhead hints at the issue. The officers had been praised for gallant conduct, fine example and excellent behaviour; successful defence was attributed to their exercise of command. Dalton, on the other hand, had 'actively superintended the work of defence', and it was to his energy 'that much of the defence ... was due'. Others who had been present were even more emphatic. It was Dalton who had forcefully argued against what would have been a doomed attempt to retreat to Helpmakkar. It was he who urged that they should fortify the Drift and explained how it could be done using his transport wagons and bags of mealie. He had also distinguished himself in the fighting, drawing on his former experience as sergeant major in a line regiment. The army found it awkward to acknowledge that an experienced non-com might contribute more to command than officers. When the Dalton recommendation came to the Duke of Cambridge for approval he commented that 'we are giving the VC very freely, I think', but this was probably less a reflection on Dalton's merits than exasperation at the tally for Rorke's Drift.[4]

Election by peers had one undeniable advantage. It implied that all were potentially deserving and that a formula governing the number of awards was the only limiting factor. Such awards could be thought of as representative, with every man sharing the glory as they had shared the danger.[5] It was, after all, unit cohesion that had saved D Company: in the fraught atmosphere it might have taken no more than a handful of men to break for panic to have set in. During the Second World War, a Canadian general defined a 'good' award as one with which the troops agreed.[6] Although it runs counter to the prevailing doctrine of rewarding only individuals, there is also a case to be made for an equivalent unit award.[7] D Company would have been a prime candidate.

Appended to the gazette notice that announced the initial awards for Rorke's Drift was a memorandum concerning 'the disaster at Isandlwanha'. Lieutenants Teignmouth Melvill and Nevill Coghill of the 24th Foot had been killed attempting to save the Queen's colour. The memorandum said that they would have been recommended for the Victoria Cross, but death had rendered them ineligible. To some their actions appeared to be an attempt to cloak dishonour with honour. Their duty was to their men, not to a piece of bunting. General Wolseley, who succeeded Chelmsford, was privately scathing of these two and of most of those who were awarded for Rorke's Drift:

> Heroes have been made of men like Melville (*sic*) and Coghill who taking advantage of their having horses bolted from the scene of action to save their lives … it is monstrous making heroes of those who saved or attempted to save their lives by bolting or of those who shut up in the building at Roorke's (*sic*) drift could not bolt & fought like rats for their lives which they could not otherwise save.[8]

In the end, the 1881 revision was minor. As noted above, it restated that deeds had to be performed in the presence of the enemy. It also extended eligibility to auxiliary and reserve forces. The wording suggested by the Duke of Cambridge had fallen by the wayside: 'conspicuous bravery', elevated from rule 6, replaced 'signal act of valour' in rule 5. Devotion to country remained as another qualification, but there was no mention of acts of duty. Nothing in the revision seemed to have made Sartorius any more eligible than he had been previously, but he was nonetheless awarded the Cross. The citation declared that he had qualified on the grounds of conspicuous bravery alone.

The change presented Sir Evelyn Wood VC with a dilemma. Two years earlier he had successfully recommended two awards for an action – strictly a retreat – fought at Inhlobane during the Zulu War. He had also considered another for a deed that closely paralleled that of Sartorius, but he had decided that it fell outside the provisions of the warrant. Like Sartorius, Lieutenant Henry Lysons of the Cameronians had attacked up a narrow defile, in his case to reach Zulus occupying a cave. Lysons's parents had subsequently lobbied furiously on his behalf and Lady Lysons assured Wood that the Duke of Cambridge himself had told her that the boy should have been recommended. The Duke's view had at least the virtue of consistency, but Wood was uneasy. He explained to the military secretary that he could not recommend Lysons without doing the same for Private Edmond Fowler, who had accompanied him. Both men had been members of Wood's personal escort and had volunteered to support Captain Campbell of the Coldstream Guards, who was leading the assault in single file when he was killed. Had he survived, Woods said, it was Campbell who would have been recommended for the Cross.[9] Was this a hint that the Queen might be expected to have reservations about making two more awards for a retreat, the more so as at least one of the candidates was alive courtesy of a dead man who had taken upon himself the primary risk? Horse Guards waved the paperwork through. The revisers had managed to create another loophole, this one not even visible, through which doubtful cases could be lugged.[10]

In the meantime, there had been indications that to reward any act relevant to duty might have adverse implications for morale. When Lieutenant Dick-Cunyngham of the 92nd Foot had seen his regiment wavering under attack at Sherpur Pass, Afghanistan, on 13 December 1879, he had ridden to the head, exposing himself to the full fire of the enemy. He rallied the Highlanders and led their charge into the middle of the opposing mass. The commander, now Sir Frederick ('Bobs') Roberts VC, mentioned him in a dispatch and that prompted a recommendation. It was not long before the War Office received an anonymous letter, signed 'A Witness To What Happened', which should have given it pause.

> If [Dick-Cunyngham] is recommended for the Victoria Cross for doing what any other officer would have done in like circumstances then the Cross is not worth striving for. Ask for the opinion of his brother officers.[11]

There is no evidence that any such opinion-gathering was undertaken. The letter was filed away and Dick-Cunyngham was awarded the Cross for 'conspicuous gallantry and coolness', but the influence of views like those of 'A Witness' can be seen in the absence of any reference to duty in the 1881 Warrant, an absence that was probably at least partly to blame for the confusion when General Buller VC came to make recommendations following the action at Colenso in 1899. His own decoration had been one of the two recommended by Wood in 1879 for

Inhlobane, where he had rescued three dismounted men of the Frontier Light Horse. That had been a display of initiative, a voluntary act. Had he been ordered to undertake the rescue, that would have made it his duty. By his reading, if the 1881 Warrant had been in force in 1879 an order would have made him ineligible, hence his position on an award for Schofield. He did not alter his view even after the military secretary advised him that that the new formulation was held to permit awards for marked gallantry in the performance of duty.[12] Buller, like all soldiers, expected instructions to be clear; in warfare lives depend on it. If that is what was intended, why didn't the Warrant say so?

Chapter 10

Brave by Choice

Aristotle's dictum – that when faced with annihilation the driving force is desperation rather than courage – lacks nuance. After all, putting oneself in harm's way for a cause is courageous even if the fight itself becomes no more than an animal struggle for survival, and this raises the question of deliberation. Aristotle conceded that the most natural form of courage was that inspired by spirit or anger, but held that it could only be called true courage when it involved deliberate choice and purpose. Major General Floyer-Acland, who was military secretary in 1941, was of the same opinion. When a sergeant of the King's African Rifles was put up for a posthumous award for attacking a succession of Italian tanks in Abyssinia, a majority of VC Committee members was supportive, but Floyer-Acland disagreed.

> Although Sergeant Leakey certainly displayed great gallantry I regard his action as of the spontaneous nature, lacking the elements of long-sustained courage and endurance which tell of the highest form of self-sacrifice.[1]

The King upheld Floyer-Acland's objection and Nigel Leakey's achievement went unrewarded until after the war, when the recommendation was resubmitted with 'further and important details' and the King approved. The citation described it as a remarkable feat and emphasized that Leakey's valour was on display 'throughout the action'.[2] There is no support for Floyer-Acland's position in the Warrant, which makes no distinction between deliberate and spontaneous acts.

Once imagination has been factored in, as required by Moran and Slim, the deliberate courageous act becomes more difficult. Deliberation gives the imagination time to conjure up fear. The more fear there is, the greater the courage needed to overcome it. It is difficult to act when a vivid imagination is forcefully bringing to your attention the probability of dire consequences. Consider Temporary Second Lieutenant Cecil Knox of the Royal Engineers. A civil engineer by profession, on 22 March 1918 he was tasked with demolishing twelve bridges over the Somme Canal to slow the German advance on Amiens. He successfully blew eleven of them, but the time fuse failed on the twelfth. Without hesitation Knox left cover under heavy fire and made for the charge set under the bridge. He lit the instantaneous fuse with German troops already on the structure, making it highly likely that he would be either shot or blown up as he tried to make his escape. As the citation for his VC drily noted, 'this was an act of the highest devotion to duty, entailing the gravest risk, which, as a practical engineer, he fully realized'.[3] Knox's is one of only a few citations in which the writer presumes to know the mental state of the recipient. In most cases we are dependent on what the recipient chooses to tell us. One of the best documented cases is among the more recent.

On 11 June 2010 Corporal Ben Roberts-Smith of the Australian Special Air Service, second-in-command of his patrol, was airlifted into Tazik on a capture-or-kill operation in Afghanistan. The patrol advanced through a fig plantation until forced to ground by three machine guns firing through crenellations cut into the top of a mud-brick wall. Roberts-Smith and two other troopers were halted at the edge of the plantation's scanty cover about twenty metres from the wall. Roberts-Smith was slightly less exposed than the others and under covering fire threw a grenade that missed. Had it been effective in at least temporarily suppressing the enemy's fire, the standard drill called for the group to charge the position. Instead, the ineffective grenade encouraged the gunners to concentrate their fire on the group, again driving it to ground. The sergeant commanding the patrol was more successful with a second grenade and eliminated one of the guns. Another shifted targets but the third, supported by two Taliban armed with Kalashnikov assault rifles, was still active. Bullets struck the rocks in front of Roberts-Smith but the gunner's attention was focused on the other troopers. Again it came down to the drill.

> At that point you have one of those moments where you think 'now I'm supposed to go'. Everything in me was screaming 'don't go!' because it wasn't like the training scenario and

they were still firing. But then what overrides that is it's not about you, it's bigger than you. You don't think about the odds, you just think 'I can get there. I can do it.' I didn't weigh everything up, but I thought I could probably get there. I knew if I don't go now someone's going to get hit, and they would have. The other blokes couldn't go. I had the cover. As shitty as it was, it was better than they had. You're not going to sit there and watch your mates die. The bottom line is, if I sit here now someone will get hit. I would rather that it be me than for me to come home and have to see their families. I've done that before and I never want to do it again. You can't possibly fathom how bad you feel losing a mate, and that's nothing compared to how the wife feels or their kids. Do you want to be the one who lives with that forever – that I could have done something? At that point I decided I'd had enough. The fact is, it took two seconds for everything to go through my head and then to think 'Fuck, I can do it, it's 50:50. I've got as much chance as he has'. I stood up and I remember looking at the wall and your adrenalin is going. The only thing in my head was 'you've got to get to the wall'.[4]

It was a toss-up. The two men with Kalashnikovs broke and ran before Roberts-Smith had taken three steps (he is a very big man). He reached a gap in the wall a few metres to the right of the gunner. The coin was still in the air. The Afghan tried to swing his weapon in Roberts-Smith's direction but was too slow. With the wall cleared, the three Australians were able to charge through the position and kill several more insurgents.

The imperative of a drill can be read as a call to duty; imagination, arguing for self-preservation, was looking for excuses to ignore it. The focus on reaching the wall was the same fixity of purpose that had been displayed by Ganju Lama in getting his PIAT within range of the Japanese tanks. Roberts-Smith claimed not to have 'weighed everything up' but he had; it had taken him all of two seconds, but in that eternity rashness had been denied and what followed was a premeditated act. It was a textbook Victoria Cross, but Prince Albert would have been mildly disappointed that Roberts-Smith had been thinking about his mates rather than the mission. It was unrealistic to have expected otherwise; the medal they pinned to his uniform jacket says 'for valour', but the tattoo on his chest reads 'I will not fail my brothers'. In the judgement of a fellow special forces soldier who knew him well, Roberts-Smith would have charged the wall even if the odds had been against survival.[5]

As a boy Roberts-Smith had been taken to the Australian War Memorial, where he was particularly impressed with the Victoria Cross citations. For him the stories were 'awesome' heroic reality, thereby amply rewarding the founders' hopes that the decoration would be prized and sought after. That inspirational aspect has been under-emphasized in recent years. Roberts-Smith's unexpurgated account is compelling, but the same cannot be said of his citation, which records but does not describe 'most conspicuous gallantry and daring in the face of the enemy while in circumstances of extreme peril'.[6]

Roberts-Smith calculated his chances as 50:50. In some cases they have been much poorer. On 21 November 1965 Lance Corporal Rambahadur Limbu, 10th Princess Mary's Own Ghurka Rifles, was with his company when they discovered an Indonesian platoon entrenched on a ridge on the Sarawak side of the Borneo border. Rambahadur killed a sentry and established a one-man foothold in the all but unassailable position. He gathered his fire group and advanced it to a better firing position. While reporting to his platoon commander he saw that two members of the group had been wounded. Under intense fire from point-blank range he returned and carried them in one at a time. He recovered their light machine gun and killed four more enemy as they attempted to escape across the border. Those who witnessed the action were incredulous that in full view of the enemy and under sustained aimed automatic fire for twenty minutes he had not been hit. The VC citation writer devoted a page and a half of the *Gazette* to a description of the action. He channelled Aristotle and did not skimp on superlatives. The Ghurka's actions had reached

> a zenith of determined, premeditated valour which must count amongst the most notable on record and is deserving of the greatest admiration and the highest praise.'[7]

The writer called it an incomparable example for his comrades: without Rambahadur's inspired conduct much less would have been achieved with greater casualties.

Rambadahur's had been the first Cross won by a British soldier since the Korean War and attracted enormous attention. When the little Ghurka visited the London Stock Exchange the trading was interrupted for three minutes by a standing ovation. In retrospect it was a model award that ticked most boxes. Prince Albert would have been pleased that the lance corporal's actions were central to military success. He might even have been prepared to concede that saving wounded under such extreme circumstances was important for morale, the *sine qua non* of unit effectiveness. The great unknown is the state of Rambadahur's mind; if he felt fear he did not show it, nor allow it to interfere with what he saw as personal responsibility for his men. Would he have agreed with the citation's description of his survival as miraculous? If so, did he feel that he was under supernatural protection? The message of his award was that no matter how impossible the situation, if you do what the circumstances require then providence or luck might still bring you through. Flashman would have agreed.

Chapter 11

England Expects

At Trafalgar Nelson had famously expected that every man would do his duty. Some of those men were mere boys, and juvenile enlistment remained a feature of naval recruitment until well into the twentieth century. Australians being towed ashore in the first wave at Gallipoli, heads down under enemy fire, were amazed to see British midshipmen coolly standing at the stern of towing launches, piping orders in voices that had hardly broken.

Boy Cornwell stood to his post although mortally wounded.

Jack Cornwell, boy first class, was sixteen years old and serving in the cruiser HMS *Chester* when it fought at Jutland. Cornwell's post was at a partly-shielded gun that remained inactive because it could not be brought to bear on the enemy. Early in the engagement it was swept by shell splinters, which killed or wounded all but two of its crew. Cornwell continued to stand alone and exposed at his station, mortally wounded, awaiting orders or relief as he had been trained to do. In a dispatch reporting the battle Admiral Beatty recommended the boy for special recognition, to acknowledge his example, but did not mention a Victoria Cross. Jutland had been a missed opportunity for the Royal Navy and a disappointment for a public expecting another Trafalgar. Cornwell died in Grimsby two days after the action, but his story went around the fleet and then around the country. It was not to be expected that generations of Englishmen who could recite by heart Mrs Hemans's poem *Casabianca* (the boy who stood on the burning deck awaiting his father's permission to leave) would be unmoved. Cornwell's corpse was exhumed from its mean grave and reburied in London.

A painting was commissioned, with a copy to be placed in every school that contributed to the cost. Queen Mary hoped that it would remind scholars of the lasting glory that attaches to doing one's duty. When accepting the original, the First Lord of the Admiralty told his listeners that he had a message from Cornwell: 'Obey your orders, cling to your post, don't grumble, stick it out'.[1] Artist Frank Salisbury misrepresented the scene to suggest combat heroism: although Cornwell's gun had not been fired, the breech was shown open and smoking. The boy's example was important as recruiting propaganda at a time when enlistments were in decline, but it was difficult to fit into the VC rules. He had clearly displayed devotion to duty, but that was expected of him. He had not absented himself from his post although mortally wounded, which was remarkable in one so young, but as it made no difference to the outcome (the gun remained out of action), what exactly was being rewarded? A conspicuous act of bravery, said the citation, which highlighted his youth and briefly outlined his situation after the gun was hit. There was no mention of duty. The epitaph above his grave referred to honourable conduct, but it was also exemplary conduct, encouraging a war-weary nation to continue the struggle. It gave force to the poet Milton's observation that 'they also serve who only stand and wait'. In a very similar incident, Ordinary Seaman John Carless was mortally wounded while acting as rammer at a gun on HMS *Caledon* during the battle of Heligoland Bight in November 1917. He had cleared casualties and tried to keep the gun in action until a relief crew arrived, after which he cheered it on until he collapsed and died. Again, the navy emphasized the inspirational aspect, while in this case being able to claim that the dying Carless had 'continued to do effective work against the King's enemies'.[2]

Public expectations also became an issue following the Battle of Britain. As the German effort fell away in the late autumn of 1940 the authorities were disconcerted to find that none of the Few had been awarded the Cross. Casting about, they went back two months to 16 August, when Flight Lieutenant Eric Nicolson of 249 Squadron had been flying his first combat patrol. His Hurricane had come under fire from a Messerschmitt 110 that wounded him and set his aircraft on fire. As he struggled to bail out, badly burnt, he saw another Messerschmitt nearby, returned to his seat and fired until the enemy fell away to crash. He then took to his parachute and descended painfully but safely. He was recommended for a DSO and was bemused to learn, months after the event, that he had been upgraded to a VC. Doubtless thinking of other pilots who had done as much and more for longer, he said 'now I'll have to earn it'. He was killed in 1945 in an aircraft ditching.[3]

Neither Cornwell nor Nicolson experienced the burden of post-conflict expectations that fell on those who lived to wear the Cross at home. It was understandable that ordinary people would be curious to the point of insensitivity to hear the circumstances from the men themselves, but there also seemed to be official expectations that a VC-winner should be present at most military occasions of honour. For many years there were enough winners to share the burden, but as their numbers thinned the calls made on the survivors increased. Keith Payne, the last surviving VC from Vietnam, was overjoyed when he heard in 2006 that Trooper Mark Donaldson, Australian Special Air Service, had been awarded the VC for saving a wounded Afghan interpreter during an ambush in Oruzgan province. At last, he said, there was someone to share the load.

Eric Nicolson baled out of his burning Hurricane after shooting down a Messerschmitt 110.

Chapter 12

Tally Ho

Eric Nicolson was the only fighter pilot to be awarded a VC for air-to-air combat in the Second World War. It was otherwise in the first war, when twelve scout pilots were honoured. The public was encouraged to hail them as chivalry reincarnated, great warriors enjoying the privilege of personalized warfare far removed from the anonymous slaughter taking place on the ground below. Many came from the cavalry and at its purest air combat was a joust, one on one, although the swirling all-in dogfights more resembled the mêleés that followed a medieval tournament's individual contests. Like the mêlee, aerial contests lacked any notion of fair play. The tactic was to stalk the enemy from up-sun, manoeuvre behind or below his tail (which was difficult to achieve if you had been spotted) and stay there firing until he went down. Captain James McCudden acknowledged the unpleasant reality that this was war by ambush:

> I hate to shoot a Hun down without him seeing me, for although this method is in accordance with my doctrine, it is against what little sporting instincts I have left.[1]

Many of the VCs went to high-scoring aces like McCudden but some were a reward for single feats of airmanship. Two were almost epitomes of knightly values, involving as they did the exercise of arms to defend civilians in distress. Far more than material damage, the airship raids on England that began in 1915 had the potential to severely depress civilian morale and against this new threat the authorities were initially helpless. Interception at night was extremely difficult and although the airships were highly flammable, tracer rounds were found to be ineffective. The first airship to be brought down by an aircraft was returning from a failed raid when it was intercepted over Belgium by Flight Sub Lieutenant Reginald Warneford on 7 June 1915. With no confidence in his gun

COURAGE
INITIATIVE INTREPIDITY
FLIGHT-SUB-LIEUT-REGINALD
ALEXANDER-JOHN-WARNEFORD
V.C.R.N.A.S.-BORN-15-OCT-1891
ACCIDENTALLY-KILLED-17-JUNE-1915

Warneford's monument in Brompton Cemetery, London, commends his courage, initiative and intrepidity.

ammunition he flew above the Zeppelin and dropped several small bombs on it, the last of which set it afire. Not only did he get the VC the following day, but Warneford's method was also recommended to other interceptor pilots, improvisation filling the gap while effective ammunition was being developed. He did not live to see it, an aircraft accident claiming him ten days after his success.

Explosive rather than incendiary rounds were thought to be the answer and on the night of 2/3 September 1916 Lieutenant William Robinson got an opportunity to use them. On patrol over London he saw airship SL 11 illuminated by searchlight. By the time he got within firing range he was above Cuffley in Hertfordshire. Strafing the length of the airship in two passes at a range of 800 feet produced no result, so he directed his third drum of explosive ammunition at a single point from 500 feet below. The airship caught fire and fell to earth, watched by large numbers of people. Robinson's own aircraft had sustained considerable damage from the airship's machine guns.

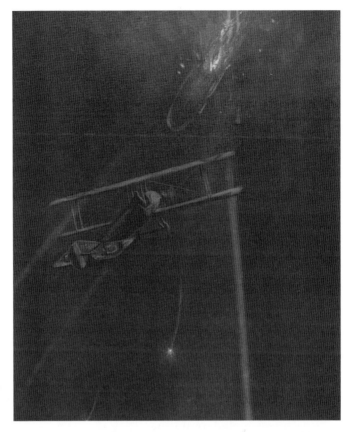

William
Robinson brings
down a Baby
Killer.

It was a triumph for the boffins, but boffins are not hero material. It was Robinson who had demonstrated that the 'Baby Killer' could be slain, and he had done so before an audience of its intended victims. Gratitude followed relief. If the War Office had reservations about awarding the VC for performance of duty it did not show; the decoration was gazetted two days later, citing most conspicuous bravery. It is difficult to see how the department could have resisted when it was clear that a range of civilian organizations would be presenting Robinson with rewards they had promised for this very achievement. He received £4,200 in total, was presented with a silver cup and found himself very popular with young West End actresses. The War Office quickly prohibited the acceptance of monetary rewards for the future and within a short space of time it became apparent that the Victoria Cross was also off the table.[2] Two more Zeppelins were brought down in the following month, but the victorious pilots had to settle for Distinguished Service Orders (and silver cups).

Another complication for those managing warfare in the air was of their own making. The ethos of the tournament engendered just as much competitiveness as it had in medieval times, but in respect of the Victoria Cross it was of no consequence while awards were for single feats of bravery. That changed when Temporary Captain Albert Ball was shot down and killed near Cambrai on 7 May 1917. His achievements to that date had been recognized by three awards of the DSO and a Military Cross. He had been recommended for the Victoria Cross but the recommendation had been downgraded to the third DSO. He was acknowledged as the leading fighter pilot of the Royal Flying Corps and had been a household name for months. The citation for his Victoria Cross credited him with forty-three aircraft and one balloon destroyed. He was said to have displayed most exceptional courage, determination and skill. Death precluded the award of a fourth DSO for the eleven victories that had followed his third. The only way to acknowledge them posthumously, other than by Mention in Dispatches, was with a VC, but by awarding one to Ball the War Office was inadvertently signalling that the highest decoration of all could be earned by piling up victories. Although Major Lanoe Hawker's VC had been awarded specifically for three victories on a single day in July 1915, by the time his decoration was gazetted he had become the first British pilot to achieve unofficial 'ace' status (five kills), creating a nexus in the minds of those interested in such things, including William Bishop.

Four other high-scoring aces were subsequently awarded the Cross. McCudden, the reluctant but resigned assassin, received one when his tally stood at fifty-two. The citation mentioned two recent 'examples' of success, but concluded by pointing to his overall record, fearlessness and great service as deserving of the highest honour. He was killed in an aircraft accident two months later, on 9 July 1918. His death deeply affected his close friend Major Edward Mannock, who by June 1918 had also been credited with more than fifty victories and had won three DSOs. After McCudden's death, it was remarked that Mannock became more ruthless and took more risks. He declared that he would avenge his friend.[3] On one occasion, having damaged a German two-seater, he followed it down until it crashed. He then strafed the wreckage, killing the crew. This was contrary to his own dictum about never risking ground fire by going down to confirm a victory, and he did it again on 25 July. While circling low over a downed DFW two-seater he was hit by machine-gun fire from the ground and crashed in flames. Like Achilles, hero of the *Iliad*, Mannock had allowed the war to become personal. Achilles was killed when an angry god exploited his weakness: Mannock's vulnerability came from allowing wrath to override discretion.

Ball's award had created a precedent for posthumously rewarding high tallies with a VC; McCudden's VC had widened the precedent to include the living. The names of William Barker and Andrew Beauchamp-Proctor, Canadian and South African respectively, were gazetted on the same day at war's end. Both had lived to record more than fifty victories. This had the appearance of acknowledging a benchmark, but Donald MacLaren, a Canadian who had scored fifty-four, ended the war with no more than a belated DSO. It cannot be assumed that had Billy Bishop been patient his name would have been up there, even had his final claimed score of seventy-two been beyond question. This was the context in which Mannock's tally, augmented but still unrewarded after his most recent DSO, had to be reassessed for final recognition. Friends who thought that he deserved a VC sought confirmation of as many victories as possible. The Minister for Air, Winston Churchill, initiated an investigation that produced a figure of exactly fifty victories, fewer than Mannock had already been credited with at the time he was awarded his third DSO.[4] Technically, he had already been rewarded for more kills than he had made. His VC, gazetted almost a year after his death, was therefore an overall career award reinforced by, but not dependent on, tally. The citation praised a record of courage, skill, devotion to duty and self-sacrifice 'which has never been surpassed'. And for fighter pilots it never would be: no British ace of the Second World War got close to fifty kills.

Cumulative awards continued in the second war, but there was only one for a flier and that went to a senior officer in Bomber Command. This was uncharted terrain. A valiant pilot in a single-seat fighter was easy to fit into the VC rules. The pilot of a bomber, on the other hand, was a leader. Was it appropriate to single him out for reward when all in the aircraft or formation would have shared the risk and contributed to any act of valour? And the more senior the leader, the more rarified his responsibilities, even if they did not preclude valiant acts. There is no evidence that the RAF considered elective or representative awards as a means of addressing the question. Indeed, it chose for its only cumulative award a pilot who was probably the most unrepresentative officer in the RAF, and one for whom his peers would never have voted.

Group Captain Geoffrey Cheshire was a particularly difficult man to manage. His 1942 book *Bomber Pilot* had offended many in the RAF, not least because a tabloid had printed extracts under headlines like 'How I Conquered Fear'. By 1944 he had survived four tours of duty, a total of 100 bombing missions, and had fiercely resisted desk jobs at the end of each tour. On one occasion he had sought the intervention of Sir John Symonds, the distinguished neurologist advising the RAF on flying stress, asking him to certify that Cheshire's nervousness was caused by too little operational flying rather than too much. Symonds surmised that he was dealing with a brilliant eccentric whose ability to deal with risk was atypical. Between fearlessness and positive courage – the latter being defined as the overcoming of fear for the sake of achieving an object – Symonds assessed Cheshire as being 90 per cent fearless and only 10 per cent courageous.

> Cheshire, although an acutely sensitive and introspective man, seemed as completely immune from apprehension as the most phlegmatic and unimaginative types, with whom the stolid quality of fearlessness is invariably associated. He had the heart of a lion and the incisive brain of the practical planner, so that risks appeared to him as impersonal obstacles to be overcome. He had the foresight courage gives with none of the fearfulness beforehand.[5]

Cheshire had much the same understanding of the distinction between the courageous and the fearless and counted himself among the latter, but he added another element to the mix.

> Two men may attend the same briefing and listen to the same intelligence report. One may conjure up a vivid picture of the defences, of what it will mean when they open up, and of how heavily the odds will be stacked against him; the other gives no thought to this, he may only be thinking what a beautiful sight it will be when the target goes up in smoke, as go it surely will. The former will require a hundred times more courage than the latter, but it will be the latter, almost certainly, who will bring off the more spectacular result. But even then only if luck is on his side.

Without luck even the bravest would not win honours. That fact, he wrote, should console the unlucky and remind the winners that the credit is not entirely theirs. Indulging the mystical side of his nature, Cheshire went on to query whether Fortune was really blind or 'has her own mysterious designs, too deep for human mind to fathom'.[6] His VC citation referred to a cold and calculated acceptance of risk over four years of operations, which none could deny was evidence of extraordinary devotion to duty. Unfortunately, the RAF felt a need to gild the lily by instancing an act of valour, and the one it chose to highlight was the Munich raid of 24 April 1944, a triumph for Cheshire's innovative low-level target-marking. This was seen by the leaders of the Pathfinder force as a reflection on their high-level marking. Even Cheshire's commander was of the view that another squadron had subsequently mastered the low approach with better results. This was just RAF politics, but the citation included a statement that to demonstrate the concept Cheshire had selected Munich for its strong low-level defences, through which he continued to fly 'until he was satisfied that he had done all in his power to ensure success'.[7] In fact, shortage of fuel had forced his Mosquitoes to leave the scene immediately after marking. The statement hardened some of his peers in the view that Cheshire was often given, or took, more than his share of any credit going. A more valid criticism would have been that the multiple runs Cheshire usually made to provide the best possible aiming point left the main force vulnerable to attack while waiting its turn. If anything, what the main force would have preferred was no more than five minutes of courage from Cheshire. The contretemps was well short of a Bishop-level bruising, but it did point up the difficulty of justifying a VC for anything other than a single act of valour.

Paradoxically, a cumulative record like Cheshire's was what Portal, chief of the air staff, seemed to be looking for when he was asked to consider a VC for Sergeant James Ward, RNZAF. When his Wellington bomber was attacked by a night fighter that set fire to the starboard wing, Ward had volunteered to attend to the flames. He had climbed on to the wing, breaking hand and foot holes in the fabric, and partly succeeded before the engine cover that he had been using as a fire blanket was blown from his grasp. He returned to the fuselage and the fire burnt itself out. Portal admired the courage displayed but …

I must say I think the VC should more often be given to a man who displayed exceptional valour in getting himself *into* great danger, than to one who shows equal bravery in getting *out* of the kind of desperate situation which is latent in all air operations. The first type knowingly raises the odds against himself in the pursuit of his duty, whereas in the latter type of case the motive of self-preservation may sometimes dominate his actions.[8]

Nevertheless, Ward had volunteered and he had saved six lives and the aircraft. He got the VC, although the Air Member for Personnel held that a Distinguished Flying Medal would have been more appropriate.

The Royal Navy's only cumulative award was for a submariner. When Commander John Linton and the *Turbulent* were lost with all hands off Italy in March 1943, the twenty-three posthumous awards for the crew included a VC for Linton. Reference was made to his service since the outbreak of war in 1939 and tallied his achievements: 100,000 tons of shipping sunk and three trains destroyed by gunfire. It also described the

James Ward climbed onto a wing to fight a fire near the engine.

hazards; in 1942 alone *Turbulent* had been hunted thirteen times and subjected to 250 depth charges. Superficially imperturbable, Linton let it slip that he was not immune to fear. He once asked his first lieutenant if he got crinkles in his fingernails when the boat was being depth-charged. 'I get them', he said. 'It's because you're scared stiff'.[9]

As submitted, the recommendation detailed no specific exploit like Cheshire's Munich raid. Instead it sought recognition for a career of conspicuous gallantry and, using the words of the 1920 Warrant, 'extreme devotion to duty in the presence of the enemy'. The navy was then asked to submit an example. It chose a night attack that Linton had carried out against a four-ship convoy. He had manoeuvred to get ahead of the ships, where the moon would be behind them, and held his aim and his nerve although a destroyer was coming down his throat. He sank two merchantmen and one of the destroyers. The exploit was featured in the citation but no date was given, probably because it would have raised questions. It had occurred ten months before *Turbulent* was lost. During the intervening period Linton had been given the DSO for 'courage and skill in successful submarine patrols'. In other words, the commander had already been given as much recognition for the cited exploit as the Admiralty thought that Linton alive deserved. There were other successful patrols after the DSO, but it is near certain that without another dramatic exploit any additional recognition that Linton might have received had he lived would not have taken the form of a VC. The authorities were clearly concerned that a citation couched in generalities about a career would invite a flood of applications, but the specific exploit with which they chose to head off the possibility undermined the logic of Linton's award.

The Admiralty had only itself to blame for this difficulty, which it had inadvertently created with its handling of an earlier award. Like Linton, Lieutenant Commander Malcolm Wanklyn was the commander of a submarine that operated in the Mediterranean. He was more successful than Linton and his overall record had been mentioned in the citation for the VC that he was awarded for sinking a heavily escorted troop-ship on 24 May 1941. Unusually, the citation also made a point of mentioning that he had earlier been awarded the DSO and had since torpedoed a tanker and a merchantman as well as the troop-ship. In other words, the VC was for additional successes, the one against the troop-ship being particularly noteworthy. Like Linton, Wanklyn and his submarine were subsequently lost with all hands. Unlike Linton, he already had a VC. For Linton to get one, the Admiralty was forced to imply that his successes after the DSO were on a par with Wanklyn's, which they were not.

Bomber pilots and submarine commanders had little scope for singular valiant acts. Their qualification came from VC-grade devotion to duty, which is what it took to sortie repeatedly in almost defenceless metal coffins, knowing that with each departure the odds against returning had shortened further. In both cases it was leadership that was being acknowledged, but in terms of risk as much was being expected of crews as of captains, and often the death of one meant the death of all. If a VC was appropriate recognition, why not for the entire crew?

VC awards based on cumulative tallies were almost unknown in the army, but there was a notable exception. During the Crete disaster of 1941 Sergeant Alfred Hulme, New Zealand Military Forces, became a sniper-stalker. On 20 May he began eliminating snipers around Maleme airstrip. Between 22 and 24 May he continually went out with one or two men and on 27 May stalked and killed five snipers that had positioned themselves overlooking Suda Bay. On the 28th, after eliminating a mortar position, he killed three snipers who were threatening the rearguard. He was severely wounded while stalking another. By then his tally was thirty-three, an achievement highlighted in the citation.

Alfred Hulme was the nemesis of German snipers on Crete.

Chapter 13

The Politics of Empire

In the nineteenth century all of Britain's settler colonies to a greater or lesser extent suffered from an inferiority complex when it came to the mother country. Admiration tinged with resentment was the prevailing sentiment. Although colonials had served in their own formed units in some of Victoria's little wars, the Second Boer War provided the first large-scale opportunity for the colonies to prove the mettle of their soldiers alongside (and by comparison with) British units. The British Army was initially disconcerted by Boer free-ranging mounted tactics that its own cavalry, less agile and more dependent on supply columns, had difficulty countering. What the army needed were Boer equivalents and it looked to the settler colonies, Australia, Canada and New Zealand in particular, to provide them. The colonial mounted units proved their worth and more than met the expectations of those who had dispatched them.

Three Victoria Crosses were gazetted on 4 October 1901. One went to Lieutenant William English of the 2nd Scottish Horse for resupplying his men with ammunition by crossing open ground under intense short-range fire at Vlakfontein. The other recipients were colonials. Lieutenant Frederick Bell of the West Australian Mounted Infantry, while retiring in the face of heavy fire at Brakpan, had noticed a dismounted man and returned to pick him up. His horse was not up to the double load and fell. Bell stayed to provide cover until the rescued man was out of danger. The exploit of Farrier Major William Hardham, 4th New Zealand Contingent, was similar: while his section was retiring from a position near Naauwpoort one of the troopers had been wounded and his horse killed. Under heavy fire Hardman put the man on his own horse and ran alongside, guiding it to safety. The Chief of Staff in South Africa, General Ian Hamilton, recommended the officers for DSOs and Hardman for its non-commissioned equivalent, the Distinguished Conduct Medal.

Hamilton had personal experience of being on the wrong side of a fence when it came to the Victoria Cross. He had been recommended while a brigade commander against the Boers, but denied on the grounds that the Cross had never been awarded to an officer of such high rank. He had not even been given the consolation of a bar to his DSO.

It was Hamilton's superior, Lord Kitchener, who upgraded the three recommendations to Victoria Crosses. When the recommendations came to Roberts, now commander-in-chief at Horse Guards and responsible for forwarding them to the War Office, he had a bob each way. He did not think that Kitchener would have so recommended unless he had been satisfied that it was deserved, but in addition: '… it seems to me desirable to show the colonials that we appreciate their gallantry and their coming forward to help us. We may require them to do so again perhaps ere long'.[1]

The same thinking was behind the arrangements made for presentation of the medals. The Prince of Wales, later George V, was to visit the troops in South Africa. He carried with him three Crosses and personally pinned the Englishman, the Australian and the New Zealander in a ceremony intended to demonstrate imperial solidarity. Roberts's concession paid off handsomely in the First World War and it is possible to read into the handling of Canadian Billy Bishop's case a similar concern for colonial goodwill. Such instances confound the popular prejudice, widely held in Australia at the time, that its forces always deserved more consideration than they were ever likely to get at the hands of the imperial authorities. The case of Private Keysor, however, might well have led the Australian government to subscribe to popular opinion.

Leonard Keysor was a son of Empire. Born in London, he spent ten years farming in Canada before joining siblings in New South Wales in 1914.[2] At the outbreak of war he joined the 1st Battalion, Australian Imperial Force, and took part in the Lone Pine assault at Gallipoli on 7–8 August 1915. For fifty hours, during which he was wounded twice, he threw bombs, smothered bombs and returned Turkish bombs. When the exasperated Turks shortened their fuses, he caught the bombs in the air 'just as if they were cricket balls' and bowled them back.[3] After he was awarded the Victoria Cross he wrote to the War Office to enquire when he might expect to receive the annuity that went with it. In response the War Office wrote to the Australian High Commissioner in London stating that all AIF charges were the responsibility of the

Leonard Keysor had better fortune returning Turkish bombs than in recreating his exploit for the camera after the war.

Australian government. The colonial secretary, Bonar Law, intervened. He was concerned to avoid anything 'which would prejudice the Imperial character of these decorations'. The War Office retorted that 'Imperial character' might be better preserved if the dominions paid the annuity. It lost that round, but was still reluctant to pay the annuity that went with the Distinguished Conduct Medal. Bonar Law was sufficiently concerned about the consequences for imperial relations that he took the matter to Prime Minister Lloyd George, who ruled that Britain should continue to be responsible for DCM annuities.[4] Keysor returned to Britain to marry after the war and drew his annuity there for more than thirty years.

By then the Empire was morphing into a Commonwealth of Nations and the arrangements for administering the Victoria Cross were constitutionally anomalous. If the Queen was the Queen of Australia, Canada, New Zealand and so on, in addition to being Queen of the United Kingdom, why was Whitehall allowed to filter the advice about decorations that came from the governments of her other realms? The issue was more theoretical than real until Vietnam, the first war in which dominions took part without Britain alongside. The Queen received recommendations from Australia to award four Victoria Crosses. They were referred, in accordance with the time-honoured process, to the Ministry of Defence. One in particular raised eyebrows. Warrant officers Kevin Wheatley and Ronald Swanton of the Australian Army Training Team Vietnam (AATTV) were with a platoon of South Vietnamese irregulars when it was ambushed in the Tra Bong valley. Swanton was hit in the chest. Discarding his rifle and radio, Wheatley dragged his mate 200 metres to cover under heavy fire. Urged to abandon the dying Swanton as the Viet Cong closed in, he refused and was last seen pulling the pins from two grenades. Two explosions and gunfire were heard. The men's bodies were recovered the following morning. The Palace pointed out that as worded the recommendation could be interpreted as describing a suicide pact. Enquiry of the Australian Army Liaison Officer elicited the information that both men had died of gunshot wounds. The recommendation was amended accordingly. Even so, a subsequent Ministry of Defence assessment doubted that the act was 'really to VC standard'.[5] The British were concerned that Australia was being too free with the Cross: all four had been won by a single unit, the AATTV, through which only 1,000 men had rotated during the entire war. They contrasted that with the 20,000 Commonwealth troops who won four VCs between them during the Korean War. A more relevant comparison would have been with the total of 60,000 Australians who served in Vietnam, awarded one VC per 15,000 as against one per 5,000 of the Commonwealth personnel awarded in Korea.

The creation of the 'Victoria Cross for Australia' and its Canadian and New Zealand equivalents during the 1990s ended the role of Whitehall in respect of non-British recommendations. Victoria, who had resented the erosion of her royal prerogative over honours and awards by British ministers, would have been pleased, but this was not restoration. Control over exercise of the prerogative had simply been transferred to Dominion ministers whose advice the Queen was equally bound to follow.

Chapter 14

Soldiers of the Queen

Only one foreign national has been awarded a Victoria Cross. His medal is inscribed to 'The Unknown Warrior of the United States of America' and was presented at Arlington National Cemetery in 1921 to reciprocate the Act of Congress that had awarded his British counterpart the Medal of Honour. There was an early attempt to have the Cross awarded to a French naval officer, M. Ducrest de Villeneuve, whose ship and marines had served alongside British units in putting down a West African rebellion in 1855. Panmure ruled that the VC Warrant did not allow for awards to foreigners, but in an empire on which the sun never set half the world was British. Soldiers of the Queen were recruited in her dominions from Bombay to Bulawayo and Montreal to Melbourne. Others, although from beyond the Empire, were not foreigners if they had taken the Queen's shilling.

The Irish always considered that they had been forcibly adopted into the imperial family. They had never served in numbers to rival the Scots and recruitment in the early days of the First World War was slow. Then Lance Corporal Michael O'Leary of the Irish Guards distinguished himself at Cuinchy. In the storming of a position he killed five Germans at the first barricade and three at the second, capturing it and taking two prisoners. In doing so he eliminated a machine gun that would otherwise have fired on the attacking party. The VC citation credited him with practically capturing the position by himself.[1]

The War Office promptly issued a recruitment poster designed to appeal to national pride. One Irishman was worth ten Germans, it said (to which the man in the Dublin pub would have added, 'and twenty English'). George Bernard Shaw thought that the appeal was misconceived and tried to say so. In *O'Flaherty VC*, subtitled *A Recruiting Poster*, he argued that it was poverty, not a thirst for glory, that drove Irishmen like him to leave home. Recruitment should emphasize the

Michael O'Leary
eliminates a
machine-gun post
unaided.

opportunities for looting the enemy and the separation allowance that
supported the families of servicemen in their absence. As for the VC,
the pension was more important than the decoration. Unsurprisingly,
the play went unperformed for the duration of the war except for an
outing by 40 Squadron's amateur dramatic society in Belgium in 1917.
O'Flaherty also had a distinctly unheroic take on what it took to win a
VC. He put it down to his mother, who had taught him to be more afraid
of running than of fighting.

> I was timid by nature; and when the other boys hurted
> me, I'd want to run away and cry. But she whaled me for
> disgracing the blood of the Flahertys until I'd have fought
> the divil himself sooner than face her after funking a fight
> … That's the way I came to be so courageous.[2]

The O'Leary poster was George Bernard Shaw's inspiration for *O'Flaherty VC*.

It was noted earlier that a revision of the VC Warrant in 1857 had extended eligibility to the officers and men of the East India Company's armies. There was no formal exclusion of native troops, but discrimination was at the very core of Indian army arrangements: no Indian, however senior in rank, could command Europeans. Separation in respect of decorations had been institutionalized in 1837 with the creation of the Indian Order of Merit, unavailable to British troops. It was awarded for conspicuous gallantry and the highest of its three grades attracted double pay. Depending on rank, the First Class was more generous than the VC annuity. Did this make the two decorations separate but equal? The question presented itself forcefully when the Government of Bombay recommended Lieutenant William Kerr and Daffadar (Sergeant)

Gunput Rao Derkur of the Southern Mahratta Irregular Horse for storming a mutineer fortification at Kolapur on 10 July 1857.

The two men had twice broken down doors to gain entry, together entered the breaches and had been lucky to avoid the concentrated fire directed at them. In a fierce hand-to-hand struggle Kerr would have been bayoneted had the daffadar not seized a musket and killed his assailant.

William Kerr and Gunput Rao Derkur – equal at the gate but not on the parade ground.

Outnumbered two to one, Kerr's seventeen-man party accounted for all the mutineers at the cost of twelve dead and the remainder wounded. The action effectively arrested the mutiny on the Malabar coast. The Governor General, Lord Canning, forwarded the recommendation but did not support a VC for Gunput Rao on the grounds that the Indian might thereby gain both Cross and Order, while Kerr was only eligible for the Cross. Sir Henry Storks, the Permanent Secretary at the War Office, thought that he detected racism and pointed out that the French did not discriminate against their non-European troops in awarding the Legion of Honour. For once Panmure did not decide the matter on his own authority. He took the matter to the cabinet, which sided with Canning.[3] When Kerr's Cross was gazetted there was no mention of the daffadar. He was just among 'some dismounted horsemen' who had helped Kerr force the gate.

It was a year before Indian affairs were sufficiently quiet for the decoration to be conferred. From on high it was intimated that the VC ceremony should

> … evince Her Majesty's sense of the noble daring displayed by Lieutenant Kerr before the enemy, to testify her wish that a distinction, in which the officer or private soldier may equally share, may be highly prized and eagerly sought after by all, of whatever rank or degree …, omitting nothing which could tend to redound to Lieutenant Kerr's honour, and enhance the value of this decoration.[4]

Among the troops who paraded in review order, heard the citation read, presented arms and marched past the stand on which the recipient stood, was Gunput Rao; one hopes that he was able to smile at the irony. The Queen's message might appear to be no more consistent than slave-owner Thomas Jefferson's declaration that all men were created equal, but there is evidence that she was concerned about discrimination and might here have been engaging in subtle criticism.[5] Thirty-five years later a similar recommendation came before her. During the Burma expedition of 1892–3 Surgeon General Owen Lloyd ran out of the post at Sima to tend its commanding officer, Captain Moreton, who had been wounded by Kachin tribesmen. With him went Subadar (captain) Matab Singh, who subsequently returned to the post under close-range fire to obtain further assistance. Five sepoys carried Moreton to safety but he died shortly afterwards. The VC citation mentioned Matab Singh, but only Lloyd was awarded. Victoria enquired whether anything was being done for the subadar. She was glad to be told that he and the sepoys were to receive the Third Class (one-third extra pay) of the Indian Order of Merit. This fact was added in parentheses to Lloyd's VC citation.[6]

It could not be argued that a Third Class award, no matter how exalted the Order, was in any way the equivalent of a Victoria Cross, but when asked in 1898 whether the Order as a whole was of equal status, the Secretary of State for India replied that it was. He focused on the pay differential and argued that the higher rate, when it occurred, was highly valued in India.[7] He did not address the esteem differential, nor the precedence of the Cross in the order of wearing. Thereafter the issue faded from attention, mainly because a period of relative peace had set in along the North West Frontier. What revived it was the need for an announcement to celebrate the accession of a new King Emperor. In 1911 George V embarked for India to attend his coronation durbar. 'For divers reasons Us thereunto moving', the King made Indian troops eligible for the VC.[8] As everyone had predicted, the announcement was very popular in India.

The complication of relative financial reward was removed by the simple expedient of abolishing the First Class of the Order and redesignating the Second and Third classes First and Second respectively, without prejudice to existing entitlements. The preeminence of the VC throughout the Empire was now formally beyond question, as it had been in public estimation for decades. Indians won two of the forty-five VCs awarded in 1914, when for the first months of the war Britain depended on the Indians to augment what the Kaiser derided as its 'contemptible little army'. The first award went to Sepoy Khudadad Khan, a Pathan serving with the 129th Duke of Connaught's Own Baluchis. On 31 October 1914 at Hollebeke in Belgium the officer commanding his machine-gun detachment was wounded and one of its guns put out of action by a shell. Although Khudadad was also seriously wounded he kept the remaining gun in action until he was the last living member of the detachment. He was left for dead by the Germans but managed to crawl to safety.[9]

When India achieved independence in 1947 most native troops ceased to be eligible for the Victoria Cross. The exceptions were the Nepalese nationals who continued to serve in those Gurkha regiments that were transferred to the British Army. Because Gurkhas are foreigners recruited with the permission of their national government they are commonly regarded as mercenaries, but as they swear allegiance to the Crown and are subject to the same rules that bind British soldiers they are not excluded from the protections of the Geneva Conventions. Of the 840 VCs awarded since 1911, when Indian troops first became eligible, thirteen native Gurkhas and three of their British officers have won the Cross, a record rivalled by only one British regiment. The fighting reputation of the little men with the big knives became legendary, built on a seeming indifference to danger, an enthusiasm for the fight and a fierce professionalism, all wrapped up in the uncompromising motto 'better to die than to be a coward'. According to Field Marshal Manekshaw, former Chief of Staff of the Indian Army, if a man said he was not afraid of dying he was either lying or a Gurkha.[10] Although none of the Gurkha regiments carried the Prince Consort's name, in their value as fighting troops these were Albert's Own.

In May 1943 the Japanese were advancing into the Chin Hills in Burma. Havildar (sergeant) Gaje Ghale, who had not been under fire before, was given a raw platoon of the 2nd Battalion, 5th Royal Gurkha Rifles and orders to attack Basha Hill East after two earlier attempts had failed. Approaching along a bare knife-edge ridge five metres wide, his platoon was met by artillery and mortar fire and machine guns firing from well-concealed positions. The havildar was wounded in the arm, chest and leg by a hand grenade. Ignoring his wounds, he led his men into a hand-to-hand fight, shouting their war cry *Ayo Gurkhali!*[11] Throwing grenades, he rallied his men to the assault several times until the Japanese were forced from the hill with heavy casualties. He then consolidated the position under heavy fire until ordered to the rear to have his wounds tended. The VC citation praised his courage, determination and leadership under 'the most trying conditions'.[12]

In Aristotelian terms the valour for which the Gurkhas are famed is anomalous. They are not actuated by patriotism, ideology or theology. They fight for money, which George Bernard Shaw had suggested was a better incentive for poor men, yet among the soldiers of the Queen their dependability is second to none. One would expect that loyalty to comrades might be particularly intense among men who spend most of their working lives away from home; Ghurka loyalty to Crown and colours, on the other hand, puts them in a class of their own.

Chapter 15

Irrespective of Rank

Although the Victoria Cross was created explicitly to reward valour regardless of rank, there was from the beginning a reluctance to award it to commanding officers. It was not a question of such officers being remote from situations where valour might be displayed. During the Persian War of 1856–7 Captain John Forbes led his 3rd Bombay Light Cavalry from the front. At Khoosh-ab the regiment performed the remarkable feat of breaking into and destroying an infantry square. Lieutenant Arthur Moore had jumped his horse over the enemy bayonets. The horse fell dead, breaking Moore's sword, and he would have been killed had not Lieutenant John Malcolmson also broken in and carried the dismounted man away at his stirrup.

Arthur Moore charged and and broke into a Persian square at Koosh-ab.

Both men were awarded the VC. Forbes was also recommended but, although only slightly senior to the others, he had been in command. This put him up against an entrenched prejudice in favour of the hierarchical Order of the Bath, a time-honoured structure into which worthy commanding officers were slotted according to rank. Horse Guards noted that Forbes had already been given brevet promotion to lieutenant colonel and admitted to the Bath.[1] He had gallantly led in a 'very desperate service, which the attack of a square of infantry formed to receive the attack of cavalry must be considered to be'. He had also, added the Duke of Cambridge, set a notable example to his regiment, but that was what duty required of him. The Bath was not only appropriate but sufficient. A ranker could not expect a double reward, so why should an officer?

There was, however, an inconvenient precedent. On 8 September 1855 Major Frederick Maude had commanded the 3rd Foot in the assault on the Redan during the siege of Sebastopol. He personally led the covering and ladder party into the fortress and held a position between traverses until lack of support forced a withdrawal, during which he was dangerously wounded. For this exploit he had been rewarded with a brevet promotion to lieutenant colonel and admission to the third class of the Order of the Bath, but subsequently he had been awarded the Victoria Cross for the same action.[2] What Cambridge chiefly feared was a retrospective rash of claims from officers who had been brevetted and Bathed but felt that they were entitled to the new decoration as well. Forbes would have to be content with what he already had.

Several officers senior to Forbes and Maude had in fact been admitted to the Order of the Bath and awarded VCs during the 1850s. In those cases the Cross had been for individual action and the Order a separate reward for meritorious service generally. Moreover, none of the army officers concerned had been in command of a unit larger than a company at the time and the naval officers were not in command of ships. During the Mutiny Colin Campbell had flatly refused to recommend senior officers at all. As late as 1900 the Cross was withheld from Colonel Ian Hamilton because he had been in command of a brigade (that is, acting as a general officer) during the relevant action. That remained the practice until late in the First World War.

On 31 July 1917 Lieutenant Colonel (temporary brigadier general) Clifford Coffin was leading the 25th Infantry Brigade in an attack on

Westhoek during the battle of Passchendaele. Enemy machine-gun and rifle fire from the front and right flank drove his men to ground in a line of shell holes. In full view of the Germans Clifford walked imperturbably from shell hole to shell hole under heavy fire, quietly advising and cheering his men. His example was widely credited with keeping the line intact and, indeed, for preventing it from being forced back. Senior he might have been, with a duty to lead, but that duty could not be held to require the 'utter disregard of personal danger' he had displayed to produce the moral effect for which he was rewarded. His VC established a precedent for general officer awards, but there have been only two since.

The award to Major (temporary brigadier general) George Grogan in May 1918 was much like Coffin's. He was in command of the 23rd Infantry Brigade when it found itself facing Ludendorff's last offensive in the west. A surprise bombardment in the Aisne sector destroyed four British divisions. For three days Grogan held his own brigade together and rallied the remnants of British and French formations, reorganizing those in disorder and leading retiring men back into the line. On the third day he rode up and down the line exposed to artillery, mortar, machine-gun and rifle fire. When his horse was shot from under him he continued on foot until another could be brought. The line held and the German offensive ground to a halt.

The last of the general officer VCs was Lieutenant Colonel (acting brigadier) John Campbell, who on 21 November 1941 was commanding the 7th Armoured Division's Support Group (artillery) and one of its tank regiments. During Operation Crusader the division had advanced to Sidi Rezegh in Libya. The 21st Panzer Division counterattacked, disabling much of Campbell's armour. To fill the place of the senior tank officers, all of whom were casualties, Campbell several times reconnoitred across the battlefield in an open car under fire and formed up the remaining tanks for counterattack. On the following day he personally controlled his guns, and twice joined crews to replace casualties. During the final German attack he was wounded, but refused to be evacuated. At the crisis, when British guns and German tanks were exchanging fire at point-blank range, causing heavy losses among the latter, he acted as a loader. It was probably this action that made Rommel wary of the fighting capabilities of the 7th Armoured in spite of its pedestrian leadership at higher level. When the commander of 21st Panzer was subsequently captured he wrote to Campbell congratulating him.

Brigadier John Campbell led his armour and guns from the front at Sidi Rezegh.

All three of the general officer VCs were acting above substantive rank and in circumstances where command was as much about inspirational leadership as control of events. Even Campbell's masterful handling of the resources at his command would probably have counted for little if unaccompanied by 'outstanding bravery and consistent determination [which] had a marked effect in maintaining the splendid fighting spirit of those under him'.[3] Conventionally, brigadiers and above manage their responsibilities from headquarters far enough in the rear to facilitate overall command and control of the battlefield without exposure to direct enemy attack. Remote from the line, there should be neither need nor opportunity for personal valour. Should such a situation arise, it would be *prima facie* evidence that the officer concerned was no longer in effective command.

As far as the achievement of high command is concerned the Victoria Cross has been either a good predictor or a self-fulfilling prophecy. Most awardees have been relatively young and junior men. If they were among the thousand-odd who survived to wear the decoration their prospects of promotion were exceptionally good: 146 eventually achieved starred rank.[4] Seven of them reached the very top: four field marshals and three admirals of the fleet. Two – Roberts and Wood – played roles in the evolution of the Cross. Gort featured as a case study in the nature of valour. The most interesting of the other four was Admiral of the Fleet Sir Arthur Wilson, who had no business winning a Victoria Cross at all.

During the Sudan campaign of 1884 his command, HMS *Hecla*, was stationed off the Red Sea port of Suakin. On 29 February the British advanced on El Teb. Captain Wilson accompanied them 'as a loafer just to see the fight', having nothing better to do that day.[5] The force advanced in a square and at times the naval machine guns at its leading corners were unable to fire, being on the move. The Dervishes seized an opportunity to attack the right half-battery, mortally wounding its commanding officer. Wilson sprang to the defence of the gun, but his sword snapped off in a spearman's ribs. With the stub of the blade he then held off the attackers, sustaining a head wound, until infantry came to his assistance. One of the brigadiers, Redvers Buller VC, wanted to recommend Wilson for the Cross. The difficulty was that he was not supposed to be there. That was hastily remedied by retrospectively appointing him to the staff of the senior naval officer on station, Admiral Sir William Hewett VC.[6] Wilson had been an official observer all the time without knowing it.

Wilson was old for a VC-winner, having already served for nearly thirty years. Like Hewett's, his award was anomalous from a service

Infantrymen came to the assistance of Arthur Wilson (lower left) after his sword broke.

viewpoint, having been won on land. Wilson claimed that it was still relevant, writing that it would not have done 'to miss such a good chance of learning one's trade'.[7] His advancement for the next ten years was steady but unspectacular, but thereafter he prospered, becoming in turn Comptroller of the Navy, commander of the Channel Squadron and commander-in-chief Home and Channel Fleets. His last appointment, from which there was nowhere else to rise, was to First Sea Lord on the Board of Admiralty. He retired in 1912. There is no obvious connection between individual valour and fitness for high rank, but for all that the most potent form of leadership is by example. Promoting authorities were unlikely to overlook it entirely.

It might be expected that a decoration open to all ranks would mainly be awarded to common soldiers and seamen, given their preponderance of numbers over officers and NCOs. In fact less than one Cross in three has gone to a ranker and some of those were standing in for their superiors.[8] Privates Walter Cook and Duncan Miller of the Black Watch were skirmishing at close quarters against large numbers of mutineers at Maylah Ghat, India, on 15 January 1859. In the fierce encounter the only officer was carried away wounded and the colour sergeant was killed. Cook and Miller went to the front, took charge of the company and directed it with 'courage, coolness and discipline which was the admiration of all who witnessed it'.[9] Conversely, many officer and NCO VCs have been awarded for personal exploits at the front of their men

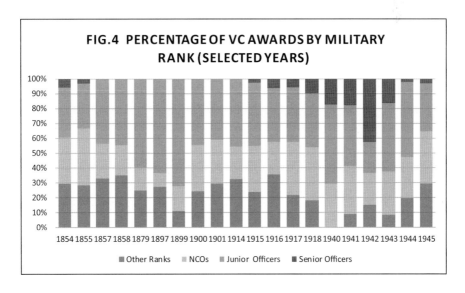

FIG.4 PERCENTAGE OF VC AWARDS BY MILITARY RANK (SELECTED YEARS)

that in less desperate circumstances would have been the task of the rank and file. The awarding authorities have been favouring hazardous leadership, not rank. It should not surprise that they have found it mainly, but by no means exclusively, among those whose duty it is to lead.

The 1942 spike in senior officer awards to 42 per cent (fourteen out of thirty-three) marked the high point of a trend that had emerged early in the First World War, largely at the expense of other ranks. The tide has since ebbed, but of the twenty awards made since 1945, 10 per cent have gone to senior officers and 15 per cent to other ranks, leaving non-commissioned officers with an all-time-high share of 75 per cent. This reflects the changing nature of the conflicts in which Commonwealth forces have been engaged. The opportunities have been for non-commissioned members of special forces rather than leaders or followers in mass formations.

Chapter 16

Death or Victory

Queen Victoria had rejected Newcastle's suggestion of a motto that punned with her name. The Latin tag referenced by the duke was *victoria aut mors*. By reversing the word order he seemed to be suggesting that dying bravely, victorious or otherwise, might itself be enough to earn a warrior the coveted decoration. This was entirely contrary to Albert's view; death, if it had to come, should advance the cause. In the Second World War the American general George Patton was as one with the Prince Consort on that score: 'No dumb bastard ever won a war by going out and dying for his country. He won it by making some other dumb bastard die for his'.[1] Newcastle's formulation was in keeping with his aim of making the decoration highly esteemed because difficult to win, but it was unlikely to become eagerly sought after if aspirants could read that death had first billing as an outcome. Had the motto been adopted it would also have cut across Panmure's interdict against posthumous awards, which made it quite clear that if you wanted a Cross you would have to live to receive it. For half a century that was the rule.

When it was overturned, Roberts was again instrumental. After the battle of Paardeburg in 1900 Lieutenant Francis Parsons had been recommended to him for bringing in a wounded man under heavy fire. Roberts had not submitted it because Parsons had been killed at Dreifontein three weeks later, before the recommendation reached him. However, the lieutenant's name came forward again for conspicuous gallantry at Dreifontein and this time Roberts recommended him. Here was no ambiguity like that in the case of Roberts's son; this would be a posthumous VC. The War Office was torn. Roberts had already blurred the boundary and now he wanted to cross it. And if for Parsons, what about Sergeant Alfred Atkinson, also recommended for Paardeburg, who had been killed while attempting to aid the wounded? The main reservation was the prospect of 'shoals of applicants' on behalf of men previously killed in action. Indeed, the War Office hoped that posthumous awards could be limited to those recommended during the South African War, but the past came up on them with a roar. Sir John Coghill wrote an 'intensely disagreeable and threatening' letter on behalf of his son, one of the would-be rescuers of the colours at Isandhlwana. Sir Ian Hamilton, who as military secretary dealt with it, cited it as an example of 'the impossibility of arguing with the relatives of a dead man'.[2]

Now that posthumous awards were an admitted fact, said the adjutant general, should the Warrant be amended to make formal provision for future cases? Colonel Cowan, the assistant military secretary, pointed out that there was nothing in the existing Warrant to preclude them. Panmure's prohibition had no statutory basis. From the position that such awards were excluded because the Warrant did not specifically allow them, it was now being argued that they were allowed because the Warrant did not exclude them.

The King had approved the South African cases, but he baulked at earlier ones like Coghill because he feared that they could open the door to many more. To preclude it he had declared that 'in future the decoration should be given at once or not at all'. The War Office, which had earlier entertained similar fears, was now more concerned with consistency. There was no logic to excluding Coghill and the other five men gazetted as 'memorandum cases' up to the South African War. For years Edward VII refused to address the anomaly until, in 1906, he abruptly changed

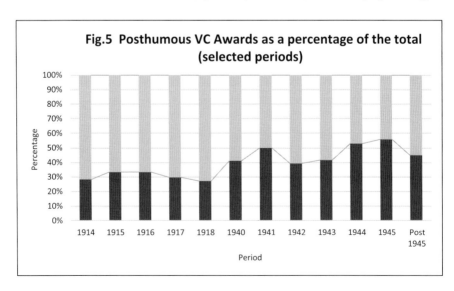

Fig.5 Posthumous VC Awards as a percentage of the total (selected periods)

his mind. After rejecting all official advice he was swayed by a petition from Mrs Melvill, the widow of the other officer at Isandhlwana. The War Office gently reminded Sir Arthur Davidson, the King's secretary, that Mclvill's case could hardly be reconsidered separately from the other five. The King conceded 'on the strict understanding that no other cases are involved in this decision'.[3] Posthumous awards became formally admissible in 1902. Since then 265 men have been killed while winning the distinction. From about 30 per cent throughout the First World War, the rate escalated to over 40 per cent in the second.[4]

The Ministry of Defence considers the likelihood of death to be a useful yardstick of quality. The same document that queried Australian standards set out as a rule of thumb that there should be 'a 90% possibility of being killed in performing the deed'. That word 'possibility' seriously understates what is more like high probability or near certainty, but more to the point the rule privileges the dead by allowing that they have fulfilled a *de facto* requirement before anything else has been taken into account. It significantly raises the bar from the actual death rate since 1902 unless one considers that many of the survivors were exceptionally lucky: i.e. by MoD accounting more of them should have died winning the Cross. And death has not been the only hazard. The ratio of killed to wounded on battlefields has historically been about 1:3. Among VCs it is more like 5:4. Add killed and wounded rates together and a VC nominee has had less than a 50 per cent chance of coming through his exploit unscathed.

In recent times the MoD has come close to its post-Vietnam standard. Since 1982 six British soldiers have been awarded the Victoria Cross. Four were killed and one was wounded, a casualty rate of 83 per cent. Two VCs were awarded for the Falklands War. Both were posthumous, but if the system had had its way even they would have been denied. The publicly acclaimed hero of that last war of empire was Lieutenant Colonel Herbert Jones, officer commanding 2 Battalion, the Parachute Regiment. At Goose Green the battalion attacked a strongly entrenched force of Argentines. Three soldiers of A Company were killed at a re-entrant called Gorse Gully. The attack stalled and Jones conducted a personal reconnaissance with the battalion sergeant major that took them to the head of the gully. Concerned that the attack was in danger of failure, he took a sub-machine gun and called on A Company to follow him in an attack on the nearest enemy trench, but only the sergeant major responded. Fired upon from several trenches, Jones fell and rolled back. Regaining his feet he charged again, disregarding the heavy fire now directed against him. He was hit from another trench on his flank and fell dying a few feet from the position he was assaulting. Shortly afterwards A Company resumed the attack and the Argentines quickly surrendered.

Viewed from a textbook perspective, Jones's action was an object lesson in what not to do. It was his duty to direct the battalion, not to act as a section leader. By removing himself from where he could exercise command and control he exposed his unit to disorganization; by risking himself he risked decapitating the battalion, which is what happened. The VC citation made much of the demoralizing effect Jones's action had on the enemy, going as far as attributing to this one incident a conviction among the Argentine forces that their defeat was inevitable. Some of the men under his command saw it differently. Corporal John Geddes was one of those who declined to commit suicide. He wrote that A Company had intended to 'sort it out in their own way and that didn't include charging into machine guns World War One style'. Even the battalion second in command, Major Chris Keeble, reflected that Jones was 'a man straight out of *Boys' Own* … who ruled by a bullwhip rather than a conductor of an orchestra'. Geddes suggested that the Cross should have gone to the man who sorted it out. Twenty minutes after Jones's charge Corporal David 'Pig' Abols used the scanty cover available to get within firing range of the strongpoint.

> Pig jumped to his feet in the middle of a howling gale of machine-gun fire, lifted the [light anti-tank] rocket to his shoulder, lined it up on the bunker opposite, breathed out and squeezed down the rubber on the top of the tube.[5]

According to Geddes it was that combination of 'nerve, balls, and superb field craft' that broke the Argentine resistance, not Jones's 'death-or-glory dash'.[6] The great imponderable in Geddes's assessment is how far the actions of Abols and the rest of A Company were motivated by shame at not having followed their leader and subsequent determination to redeem the company's honour. Had Jones deliberately sacrificed himself in the hope that it would inspire his men? We cannot know, but if so the eventual victory was vindication and he deserved the Victoria Cross. However, had he survived but lost the battle he might well have been called to account for irresponsibility.

After the Falklands campaign a Special Honours Committee (SHC) with tri-service representation was formed to recommend honours and awards. The list forwarded to 10 Downing Street was returned with a query: 'Where are the Victoria Crosses?'. It did not seem to occur to the Prime Minister that the absence of VCs was a matter for rejoicing – evidence that extreme valour had not been necessary to obtain victory. To Mrs Thatcher's way of thinking the Victoria Cross was an accessory to triumph. Clearly, none of the recommendations sent up the chain of command had satisfied the committee, but the Prime Minister wanted VCs so the question became how many. SHC consulted the VC Committee. The military secretary, replying on its behalf, was cautious.

> It was not for the VC Committee to make any judgement on what would be the appropriate number of VCs to award for this campaign in comparison with the numbers that have been awarded in past campaigns. However there will inevitably be great public interest over whether the award is in any way being cheapened if an excessive number are awarded.[7]

So, not many. The idea that there might be a limit had no basis in the Warrant and was indeed contrary to the stated intentions of Newcastle and Prince Albert. The reservations that at least a majority of the SHC members had about Jones could have been finessed, once the Prime Minister pressed for nominations, by calling for a ballot of 2 Para, but that would have produced at least four names, presumably too many for the misers of the VC Committee. Fortunately, the public had already decided that Jones was a hero. They did not care about neglect of command responsibilities; this was an exploit on a par with those celebrated in the war comics. A Victoria Cross for Jones then, and perhaps one other. The SHC selected a candidate whose exploit superficially paralleled that of Jones. During a night attack on Mount Longdon Sergeant Ian McKay's 3 Para platoon and another were exposed to heavy fire from a ridge. He and a few men went forward with their platoon commander to reconnoitre. The platoon commander was wounded and McKay assumed command. Judging that the attack could not proceed until the threat to the exposed platoons was eliminated, he decided to turn the reconnaissance into an attack. With three men he charged the Argentine position. One man was killed and two wounded, but McKay reached the position and killed its occupants with grenades before falling dead on the bunker. The platoons were able to redeploy in relative safety. If Jones was to get the VC it was hard to see how McKay could be denied, but his exploit had the additional value from a military viewpoint of offering a commentary on the other. Jones had abdicated command responsibility; McKay had assumed it. Jones had been unable to get his men to follow; McKay had inspired his men although all were risking, and indeed suffered, death or wounds. Unlike the uncertain and at best indirect outcome of Jones's heroism, McKay's 'was instrumental in ensuring the success of the attack'.[8]

For survivors, the possibility-of-death rule is a major hurdle. Only two British soldiers have so far cleared it, one during the Iraq conflict and the other more recently in Afghanistan. In May 2004 Private Johnson Beharry, 1st Battalion, Princess of Wales's Royal Regiment, was driving a Warrior armoured personnel carrier through Al-Amarah. His carrier platoon was ambushed and his vehicle sustained multiple hits from rocket-propelled grenades. They wounded the platoon commander, the vehicle's gunner and several men inside. With no communications or orders, Beharry closed his driver's hatch and moved the vehicle forward until blocked by a barricade. Hit again by RPGs, the carrier caught fire and filled with smoke. Conscious that he was the lead vehicle of a six-carrier convoy, Beharry opened his armoured hatch to see and drove through the barrier without knowing whether or not it was mined. As the smoke began to clear he could see another RPG in flight towards him. He pulled down on the hatch but blast pressure sent flames and blast over his head into the turret where they further wounded the gunner. With his periscope disabled he drove on head out, exposed to small arms fire. A round hit his helmet and lodged inside it. He led the convoy through fire for 1,500 metres to get clear of the ambushes to a point where he was able to join up with another company carrier and follow it to an outpost that was itself under attack. There, under fire, he recovered the platoon commander and gunner from the turret and returned a third time to guide to safety the wounded and dazed men in the rear of the carrier. Remounting, he drove the still-burning carrier to a point beyond the possibility of capture and only then triggered the extinguishers that also immobilized the engine. He took refuge in another carrier, where he collapsed from physical and mental exhaustion.

It remains an open question whether the MoD would have considered Beharry's life to be sufficiently threatened to merit a VC for this engagement. What it would have found difficult to ignore was that six weeks later his life was most definitely on the line. In another ambush, when he was again driving the lead Warrior, Beharry was seriously injured by an RPG that exploded on the front armour fifteen centimetres from his head. Other grenades incapacitated the commander and injured several of the crew. Although partly blinded by blood Beharry skillfully reversed his vehicle out of the ambush until it struck a wall. He then collapsed from his wound, but other carriers were able to rescue the crew. Although he was listed as very seriously injured and in a coma for some time, Beharry recovered. In the first incident he had taken the initiative and saved his unit from a critical situation with complete disregard for his own safety. In the second he had continued to perform his duty although badly wounded, again saving his fellow crewmen by taking the initiative. And a grenade exploding barely a hand's width from your head is a near certainty to kill you. Both incidents were mentioned in the citation.[9]

On 22 August 2013 Lance Corporal Joshua Leakey, 1st Battalion, the Parachute Regiment, was participating in a joint US/UK operation to disrupt Taliban activities in Helmand province, Afghanistan. After dismounting from helicopters the command group was pinned down on an exposed slope under heavy fire. While attempting to extricate themselves a US Marine captain was wounded and communications were lost. From the reverse slope Leakey broke cover and under heavy fire crested the hill. He could see that two machine guns and a mortar section were surrounded, depriving the force of fire support. Leakey first initiated evacuation of the wounded officer and then went under fire to one of the machine guns. With enemy rounds striking the frame of the gun he changed its position and got it back into action. He then retrieved the second gun, although he was now attracting most of the enemy fire. When he re-sited the gun and began returning fire the balance shifted and the allied force began to fight back. Leakey handed over the gun and completed extraction of the wounded officer. The Taliban lost eleven killed and four wounded.

Presumably the account of rounds ricocheting off a carried weapon was enough to persuade the MoD that for some time Leakey had been within centimetres of death. That threshold crossed, the VC citation praised 'gritty leadership' that single-handedly had regained the initiative and prevented considerable loss of life. Curiously, it patronizingly added that his leadership was 'well above that expected of his rank' and, rather insipidly, that his act of valour was 'highly deserving of significant national recognition'. Perhaps the writer meant significantly deserving of the highest national recognition.[10] At the award announcement, in a break with tradition that would not have done for the Duke of Wellington, sir, the Chief of the General Staff gave the lance corporal a hug.

Queen Victoria would have been pleased that the integrity of Albert's cross was being upheld, but at the time of writing Britain has only four living recipients of the VC, two of whom won their laurels over fifty years ago.[11] As exemplars of values that the state presumably wishes to perpetuate, this dwindling band is in sore need of reinforcement. In a few years Beharry and Leakey will be the sole survivors. If the Victoria Cross is not to fade from public knowledge for want of living recipients, the MoD will have to modify the 90 per cent rule.

Chapter 17

Fighting Mad

Alcohol can instill Dutch courage.[1] Adrenaline can numb the pain of appalling wounds before shock sets in. Anger, frustration and desire for revenge can override rational behaviour. A berserker can will himself into a state of fighting frenzy and indifference to his own safety. A number of armies, including the German and the American, have experimented with drugs designed to make soldiers indifferent to risk. To regard these altered states as capable of sustaining no more than five minutes of courage, as Slim did, is to undervalue them given that five minutes can be the difference between victory and defeat. Indeed, Corporal Ernest Egerton, 16th Battalion, Nottinghamshire and Derbyshire Regiment, did not need even that much. On 20 September 1917 his unit attacked through fog and smoke at Bulgar Wood near Ypres, leaving enemy dugouts unseen in its rear. These began causing casualties and Egerton volunteered to help clear them. Under heavy fire he went back and charged the dugouts, killing a machine-gunner and two other Germans. When support came up twenty-nine prisoners were taken. A few days before the action Egerton was told that his brother had been killed. He later said that he was longing to get back into action 'to pay back a debt'.[2] The VC citation described the exploit as reckless bravery and gallant beyond all praise, which in thirty seconds had relieved an extremely difficult situation.[3]

There is no recorded instance of a VC won while drunk, but well into the twentieth century British units would issue a rum 'stiffener' before combat. Adrenaline, on the other hand, has fuelled many a seemingly superhuman act that defied belief, none more than that of Lieutenant George Cairns during Orde Wingate's second Chindit expedition. On 13 March 1944 the 77th Indian Infantry Brigade was fighting to block Japanese road and rail communications with Mandalay. As Cairns was attacking a hilltop position a Japanese officer wielding a sword hacked off his left arm. Cairns killed his assailant and picked up the weapon.

Slashing while advancing, he killed or wounded a number of the enemy before collapsing. His actions inspired his men and unnerved the Japanese, leading to their complete rout. Cairns later died of his wounds. He was recommended for a VC but the papers were lost in the plane crash that killed Wingate. An attempt to revive the recommendation after the war foundered. It was not for doubts about the credibility of such a thing, because there had been a similar incident on 2 March 1945. Acting Naik [Corporal] Fazal Din, of the 10th Baluchis, pierced right through the body by a sword-wielding Japanese officer, had seized the weapon when it was withdrawn and used it to kill his attacker and another Japanese soldier. He then went to the assistance of one of his men and cut down a third Japanese soldier. He collapsed after reporting to platoon HQ and died at the regimental aid post.[4] There were many witnesses to Fazal Din's feat, but two of Cairns's witnesses had since been killed. It was not until 1949 that agitation by Cairns's widow led to an award, the last for the Second World War.

The Burma campaign was one of many extremes, religious diversity being not the least of them. A few weeks after Cairns had demonstrated that a fatal wound could not protect the enemy from him, Jemadar [Lieutenant] Adbul Hafiz of the 9th Jat Infantry showed that fanaticism could be equally potent. The Japanese had taken a hill north of Imphal and on 6 April 1944 the jemadar was ordered to retake it. He drew up two sections and told them that they were invincible. They would kill or drive off all the enemy. Inspired, his men vigorously followed him up the hill under cover of an artillery barrage. It ceased when the sections were a few metres below the crest, at which time machine-gun fire and grenades were rained down on them. There were casualties but Hafiz, shouting the Muslim war cry 'God is great', led a charge onto the crest. Wounded in the leg, he dealt with a flanking machine gun by seizing its barrel while one of his men killed the gunner. Taking up a Bren gun, he killed several of the enemy as he advanced.

> So fierce was the attack, and all his men so inspired by the determination of Jemadar Abdul Hafiz to kill all enemy in sight at whatever cost, that the enemy, who were still in considerable numbers on the position, ran away down the opposite slope of the hill.

Thus ran the citation for his Victoria Cross. Hafiz pursued the fleeing enemy down the hill, although again under machine-gun fire from a nearby feature. Hit in the chest, he collapsed while still attempting to fire on the retreating enemy. His last words were 'reorganize on the position and I will give covering fire'. The enemy casualties alone amounted to several times the size of his own little force.[5]

Aggression itself is second nature to some people. Private James Stokes was only serving in the 2nd Battalion, King's Shropshire Light Infantry, because a judge had said it was that or a lengthy sentence for inflicting grievous bodily harm at a dance hall in Glasgow. At Kervenheim in the Rhineland on 1 March 1945 his platoon came under intense rifle and machine-gun fire from a farm building. Without orders Stokes rushed the building. The enemy fire ceased and he emerged with twelve prisoners. He had been wounded in the neck, but when ordered to the aid post refused to leave his platoon. At the next objective there was heavy fire from a house. Again Stokes did not wait for orders and rushed it. He fell wounded but recovered his rifle and continued to advance in the face of intense fire directed at him and the platoon. He reached the building, the fire ceased and he brought out five prisoners. In the next assault, on a strongpoint, for a third time he took the initiative and attacked alone, although now severely wounded and suffering from loss of blood. After a dash of 60 metres under intense fire he was brought down 20 metres from the enemy position, firing his rifle to the last. As the platoon charged past him he raised his hand in farewell and shouted goodbye. His upper body was found to have eight wounds. The VC citation did not mince words about his motivation: 'Private Stokes' one object throughout this action was to kill the enemy, at whatever personal risk'. It added that he had inspired all those around him, ensured the success of the attack and saved his platoon and company many serious casualties.[6] This was Aristotelian rashness, and perhaps mania, but certainly useful in the cause.

Sometimes, the commitment defies explanation. What was it that sustained Private Adam Wakenshaw, aged eighteen, of the Durham Light Infantry at Mersa Matruh on 27 June 1942? The Germans had towed a light gun to within short range of Wakenshaw's light anti-tank gun, which was in an advanced position covering infantry. A round fired into the enemy tractor immobilized its engine, but a second German gun

The last survivor of its crew, Adam Walkenshaw kept his anti-tank gun in action even after losing an arm.

scored a hit that killed or seriously wounded all of Wakenshaw's crew. Duty done, one might think, but Wakenshaw, who had had his left arm blown off above the elbow, could see that the Germans were attempting to bring the stranded weapon into action against his company, which was only 200 metres away. Under intense fire he and the aimer crawled back to their own gun. With one arm Wakenshaw loaded and fired five more rounds, setting the tractor on fire and damaging the towed gun. A near miss killed the aimer and again wounded Wakenshaw, blowing him away from the 2-pounder. He crawled back to it a second time and began loading again. Had this become a personal duel between gunners? Then a direct hit exploded the ammunition. The gun was destroyed and Wakenshaw was killed, but the infantry were able to withdraw to safety.[7]

More than one recipient of the Cross, reflecting on his actions, likened them to insanity. At Gavrelle on 29 April 1917 Second Lieutenant Alfred Pollard of the Honourable Artillery Company saw that units disorganized by shellfire on his battalion's left flank were retiring in confusion in the face of a German attack. With four men he launched a bombing counterattack that held the enemy advance, retook the lost ground, gained more, and inflicted heavy casualties on the now disordered Germans. His VC citation attributed his success to 'force of will' (fortitude), dash, splendid example and utter contempt of danger. It mentioned that he had already won a Distinguished Conduct Medal and two Military Crosses.[8] It could have added that the DCM had been awarded in place of an earlier VC recommendation. In his memoirs Pollard described himself as a fire-eater:

> I enjoyed the War, both in and out of the line. Despite the discomfort and hardships of life in the trenches, I found pleasure in wandering about no man's land at night. 'Going over the top' struck some chord in my nature which vibrated strongly to the thrill of the attack. Men called me mad. Perhaps I was.[9]

It was much the same for Lance Corporal Albert Jacka, 14th Battalion, Australian Imperial Force, at Courtney's post, Gallipoli, on the night of 19/20 May 1915. The Turks had got into a communications trench and Jacka was holding them back single-handedly from behind a traverse. An officer asked Jacka if, with support, he could charge them. Volunteers came forward, but the attack was repulsed. Jacka then said 'keep [the Turks] here and I will take them at the other end of the trench'. He left the trench and crawled over open ground under fire until he was behind the Turks. When his comrades threw bombs as a diversion, Jacka jumped into the

Albert Jacka 'did his nut' while repelling a Turkish attack.

119

trench, shot five Turks and bayonetted two others. As they scattered, he shot another two. Congratulated by one of the volunteers for 'a big thing', all Jacka said was 'I think I did my nut'.[10] Lieutenant Joseph Maxwell, 18th Battalion, Australian Imperial Force, who won his VC near Estrées in October 1918, put it down to collective mental disturbance: 'If I hadn't gone mad I could never have done the things I did. But they called it heroism. We all went mad. The whole world was mad.'[11]

Where Pollard and Maxwell had been reflective and Jacka had been puzzled, Captain Neville Howse of the New South Wales Medical Staff Corps was clinical. On 24 July 1900 he had ridden out to assist a wounded trooper during the action at Vredefort, South Africa. When a shell exploded near his horse he was thrown on to his head. Concussed, he went to the trooper on foot and brought him in. Howse pleaded temporary insanity, claiming that in a dazed state he had not known what he was doing. Such modesty was unacceptable to friends at home, one of whom complained that it was impossible to get a straight answer from him about the incident.[12]

Although each expressed it differently, all four men concluded that their actions were irrational responses to the circumstances in which they found themselves. Pollard and Maxwell used the word 'mad', but in colloquial speech it means angry as well as insane and the angriest man of them all, to judge from his VC record, was Charles Upham of the 20th Battalion, 2nd New Zealand Expeditionary Force. As a schoolboy he had been given the nickname Pug, short for pugnacious, but this was a reference to single-mindedness and obstinacy rather than aggression. As an adult he was notorious for fixity of opinion, powers of physical endurance and indifference to personal comfort. By the outbreak of the Second World War he had decided that Germany was a threat to the things he held dear and volunteered immediately. After the debacle in Greece the New Zealand Division was called on to resist the invasion of Crete. In an attempt to retake Maleme airfield from German paratroops, Upham's infantry platoon had four men knocked over at the outset. Upham personally stalked and destroyed the machine-gun nest responsible. Later one of his men was shot in the stomach and again it was Upham who responded, killing the German and subduing another with the butt of his revolver. He was asked why he had not just shot the man. Why was he so savage? His only response was to resume the advance with grim determination until no further progress was possible.

SECOND LIEUTENANT **C. H. UPHAM,** NEW ZEALAND MILITARY FORCES

CRETE, 22-30 MAY, 1941

On May 22nd Second Lieutenant Upham fought his way forward three thousand yards at Maleme, and his platoon destroyed numerous enemy posts. When his company withdrew from Maleme he carried back a wounded man under fire, and also guided back a company which had become isolated. During the next two days his platoon held an exposed position under fire. Blown over by a mortar shell, painfully wounded in the shoulder by shrapnel, and with a bullet in his foot, he remained on duty. At Galatos, on May 25th, his platoon killed forty Germans, forcing the enemy back. Ordered to retire, he sent his platoon back, and when fired on by two Germans he shammed dead. Only able to use one arm, he killed them. On May 30th at Sphakia he cleverly fought off an enemy attack, killing twenty-two Germans at a range of five hundred yards. Second Lieutenant Upham was born in 1910, and his home town is Christchurch, New Zealand.

Charles Upham, who went on to win a second Victoria Cross, the only combat soldier to do so.

While he was so driven it was noted that he could be as harsh with his own men as with the enemy, but invariably with protective intent: he would not allow them to take risks that he willingly imposed on himself. He was awarded the VC for 'a series of remarkable exploits, showing outstanding leadership, tactical skill and utter indifference to danger'. He was also commended for recovering wounded men.[13]

A year later Upham was commanding a company in Egypt, where in actions at Minqar Qaim and Ruweisat Ridge he skillfully led from the front, disregarding danger and functioning as a one-man spearhead. He refused to relinquish command although severely wounded. Overwhelmed by German armour, his company surrendered and Upham became a prisoner of war. An inveterate escaper,[14] he was eventually transferred to Colditz, where other New Zealanders tried to get him to talk about his military exploits. Fred Moody, a medical officer, took a clinical interest in Upham's indifference to danger. Did he feel no fear? Upham spoke as though he had not understood the question, but ended by saying 'I got so bloody angry with them nothing else seemed to matter'.[15] He had earlier discussed the enemy with fellow prisoner and friend Neil McPhail.

> The Huns caused the war, they began it, and they'll start another war unless we wipe all their industry off the face of the earth. No armistice terms, just destroy the whole ruddy lot. There's never been a good German yet.[16]

When McPhail gently disagreed Upham refused to talk to him for a week. In 1971 he was against Britain joining the Common Market, saying 'they'll cheat you yet, those Germans'.[17] To the end of his days he would not allow German cars or German machinery onto his farm. It was as though hate was an unquenchable ember, ever ready to be fanned by any incident that validated the emotion. In action, the result was wildfire. It would have puzzled the Roman poet Horace, who held that anger was only a short madness.[18]

Before he went into the bag the senior officers of Upham's division had considered recommending him for a second VC (Minqar Qaim) and a third (Ruweisat Ridge). The chief obstacle was that as a prisoner of war Upham was theoretically subject to an enquiry that would establish whether any blame attached to him for having fallen into enemy hands.[19] Since 1917 it had been army policy not to make awards for actions connected with the circumstances under which the potential awardee had been taken prisoner, but in 1945 Upham's claims were reconsidered, consolidated and submitted. George VI sought reassurance that this second award was up to standard, it being unprecedented for a combat soldier.[20] He wanted to meet the New Zealander, but Upham had already gone home. Instead, the King interviewed General Kippenberger, the ranking NZ officer in London, and asked him whether Upham deserved the award. The general, conscious that Minqar Qaim and Ruweisat had been rolled into one recommendation, replied that in his respectful opinion Upham had won the VC several times over.[21]

The citation writer for Upham's second VC did him less than justice. Only the action at Ruweisat Ridge on 14/15 July 1942 was mentioned. A single paragraph relating to the action at Minqar Qaim was included without mentioning the place, leaving an impression that it also related to Ruweisat. The historical record had been distorted for the saving of a few column inches.[22]

Chapter 18

Happy Warriors

In the heyday of Victoria's little wars it was likely that one or two Victoria Crosses would be awarded no matter how small the affair. Some were earned by defeating large numbers of technologically disadvantaged and undisciplined tribesmen. Indeed, such victories were so common that even a feat of arms like that reported to his mother by Captain Alexander Hore-Ruthven of the 3rd (Militia) Battalion, Highland Light Infantry, was unremarkable. He was serving with an Egyptian Army column at Gedaref in the Sudan on 22 September 1898 when it encountered more than 5,000 Dervishes.

> We had a clinking good fight yesterday, which for twenty minutes looked like going the wrong way, but we got out all right and obtained a brilliant victory … My bugler and orderly were both shot alongside me. We got four fine Dervish flags, and they afterwards counted 140 dead around the rear of the baggage train. The Dervish fire was disgracefully bad, luckily, and ours very good indeed; my old chaps down on their knees downing a head every shot. Our force was only 1,400 strong, so it wasn't a bad little show. There were only seven British altogether, so the clasp [to the Sudan campaign medal] will be rather worth having … I am very fit, never been sick or sorry all the time, and enjoyed myself thoroughly. We are all rather pleased with ourselves, and more than reconciled at not being at Omdurman. We have had better fun than they had, and stiffer fighting, if you compare our butcher's bill with theirs … I have never had a better time in my life than the last few months, but I am afraid it's about over now.[1]

Hore-Ruthven hoped to get a regular commission (he did) and thought the clasp would be an unusual distinction (it was) but clearly found his greatest satisfaction in the joy of battle. In that long letter to 'dear mama' he neglected to mention that he had seen an Egyptian officer lying wounded fifty metres in front of the advancing Dervishes and had gone out under fire to bring him in, pausing once or twice to check the tribesmen with his revolver. For that, and not for victory, he was awarded the Victoria Cross.[2]

Hore-Ruthven was lucky to be presented with several opportunities for *Boy's Own* enthusiasm during the early years of his distinguished professional career. It was otherwise for Arthur Borton. He went to Eton and Sandhurst but found a subaltern's life uninteresting after the Second Boer War. He resigned his commission, failed dismally in American business ventures and sank into drink and depression. The Kaiser saved him. As lieutenant colonel commanding the 2/22nd Battalion, London Regiment, he led it against a Turkish line of defence in Palestine on 7 November 1917. Disconnected from the other battalions detailed to attack he opted to press on, although assailed by machine-gun fire from both flanks. More than fun, this was sport.

> One of the men had a football. How it came to be there goodness knows. Anyway we kicked off and rushed the first guns, dribbling the ball with us. I take it the Turks thought we were dangerous lunatics, but we stopped for nothing, not even to shoot and the bayonet had its day. For 3,000 yards we swept up everything finally capturing a field battery and its entire gun crews. The battery fired the last round at us at 25 yards ... I wouldn't have missed it for worlds, [and] except for the thought of the good fellows gone would be too happy for anything.[3]

Borton thought that he would be recommended for a bar to his DSO, but his battalion had done the work of two brigades in securing a vital objective, the water supply at Shiera. This was a VC-standard victory and the high point of his life. Alas, the war ended, his depression intensified, alcoholism set in and he died disinherited in 1933. He was one of many who discovered that they were meant to war. It gave purpose and focus to their lives and without it they were lost. Joseph Maxwell was another. He had been an apprentice boilermaker in 1914, but after the war found work as a journalist. He married but his wife soon divorced him for drunkenness and cruelty. His frank memoir *Hell's Bells and Mademoiselles* contrasted the emptiness of his civilian life with what had gone before.

> One has lost that sense of freedom, paradoxical as it may seem, the freedom of being unfettered to office or desk, the freedom of scorning the passage of the hours to whose march life sets its measured tread.[4]

For decades Maxwell drifted in and out of jobs, prison and mental hospital. In war he had found his calling, but there was no place for a warrior in peace-time Australia. At the outbreak of the Second World War he again enlisted, under an assumed name, but he was too far gone for the only role he coveted, that of a combat soldier. In his latter days he remarried and found a measure of contentment, but the only years he valued were those in which he had lived on the edge and defied the odds. He characterized them as madness, but perhaps exhilaration was closer to the mark. He had tasted the intoxication of battle and without it life was altogether too sober.

Professional officers often took pride in overcoming the trials and hazards that active service brought their way. In 1914 Captain Adrian Carton de Wiart lost an eye on operations with the Somaliland Camel Corps. In Flanders he lost his left hand at Zonnebeke (having bitten off two fingers that the medical officers refused to amputate). In the Battle of the Somme he single-handedly took control of four battalions to hold La Boiselle after the commanders of the other three had become casualties. The VC citation credited him with averting a serious reverse.[5] In all, he received eight wounds during the first war, at least two of which would have warranted an honourable retirement. With his eye patch and empty cuff he cut a Nelsonian figure. 'Frankly, I had enjoyed the war' he later admitted, and he served again in the second.[6] He is supposed to be the model for over-the-top Brigadier Ritchie-Hook in Evelyn Waugh's *Sword of Honour* trilogy.

To many around them, for whom the war was a purgatory to be endured with fingers crossed, such attitudes in a leader were not only incomprehensible, but also dangerous. Acting Lieutenant Colonel James

Adrian Carton de Wiart rallied three battalions to prevent a serious reverse at La Boiselle.

Marshall was killed a week before the end of the war while leading the 16th Battalion, Lancashire Fusiliers, across the Sambre-Oise canal over a floating bridge. He had encouraged volunteers to repair it under fire by exposing himself to the same risks. Some of those who completed the work were only saved from becoming casualties themselves because they were shielded by the dead bodies of others. Six Crosses were awarded for the crossing, including one for Marshall. He was an eccentric martinet who considered himself, as he delighted in telling others, the bravest man in the British Army. Two Military Crosses and nine wound stripes supported the claim. Captain Brockman, a fellow officer of Marshall's regiment, put him in perspective.

> There are some people, incredible people, who, I think, *like* it. There are some people, I'm sure, who have no fear at all. I've met them. They're an absolute menace to everybody else. There was a chap we had, commanded a battalion in our brigade, a fellow called Marshall, who was the bravest of the brave. He finally got himself killed in the end; got a VC and everything you can think of. There were those types.[7]

Chapter 19

Shadows

A soldier awarded the Victoria Cross can be assumed to have had a more intense experience of combat than most of his comrades. It follows that he might also be more vulnerable to what today is referred to as post-traumatic stress disorder. In the absence of records acknowledging the condition before the First World War, when it came to be known as shell-shock or war neurosis, it is necessary to look for other indicators that might shed some light on the post-combat mental condition of Victoria Cross recipients. Suicide is one such. Of the 111,313 British troops who served in the Crimean War, eighteen committed suicide during the conflict, an annualized rate of 8–16 per 100,000.[1] The comparable mid-century rate for adult males in England and Wales was 20 per 100,000, so the soldiers were less likely to commit suicide than their civilian counterparts.[2] The picture is far different for the members of the VC sub-set.

Of the 293 VC winners from the Crimean War (1854–55) and the Indian Mutiny (1857–59) none committed suicide during the conflicts, but five had taken their own lives by 1864. The number had risen to nine by the time the last veterans died in the 1920s.[3] One was Sergeant Major Wooden, who killed himself with a shot to the mouth in what was said to be an attempt to remove a diseased tooth; a coronial verdict of temporary insanity allowed him to be buried in consecrated ground.[4] These nine were only the cases in which the coroner recorded suicide as the cause of death. There were in addition two solo shooting accidents in suspicious circumstances, an 'accidental' swallowing of vitriol and a defenestration. By way of comparison, from the thousand-plus awardees since the end of the Mutiny only twelve suicides have been reported, which is broadly comparable with the rates experienced in the community at large over the intervening 159 years.[5] To compound the mystery, three of the VC suicides from the Crimea and Mutiny cohort had a direct connection with the Cross.

Private John Byrne of the 68th Foot saved a comrade at Inkerman and killed a Russian in hand-to-hand combat at Sebastopol. He later served in the Second Maori War. In 1879 he was working for the Ordnance Survey at Caerleon when a younger employee made disrespectful remarks about the Victoria Cross. Byrne shot him in the shoulder. When the police attended the incident Byrne turned the revolver on himself. At Lucknow on 13 June 1858 Private Samuel Shaw of the Rifle Brigade was pursuing a *ghazi*, a Muslim fanatic, when his quarry turned and struck him on the head with a sabre-length *tulwar*. Shaw was so enraged that that he fell on the assailant and sawed him to death with the serrated edge of his short sapper's sword. Eighteen months later, returning to Britain on a troopship, he jumped overboard. It was said that he could not stand the jibes of his comrades about the Victoria Cross he had been awarded.[6] Was he being teased about manic behaviour? He could also have been vulnerable to depression as a result of his head wound. The third case, that of Private Valentine Bambrick of the 60th Foot, will be treated more fully in a later section. Suffice it to record here that when he was imprisoned for theft in 1864 the War Office asked the governor of Pentonville to take from him his Victoria Cross. Overwhelmed with shame at the forfeiture, Bambrick hanged himself in his cell.

One experience common to many of the early recipients was presentation at the hands of the Queen. Sixty-two Crosses were conferred at the inaugural parade in Hyde Park. Contemporary accounts noted the heightened atmosphere among participants and spectators alike and Victoria recorded that she too was 'full of agitation'.[7] As described earlier, so highly was the royal connection valued that some of the awardees were reluctant to surrender their Crosses for engraving. Over the next three years the Queen presented another forty-four Crosses in three mass conferrals, but for fourteen years thereafter all presentations were done by others. The influence of what might be called a 'Victoria effect' on the mental and emotional state of some of these early conferees has to be considered. It had a precedent in the beliefs of earlier centuries, when the Queen's predecessors had touched subjects to cure them of scrofula, the 'King's Evil'. What might have uniquely impressed itself on the earliest recipients was that national honour was somehow bound up with the Cross, and that on it hung their own honour and sense of self-worth.

Fusilier Francis Jefferson was twenty-two when he destroyed one German tank and forced a second to withdraw at Monte Cassino. With a VC on his chest he was sent on a Victory Bond tour of Britain.

Queen Victoria presented the first VCs from horseback.

For decades he lived with the honour and fame of the Cross until it was stolen from his mother's house in 1982. He fell into depression and later that year threw himself under a train. The person who stole his VC might just as well have taken his life.

Chapter 20

Instruments of War

For millennia musical instruments have been used on the battlefield to transmit orders and maintain formation, practices that persisted well into the era of the Victoria Cross. When better means of exercising command and control became available, other combat functions were found for bandsmen. As stretcher-bearers, particularly during the First World War, they discovered that a Red Cross armband was poor protection against indiscriminate fire. Five drummers earned their VCs for saving the wounded. Another got his for defying a regulation that said instruments

Drummer Walter Ritchie rallied wavering men by sounding the charge on a bugle rather than beating a drum as shown in Howard Elcock's painting.

were to be left in the trenches: Drummer Walter Ritchie took his bugle along when the 2nd Battalion, Seaforth Highlanders, went over the top at Beaumont-Hamel on 1 July 1916. By the time the attackers reached the enemy trenches they were reduced in numbers, disorganized and uncertain. Ritchie mounted the parapet under heavy machine-gun fire and repeatedly sounded the charge, which rallied men from various units who had lost their officers and were beginning to retire. For the remainder of the day he carried messages over fire-swept ground.[1] He later said that if things had turned out differently he would have been court-martialled instead of decorated. The artist Howard Elcock, who painted the scene, seems not have known about the regulation: he showed Ritchie playing his drum, a rather large piece of contraband to be smuggled on to a battlefield.

Ritchie was the last of only three buglers awarded. During the retaking of Delhi in 1857 Bugler William Sutton of the 1st Battalion, 60th Rifles, had seen mutineers forming up to attack in force. He rushed their trenches and killed his opposite number, who was about to sound the charge.[2] A month later Bugler Robert Hawthorne of the 52nd Foot was attached to a small party tasked with blowing up the Kashmir Gate. When it was blown he was to signal the advance, but the firing was so heavy that neither the explosion nor

Hawthorne could not make his bugle heard at the Kashmir Gate.

the call was heard. Twice more he blew without response, but the supports judged that sufficient time had elapsed and advanced anyway. Three of the four members of the party received VCs, including Hawthorne.[3]

Which leaves the pipers. By legal definition, established in the treason trial of a Scots piper after Culloden, bagpipes were classified as instruments of war. Although Scottish regiments had carried pipers on strength for a century, it was not until 1854 that the War Office officially acknowledged them for their inspirational quality. During the North West Frontier War of 1897–8 the 2nd Battalion, Gordon Highlanders, was committed to an assault on the Dargai Heights after three other regiments had failed. George Findlater was one of six who stepped forward on the order 'pipers to the front'. The tune would be *Cock o' the North* said Piper Lance Corporal Milne, who was in charge, but Findlater claimed not to have heard him.

> Using my own judgment I thought that the charge would be better led by a quick strathspey, so I struck up *The Heaughs o' Cromdale*. The *Cock o' the North* is more of a march tune and the effort we had to make was a rush and a charge. The battle fever had taken hold of us and we thought not what the other was feeling. Our whole interest being centred in self.[4]

Men began to fall and Milne was hit in the chest, which left him unable to play. Findlater felt a bullet graze his foot. Another bullet struck his chanter, but the pipes remained playable and play he did until a third bullet went through his right ankle, throwing him to the ground and the pipes from his shoulder. He found a rock that he could sit against and played his own selections until the Highlanders had taken the heights.

Piper Daniel Laidlaw also suited the tune to the occasion. While waiting to attack at Loos on 25 September 1915 the 7th Battalion, King's Own Scottish Borderers, was subjected to gas bombardment. Laidlaw's company was shaken so he mounted the parapet and raised his gas mask so that he could play. Marching up and down he played the company out of the trenches.

> … they never wavered but dashed straight on as I played the old air they all knew, *Blue Bonnets over the Border*. My, but there's some fire in that old tune. I ran forward with them, piping for all I knew, and just as we were getting near the

Daniel Laidlaw, who was hailed by the *Illustrated London News* for 'emulating the heroism of Piper Findlater at Dargai'.

German lines I was wounded by shrapnel in the left ankle and leg. I was too excited to feel the pain just then, but scrambled along as best I could... I changed my tune to *The Standard on the Braes o' Mar*, a grand tune for charging on. I kept on piping and piping, and hobbling after the laddies until ... the boys had won the position ...[5]

James Richardson was sixteen years old when he joined the Canadian Expeditionary Force as a piper in 1914. Two years later he volunteered when there was a call for pipers to play the battalion over the top at Morval on the Somme in October 1916. When the advance was held up in front of the German wire and heavy casualties caused the battalion to falter, Richardson strode along the line playing. According to his VC citation:

> the effect was instantaneous. Inspired by his splendid example, the company rushed the wire with such fury and determination that the obstacle was overcome and the position taken.[6]

Richardson was afterwards detailed to take back a wounded comrade and some prisoners, but after proceeding 200 metres realized that he had left his pipes behind. He returned to look for them and was not seen again. In a letter to his mother written five months earlier he had declared his faith in the military value of bagpipes:

> I have not composed a tune yet. The old ones are sufficient for me yet. We are going to strafe Fritz some of these fine days, and I sure mean to let him hear the *Braes o' Mar* if I get the chance. I can assure you if I get the pipes going Fritz will get it on his neck.[7]

George Findlater was discharged unfit for further service as a result of his wound. To earn a living he began making public appearances playing the airs that had echoed across the Dargai Heights, but when the War Office heard that he was about to appear at the Alhambra it objected, holding that it was 'repugnant to military feeling that an exhibition should be made at a music-hall of a soldier who had so recently been decorated by the Queen'. There was parliamentary and public indignation at the interference and the authorities quickly backtracked. Instead, the exposure of Findlay's financial plight was instrumental in having the annual pension for Victoria Cross winners raised from the standard £10 to a maximum of £50 at the discretion of the Secretary of State for War.[8]

Chapter 21

Comrades in Peril

Neville Howse had been one in a long line of Victoria Cross-winners honoured for saving comrades in the field. It is arguable that his medical duties did not extend to rescue and that his Cross can therefore be read as endorsement of a gallant act undertaken at his own initiative. As we have seen, Prince Albert held that such recoveries contributed nothing to military success, but his own frame of reference had been the Crimean War. He seems to have naively assumed that in warfare between civilized nations each side would at least spare the lives of enemy wounded who fell into their hands. The carnage at Solferino in Italy a few years later proved him wrong, but even Albert could have had no such expectations of the Indian Mutiny. European civilians were

John Buckley supervised the execution of mutineers by artillery.

butchered and captured mutineers were made to lick the blood of their victims from walls before being blown to pieces from the muzzles of cannon. Among the men who supervised these atrocities was Deputy Assistant Commissary John Buckley, one of four men awarded VCs for suicidally blowing up the Delhi magazine to deny munitions to the rebels. The mutineers who captured him told him that they had killed his wife and children. He pleaded for the same fate, but they would not kill such a brave man. After he escaped, he volunteered again and again for hazardous assignments but was doomed to survive them.[1] On both sides the Mutiny might be said to have entrenched the 'no quarter' style of warfare that characterized colonial conflicts for another century.

Jean-Henri Dunant's description of the aftermath of the battle of Solfrino horrified Europe. Soon there would be a Geneva Convention and a Red Cross to protect the wounded and the medical staffs that tended them, but in India it was war to the knife and the only protection was self-protection. Surgeon Herbert Reade was tending the wounded of his regiment when a party of mutineers began firing on them from nearby rooftops. He picked up his sword, gathered a few men and dislodged the rebels. Eight of the ten in his little party were killed or wounded. Two days later there was no mistaking him for any sort of non-combatant when he participated in storming the breach at the Delhi magazine and spiked one of the guns. At Lucknow Surgeon Anthony Home took time off from tending the wounded to shoot at rebels. These extra-curricular activities won both of them the Victoria Cross.

Attempts to impose notions of civilized warfare on native troops were not in evidence even when both sides were led by European officers. During von Lettow-Vorbeck's masterly guerilla campaign in East Africa during the First World War he had few German troops; most of his men were Tanganyikan askaris. On 3 September 1915 they ambushed a mounted patrol near Maktau. Temporary Lieutenant Wilbur Dartnell, 25th (Service) Battalion, Royal Fusiliers, was wounded in the leg. While being carried from the field he saw that the enemy were nearing severely injured men who could not be got away. Knowing that the askaris would murder them he twice refused to withdraw and demanded to be left. He was last seen firing on the enemy at very close range. His body was found with seven of them lying close by. The VC citation acknowledged that he could only have 'hoped' to save the wounded and deliberately gave his own life in the attempt.[2]

John Smyth VC took part in several grim colonial struggles between the world wars. In 1920 he was commanding an Indian brigade on the North West Frontier. In the course of withdrawing the 4/39th Garhwal Rifles from the vicinity of Khot Kai in Waziristan, he detailed Lieutenant William Kenny's company to hold an exposed covering position. For four hours the company held out against greatly superior numbers of Mahsud tribesmen. Once the main force was clear Kenny skillfully withdrew three of his platoons, but observed that they were hampered by their wounded and in danger of being overrun. Without hesitation he turned his last rearguard party and with bayonets fixed charged the pursuers. The wounded were all carried to safety but Kenny and his men, whom Smyth said would have followed him anywhere, were all killed. In paying tribute to his subordinate, who was awarded the VC,

Wilbur Dartnell in fact died fighting. Seven enemy dead were found near his body.

Smyth explained that in that type of warfare no good battalion would leave a wounded man on the hillside if rescue were humanly possible.[3] He quoted Kipling in support.

> When you're wounded and left on Afghanistan's plains,
> And the women come out to cut up what remains,
> Just roll to your rifle and blow out your brains,
> And go to your Gawd like a soldier.[4]

For Smyth, saving the wounded under such conditions was a military necessity, essential for the morale of the entire force.

Sometimes saving the wounded was not humanly possible, but the attempt was made anyway. On 23 June 1944 the platoon of Corporal Sefanaia Sukanaivalu, 3rd Battalion, Fijian Infantry Regiment, walked into a Japanese ambush on Bougainville. He crawled out three times to bring in wounded men but while returning with the third was hit in the groin and thighs, which left him unable to move his lower body. Several attempts were made to reach him but they only produced more casualties. Sukanaivalu called on his comrades to stay back as he was in too exposed a position. They shouted back that they would never leave him to fall into Japanese hands. Accepting that they would not withdraw while he was alive, and knowing that if they stayed more casualties were inevitable, he raised his body to expose himself to Japanese machine-gunfire, which killed him. The VC citation spoke of annihilation for the platoon had he not acted as he did.[5]

Similar efforts were sometimes made to retrieve the bodies of the dead. Indeed, during the Indian Mutiny it reached epidemic proportions in the British attack on the fort at Ruhya on 15 April 1858. Five VCs were awarded on that occasion, all for recovering dead and wounded from under the defended walls. Most of the cases were wounded who died before they could be rescued, but the bodies were nonetheless brought in, under fire, to avoid mutilation. Private James Davis of the 42nd Regiment was only present to point out the location of the fort gate to an engineering officer, but with another private he volunteered to carry back a mortally wounded lieutenant. As they lifted him the second private was shot dead. After taking back the officer Davis returned for the body of the private. In an ill-chosen phrase the citation-writer referred to it as 'the duty of danger and affection'.[6] Davis had volunteered, so his

Charles Lucas saves his comrades from a Russian shell at Bomarsund.

was not an act of soldierly duty, and although affection for comrades might create moral obligation it found no authority in the statutes of the Victoria Cross.

Prince Albert had also downplayed protective exploits that defused enemy action, arguing that throwing live shells out of entrenchments did not contribute to victory.[7] His narrow viewpoint ignored the casualties and equipment damage that might thereby be avoided, as was amply demonstrated by the earliest VC awarded. Boatswain's Mate Charles Lucas was serving on HMS *Hecla* during the bombardment of Bomarsund in the Baltic Sea on 21 June 1854 when a shell, fuse smoking, landed on the deck. 'Down' was the word, but Lucas picked up the shell and threw it overboard, where it exploded without doing damage.

Saving comrades from explosive devices became a VC staple. By the time of the First World War hand grenades had become the most challenging of 'returnable' explosive devices. Those used on Gallipoli were often improvised devices and as much danger to the thrower as to the target. Of the thirty-five VCs won during the campaign five went to 'bombers', two of whom payed dearly for mistakes. At Cape Helles on 15 August 1915 Private David Lauder of the Royal Scots Fusiliers threw a bomb that failed to clear the parapet and rolled back into the sap

Alfred Smith saving his men from the consequences of his mistake.

that his bombing party was retaking. As there was insufficient time to smother the bomb he stood on it. It blew off his foot but no other man in the party was injured. Four months later, also at Cape Helles, Second Lieutenant Alfred Smith, East Lancashire Regiment, dropped a bomb

William Hackett refuses to save himself by leaving an injured comrade.

that he was in the act of throwing from a crowded trench. He shouted a warning and jumped away but, seeing that others had not responded, returned and threw himself on the bomb. He was instantly killed, but his selfless action saved many lives.

Lauder and Smith were taking personal responsibility for their mistakes. In the case of Sapper William Hackett, 254th Tunnelling Company, Royal Engineers, there was no mistake. Before the war he had been a miner, an occupation with more than its share of daily hazards and a correspondingly strong ethic of solidarity. In June 1916 his company was undermining an enemy position at Givenchy when the Germans exploded a counter-mine, sealing Hackett and four others in a gallery. After twenty hours digging the trapped men were able to open a narrow unstable hole and join hands with a rescue party. Hackett was urged to pass through but refused, saying 'I am a tunneller, and must look after the others first'. Three of the men got out and Hackett could have followed, but he refused to leave the last man, who had been seriously injured by the explosion. The gallery collapsed, closing the hole. For four days the rescue party tried to reach the buried men but failed. Evelyn Wood, who had been present when Charles Lucas won the first Victoria Cross and who for more than sixty years had been intimately connected with the decoration as recipient, recommending officer and administrator, described Hackett's decision as 'the most divine-like act of self-sacrifice of which I have read'.[8]

The War Office was not interested in self-sacrifice that did not contribute to the war effort. In 1917–18 it set out to tighten the rules. Recovery of buried men was one of three exceptions to its instruction that no one, apart from those whose duty it was, was to be rewarded for rescuing the wounded. The other exceptions were bringing back wounded from a raid (to prevent unit identification by the enemy) and acting under orders to assist stretcher-bearers. The reasons for the general prohibition were threefold: to ensure that rescue efforts did not 'interfere with the employment of every available man for the operations in course of execution'; to avoid 'unnecessary' loss of life; and 'to discourage attempts to win honours for the sake of the honours themselves'.[9] To which Wolseley would have added: 'to avoid rewarding those who use rescue as an excuse for shirking duty'. Wolseley might have been less judgmental had he lived to experience recovery conditions on the Western Front. It was no coincidence that the most highly decorated British NCO of the First World War was a stretcher-bearer, Lance Corporal William Coltman VC, DCM and bar, MM and bar. He was a pacifist.

The War Office prohibition was, on the face of things, highly successful. In the first three years of the war about one-third of the

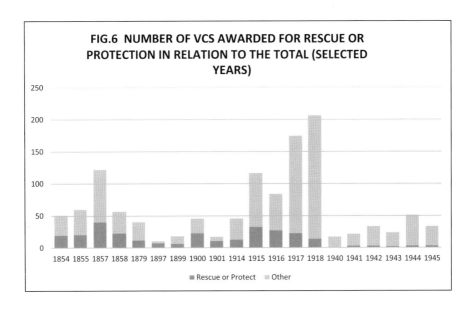

FIG.6 NUMBER OF VCS AWARDED FOR RESCUE OR PROTECTION IN RELATION TO THE TOTAL (SELECTED YEARS)

VCs awarded were for rescue or protection, continuing a pattern of distribution that had generally prevailed since the Crimean War. In 1917 the proportion fell to one in 7.5 and in 1918 to one in 15, half of which were awarded to medical personnel, but the figures do not tell the entire story. A number of citations from this time begin with praise for a military exploit but go on to mention that the awardee also assisted wounded comrades in the course of the action.

The new policy did not go unnoticed or unremarked. The writers who compiled stories of Canadian VC winners for their War Records Office offered a rationale. They claimed that in the wars of the past the Cross had been more frequently awarded for rescuing the wounded than for acts with 'more material and purely military advantages' (an exaggeration, although it had occurred in several years at the end of the nineteenth century). Gone, however, were the days of small armies, long marches and short battles, when total defeat could not hang on the outcome of a single engagement and a soldier was something more than a unit of manpower. What had changed was the length, ferocity and scale of war.

> The deed of valour must show material rather than sentimental results; the duty that inspires the deed must show a military rather than a humane intention. The spirit of our heroes is the same today as it was yesterday, whether the courageous act results in the holding of a position, killing a score of Germans, or the saving of one comrade's life. Only the spirit of official appreciation has changed; but this new spirit is logical.

Having upheld the case for the change of policy the compilers then proceeded to undermine it. They had written the apologia by way of a preamble to their account of the VC won by Sergeant Major James Hall of the 8th Canadian Infantry Battalion at Ypres on 4 April 1915. Twice under cover of darkness he had brought in men wounded in the course of a confused relief. In daylight another wounded man was heard and Hall took two volunteers to bring him in. Both of the volunteers were wounded in the failed attempt, but Hall resolved to try again alone. The writer acknowledged that duty and humanity were at odds.

It was his duty as a non-commissioned officer to avoid making the same mistake twice. He had already permitted the risking of three lives in the attempt to save one life and had suffered two casualties; but doubtless he felt free to risk his own life again in the same adventure as he had already successfully accomplished two rescues over the same ground. He may be forgiven, I think, for not pausing to reflect that his own life was of more value to the cause than the life of the sufferer lying out behind the trench.[10]

Hall was mortally wounded and the wounded man was killed. It is unlikely that his sacrifice, made in the old spirit, would have earned him a VC in 1918 or subsequently. Only fifteen of the 182 VCs awarded during the second war were for rescue or protection. Of the twenty awards made since, only three can be so categorized.

Chapter 22

Writing It Up

It was clear to the founders of the Cross that if it were to be highly prized and eagerly sought after there would have to be widespread publicity of awards. The Warrant provided for public decoration in the presence of the recipient's unit and the issue of a General Order setting out the name of the recipient and 'the cause of his especial distinction'. The wider public would be informed, as they were of all honours, by the *London Gazette*, a vehicle for government announcements since the seventeenth century. The first awards, eighty-five in number, were published on 24 February 1857. The naval citations quoted at length from the dispatches that had brought the awardees to the attention of higher authority. They were often animated and occasionally adjectival. The army's citations were dull, bearing the stamp of staff writing. They reached epigrammatic brevity in the case of Private F. Wheatley of the Rifle Brigade: his award was said to be 'for throwing a live shell over the parapet of the trenches', date and place unspecified.[1] Even when they were more forthcoming they did not tell the whole story. Gunner Thomas Arthur of the Royal Regiment of Artillery had been in charge of a magazine during the attack on the Sebastopol Quarries. 'Of his own accord', said the citation, he carried ammunition across to the 7th Royal Fusiliers under fire.[2] It neglected to mention that shortly thereafter he was being marched away for leaving his post until the commanding officer of the Fusiliers intervened. An impending disciplinary charge became a recommendation for the Victoria Cross. Arthur's action was applauded by military writer Henry Knollys as 'heeding neither the responsibility nor the danger'. Initiative had triumphed over duty, but it could just as easily have gone the other way.[3]

Aware that its descriptions looked pale beside those of the senior service, the army sought to improve. Its citations in the second gazettal ten weeks later were more expansive, but still cautious, and for good reason. Assistant Surgeon Thomas Hale of the 7th Royal Fusiliers had been recommended for remaining with a wounded officer at the Redan on 18 June 1855 when neighbouring troops had retreated 'during a panic'.[4] The quoted words were omitted from the gazette notification; retreat might be admissible, but panic was not. Hale might have kept his head when all around were losing theirs, but it would not do to say so, however much the contrast would have emphasized his merit. Some later citations were slightly more forthcoming, hinting that the bravery of others present might have left something to be desired. In the assault on the *pa* at Rangiriri on 20 November 1863 Lieutenant Arthur Pickard of the Royal Artillery carried water to the wounded several times under intense fire 'when none of the men could be induced to perform this service'.[5] The admission was acknowledgement that valour is easiest to identify when it can be compared with the response of others exposed to the same fear-inducing threat, but in one case at least the comparison was too stark.

A few minutes earlier, George Moor had found it necessary to shoot four of these soldiers to halt a rout.

On 15 June 1915 Second Lieutenant George Moor, unexpectedly in command of a battalion at Gallipoli after his superiors had become casualties, saw leaderless men on his left rapidly withdrawing from their trench in the face of a Turkish attack. According to his VC citation, Moor immediately grasped the danger to the remainder of the line, 'dashed back some two hundred yards, stemmed the retirement, led back the men and recaptured the lost trench'. He did his stemming with a revolver and had to shoot four Tommies before the rest turned around.[6]

Another example of something best left unsaid was the award for honorary Captain John Foote, a Canadian chaplain who tended the wounded on the beach at Dieppe during the raid on 19 August 1942. The citation referred to his tireless efforts to carry the wounded to the aid post and back to the landing craft under heavy fire with minimal cover. It honoured his decision to stay on the beach to be captured with the wounded who could not be evacuated.[7] What it omitted to say was that towards the end he had taken a Bren gun and used it in the line in violation of his non-combatant status.[8] Internationally-covenanted practice had changed a great deal since the first relief of Lucknow, when Surgeon Anthony Home had gathered wounded from the streets and tended them in a house that was under attack. His citation had mentioned that 'at last only six men and Mr Home were left to fire'.[9] Home knew that as far as the mutineers were concerned there was no such thing as a European non-combatant, but Foote's action ran the risk of undermining observance of the Geneva Convention.

In rare cases it was not possible to exploit the full propaganda value of citations because of the need for secrecy. Ongoing operations were protected by keeping citations short and vague, notably for the awardees on the Q-ships of the First World War. These apparently unarmed merchant vessels were sent out by the Admiralty to offer themselves as targets to U-boats. If the deception was successful the U-boat would save its torpedoes and surface with the intention of sinking the ship with gunfire or scuttling charges. The Q-ship would then unmask its guns, hoist the White Ensign and engage. The *Gazette* blandly reported that Harold Auten, lieutenant, Royal Naval Reserve, had been awarded a VC 'for services in action with enemy submarines'.[10] None of the other citations for Q-ship service was any more forthcoming. When Auten attended Buckingham Palace for the presentation the band played *Hush, hush, hush! Here comes the Bogey Man*, much to the amusement of the

Harold Auten aboard a Q-ship, wearing his civilian disguise.

King. The relevant action had taken place in the English Channel on 30 July 1918, when Auten had been doing his best to offer HMS *Stock Force* as an easy target. The U-boat that came along took no chances. It remained submerged and sent a torpedo. As *Stock Force* had been filled to the hatchways with timber against just this eventuality it settled slowly. A 'panic party' abandoned the sinking ship to allay any suspicion that it might pose a threat, but the U-boat failed to rise to the bait. Only when the panickers turned back to the ship did the U-boat surface and follow, to be severely damaged when Auten opened fire at 300 metres. The U-boat sank almost immediately and *Stock Force* four hours later. Auten and his crew were rescued by a torpedo boat. The need to keep tactics secret was ample reason for reticence. One successful Q-ship was subsequently lost to another U-boat after the crew of its victim made it back to Germany and reported the manner of their undoing. A week after the conclusion of hostilities the *Gazette* published amplifying citations for all eight of the Q-ship VCs. The *Stock Force* action was described as 'one of the finest examples of coolness, discipline and good organization in the history of Q-ships'.[11]

George V took a close interest in the wording of *Gazette* notices. When the recommendation for Lieutenant Charles Rutherford of the Canadian Expeditionary Force came before him he objected to its use of the word Hun as inappropriate language for a 'more or less' official document. He also queried the word pillbox, presumably because it was colloquial. On 26 August 1918 at Monchy Rutherford had dealt with two of them. The first he approached alone and bluffed its 45-man garrison into surrendering; the second he attacked with a Lewis gun section and took another thirty-five prisoners and their machine-guns.[12] The Military Secretary explained to the King that after he had approved a recommendation it was carefully edited before gazettal: 'Hun' would be replaced with 'enemy', but there was not much that could be done about pillbox; it was in universal use and there was no other expression that described it.[13] Would placing inverted commas around the offending word make it more acceptable? His Majesty agreed that it would.[14]

If Albert Jacka had been asked to write his own VC recommendation it is unlikely to have gone far up the line. His diary entry for 19 May 1915 is unadorned to a fault:

> Great battle at 3am. Turks captured large portions of our trench. D Coy called into the front line. Lieut. Hamilton shot dead. I led a section of men and recaptured the trench. I bayonetted two Turks, shot five, took three prisoners and cleared the whole trench. I held the trench alone for 15 minutes against a heavy attack. Lieut. Crabbe informed me that I would be recommended.[15]

To judge from the citation, Crabbe's recommendation had been nearly as terse as Jacka's diary entry. The citation writer had added the by-then standard formula of 'most conspicuous bravery', which brought the act within the terms of the Warrant, and explained that Jacka had most gallantly attacked single-handed. Other recommendations were not afforded such an easy passage. Colonel Rowland Fielding wrote to his wife that he knew of a man whose commanding officer had recommended him for a Military Medal. When the recommendation was rejected the officer tried again, using the most extravagant language at his command. His candidate was awarded a VC. Fielding decried it as 'Penny Dreadful' writing, but blamed a system whereby staff officers behind the fighting line were passing judgement without first-hand knowledge of the men recommended or of the conditions they faced.

> I have known good men eating their hearts out through want of recognition. A ribbon is the only prize in war for the ordinary soldier. I wish that this form of reward did not exist, seeing that ribbons must be distributed by men, not by gods. If they were given by God, how many an iridescent breast would cease to sparkle – and the contrary.[16]

And Penny Dreadful writing could be counter-productive. Major Irwin of the East Surreys was writing up a VC recommendation for the Regimental Medical Officer, Captain Gimson, when the divisional commander came by. General Maxse was of the view that it was insufficiently 'journalistic' and undertook to rewrite it. Irwin believed that the rewriting cost Gimson the VC.[17]

We are fortunate to have a line-by-line commentary on one citation by its subject. In 1945 Corporal Edward Chapman, 3rd Battalion, a Welshman serving in the Monmouthshire Regiment, was awarded for holding the position of his isolated section near the Dortmund-Ems canal. Towards the end of the action he had carried in a wounded officer and was himself wounded by a sniper during the carry. After the war he was interviewed and taken through the citation. He corrected a number of minor factual errors, which he put down to the inexperience of the witnesses. These were the 18-year-olds of his section, who had been interviewed at battalion headquarters to find out who had brought in the officer. Chapman took exception, however, to a description of him rising to repel the advancing Germans with his Bren gun. 'I got up a couple of times. But when they say I got up, it was only bloody knees up. You can imagine: you see two hundred or a hundred men in front of you, you don't bloody stand up'. He did not dispute the accuracy of the summing-up, which spoke of his single-handed repulse of well-led, determined troops that gave the battalion time to reorganize on a vital piece of ground, but …

> See, this is all right to read, but there was a whole battalion there. You could write this for every bloody man who was up there. They picked on me because it worked that way but

there was hundreds of blokes there who got nothing. I think it's been highlighted because I took the officer; I think that's what highlighted it. And I had to take him back. He was alive when I picked him up but I think he was shot the second time, on me.

Another member of the regiment estimated that Chapman and his Bren gun had accounted for twenty or thirty of the enemy.[18]

In that second war, when propaganda reached a new pitch on both sides, the Ministry of Information found a new way of advertising the exemplary deeds of VC winners. In 1943 it published a slim pamphlet of sketches and text describing all VC actions of the war to date.[19] Produced to wartime standards and lacking much in the way of official attribution, it was a one-off. There was no second edition to record Edward Chapman's knees-up.

Chapter 23

Struck Off

As discussed earlier, the survival of some Victoria Cross winners has verged on the miraculous. Saints too acquire their status through miracles, but there the comparison ends. Soldiers are common clay, and even heroes have their flaws. It is a quirk of human nature that we expect persons admired in one respect to be admirable in all. To prevent contamination of the Cross by bad behaviour, Newcastle had wanted to provide for forfeiture of the decoration in the event of conviction by court martial for a serious offence, and for desertion. In Panmure's Warrant the grounds were enlarged into the civil sphere to embrace conviction for 'treason, cowardice, felony or of any infamous crime'.[1] The last category, distinct from felony, was intended to cover the common law offences of fraud or dishonesty and, as desertion was not otherwise mentioned, perhaps that as well. In all cases, decision to erase from the register was reserved to the Sovereign alone, as was discretion to restore.

The formula immediately threw up a problem. The first gazettal included Private William Stanlack of the Coldstream Guards, who at Inkerman had volunteered to reconnoitre. He had crawled to within metres of a Russian sentry, having been warned of the risk, and brought back such useful information that his officer had been able to launch a surprise attack. The Queen had approved Stanlack's award and he was to have received it at the great inaugural parade, but between the two events he committed a theft, which was summarily dealt with by his commanding officer. Panmure was concerned that because there was no conviction, and now no possibility of a trial to obtain one, there were no grounds for withholding the Cross. Equally, the Queen could not be expected to decorate a thief. All he could suggest was that Stanlack be told that he would not be receiving the medal from the Queen's hand, and why. The commander-in-chief, the Duke of Cambridge, suggested that the matter be deferred until Stanlack had been given time to redeem himself, but the

War Office advised that it was not possible. Stanlack got his Cross, but missed the parade. The first case to fall formally under the provisions of rule 15 was that of Edward Daniel. In the Crimea he had been one of two midshipman aides-de-camp to Captain William Peel RN, the other being Evelyn Wood. They had followed their leader through several scrapes that earned both Peel and Daniel (but not Wood, unfairly) the VC. Daniel had especially distinguished himself by tending the wounded captain under heavy fire at the Redan.[2] While afterwards serving at sea he was accused of 'taking indecent liberties with four subordinate officers'. He deserted to evade enquiry, but could not escape the long arm of the Warrant: 'if he be accused of any such offence (Daniel's was described as disgraceful) and doth not after a reasonable time surrender himself to be tried for the same' his Cross would be forfeit. The Queen signed the warrant of forfeiture on 4 September 1861.[3]

Since the Cross was instituted there have been eight forfeitures, chiefly for theft. One, which ironically involved another man's medals, was nothing short of a tragedy. Private Valentine Bambrick had won the Cross during the Indian Mutiny. At Bareilly on 6 May 1858 three mutineers cornered Bambrick and his company commander in a narrow street. Although twice wounded he killed one of their assailants while saving the officer, who recommended him. He took his discharge at Aldershot in 1863 but while celebrating in a local hostelry heard screams coming from the room above. Investigating, he found a sergeant beating a woman. Bambrick rescued the woman, but next day was accused of assault by the sergeant, who additionally claimed that Bambrick had stolen his medals. The sergeant enlisted his cronies to testify and the woman disappeared. In court Bambrick lost his temper as the conspiracy became obvious to him. The outburst convinced the court that he was capable of assault and earned him three years' imprisonment. As he had been convicted of a felony, the War Office took steps not only to erase his name from the VC register, but also to recover his medal. This was done by writing to the governor of the prison where Bambrick was serving his sentence. It was one injustice too many. Three months after entering Pentonville he hanged himself in his cell, leaving a note expressing despair at the loss of his award.[4]

The most curious forfeit, and to modern eyes a case of overreach, was the man who had his VC taken away because he was a bigamist. Gunner James Collis of the Royal Horse Artillery had won his Cross during the retreat to Khandahar in the Second Afghan War. On 28 July 1880, riding the No.2 gun of his battery, he saw his commanding officer being threatened by enemy cavalry as he was attempting to bring in a limber with wounded men. Collis ran forward and provided covering fire. The enemy cavalry, unaware that they were facing one man, dismounted and engaged him. The limber escaped and Collis killed two Afghans before being relieved. He was invalided from the army in 1893 and two years later sent to prison for bigamy, which was a felony. He had pawned his medal and the War Office asked if the Metropolitan Police could redeem it for the eight shillings lent. Concern for the integrity of this particular medal did not last: fifteen years later the War Office sold it at auction.[5]

In cases of forfeiture, as with most things to do with the Cross, the Queen was not a passive instrument. Private Edmund Fowler, for whom Wood had obtained the decoration during the lobbying done for Henry Lysons, was court-martialled for embezzlement from a comrade. In the opinion of the Assistant Adjutant General this was a felony and he submitted a warrant of forfeiture. Ponsonby, the Queen's secretary, informed him that 'the Queen cannot bring herself to sign this submission'. Her Majesty had recalled Fowler's bravery in the efforts to save Captain Ronald Campbell at Inhlobane, and noted that his offence could not have been too serious as his only punishment was to be reduced to the ranks. 'He is still fit to serve the Queen and HM thinks he should retain his VC'.[6]

The last man to forfeit the Cross was one of the seven who had saved the guns at Colenso. In 1908 George Ravenhill, formerly of the Royal Scots Fusiliers, was released from prison after serving a sentence for stealing iron. As a convicted felon his Cross had been forfeit and the recommendation to erase had received royal approval. The War Office, which had missed the opportunity of recovering the medal itself while Ravenhill was in prison, stirred when it saw that his VC was to be auctioned by Sothebys. Can he do that? it asked the Treasury Solicitor. The substance of the reply was that there was nothing in the Warrant about forfeiture of the hardware. As a civilian his medal was his to do with as he pleased.[7] Including keeping it in prison, protests Valentine Bambrick from his unhallowed grave. The solicitor also suggested that the auctioneers be advised that the Ravenhill medal 'is not a genuine VC now'.[8] The advice was unwelcome to the War Office on two counts. Had it sold the Collis VC under false pretences about its authenticity; and should it now try to restore that medal to its legal owner? The Military Secretary favoured masterly inactivity: no action would be necessary unless and until Collis raised the matter.

Collis never did, although at sixty-odd years of age he served again during the First World War. His death in 1918 of heart disease should have been the end of the matter, but his widow, she for whom he had sacrificed his liberty and his decoration all those years earlier, wrote to the King asking for her husband's name to be restored to the register. It was probably this request, which was not granted, that prompted the King to make clear his views about recovery of the medal itself in the event of forfeiture of the Cross. His private secretary advised the Army Council that

> The King feels so strongly that, no matter the crime committed by anyone on whom the VC has been conferred, the decoration should not be forfeited. Even were a VC to be sentenced to be hanged for murder, he should be allowed to wear the VC on the scaffold.[9]

Thereafter, although offences covered by the Warrant continued to come to attention and the King was kept informed, the Army Council did not recommend forfeiture. So far did tolerance now extend that when one recipient was discharged from the Army for bad character and sought to 'resign the VC' the War Office did not answer his letter. In the 1920s an interdepartmental committee recommended that all gallantry awards should be irrevocable except in 'very exceptional cases of extreme infamy', which it listed as treason, sedition, mutiny, cowardice, desertion during hostilities and disgraceful conduct of an unnatural kind. As the list did not fully align with the forfeiture provision of the VC Warrant, the solution adopted when the latter was revised in 1931 was to exclude reasons for forfeiture altogether. Instead, the new Warrant reserved to the Sovereign the right to cancel and restore on grounds unspecified. In the internal debates which had led to the reformulation it had become clear that for recipients who had returned to civilian life, treason and sedition would be the only actionable offences.[10] The other offences, with one exception, were exclusively military in nature. That exception was unnatural conduct, which was a criminal offence as well as a military one. Had the 1931 Warrant continued the previous practice of listing forfeiture offences it would have contained a glaring anomaly: a serving VC would have been liable to erasure from the Register if convicted of homosexual practices, while a discharged VC would not.

In the literature of the Victoria Cross forfeiture has been a sensitive matter. The exhaustive record of winners that was compiled and published in the 1920s by Creagh and Humphris included those who had been erased and made no mention of forfeit. The authors seem to have decided, without admitting as much, that once a VC always a VC. At the request of the Ministry of Defence Michael Crook went to some lengths in the 1970s to avoid identifying those whose names had been erased, which made his treatment of misconduct less coherent than it might have been. Not until the books of Max Arthur and Kevin Brazier appeared in 2004 and 2010 respectively was forfeiture treated as a legitimate aspect of the history of each relevant award. Long before that, however, the Creagh and Humphris practice of putting the telescope to a blind eye had been tacitly accepted in official circles. The erased names appeared in the official list of VC awards published by the Ministry of Defence in 1953. As Crook noted, time had effectively annulled the expulsions.[11]

The 1931 Warrant left unlimited discretionary power in the hands of a Sovereign who had already imposed a self-denying limitation. It is fortunate that the tolerance of George V was not tested by, say, an Irishman named O'Flaherty convicted of treason or desertion during the Troubles. His name would certainly have been erased from the Register, but would he have been allowed to make his VC an aiming mark for the firing squad?

Chapter 24

Under the Eye of the Commander

A deed unseen was a deed not done. The valiant act was insufficient to win a Victoria Cross; it had to be noticed and by someone who counted. At the outset, warfare was still intimate enough for rule 7 of the Warrant to give admirals and general officers commanding the right to confer – subject to confirmation by the Sovereign – when the act of valour had been performed under their 'eye and command'. Two Crimean VCs appear to fall into this category, although the Warrant had not yet been promulgated when the relevant actions occurred.

Major John Conolly and his company of the 49th Foot were the outlying picket of the Second Division in front of Sebastopol when the Russians attacked on 26 October 1854. 'He came particularly under the observation of the late Field Marshal Lord Raglan, while in personal encounter with several Russians, in defence of his post …', eventually falling, severely wounded. At Inkerman on 5 November 1854 Colonel Henry Percy, Grenadier Guards, found that he had charged too far and with men from a number of regiments was in danger of being surrounded by Russians. The redcoats had no ammunition so Percy, although wounded, used his knowledge of the ground to extricate the party and find an ammunition point. Fifty men were then able to return to the fight. 'He received the approval of HRH the Duke of Cambridge, for this action, on the spot'.[1]

Inherent in the power of bestowal conferred by rule 7 was power to initiate an award. As the attention of these august personages might often be elsewhere, rule 8 provided a default procedure. Ships' captains and regimental commanders were authorized to pass recommendations up to admirals and general officers commanding for consideration but, remarkably, power of initiation lay with 'the claimant', not the captains and colonels. The Warrant was quite clear that the claimant would be self-nominating and advised him that he would be asked 'to prove the act to the satisfaction' of his superior.

The first selection process, at the end of the Crimean War, was perforce retrospective. No general call went out for claimants to self-nominate. Instead, the commanding officers of returning regiments were ordered to submit names. Some circulated the order and invited those who wished to be considered to appear before a regimental board convened for the purpose. The CO of the 44th Foot made a half-hearted attempt at Albertian selection, polling all men in the regiment who had received the Distinguished Conduct Medal or France's *Médaille Militaire*. Colonel Warre of the 57th Foot forwarded all the names that had been considered by his board and for good measure threw in his own: 'I should feel gratified in being permitted to wear a decoration so entirely military and one for which all soldiers will eagerly seek'. At the other end of the spectrum the colonels of six regiments, one of which had fought at both the Alma and Inkerman, submitted nil returns. Crook has suggested that this was evidence of their own lack of energy rather than undistinguished conduct on the part of their men.[2] The regimental lists were sifted and culled at Horse Guards, passed to the War Office for scrutiny, returned if there were queries and finally submitted to the Queen for approval which, as we have seen, was not a foregone conclusion.

The direct supervision exercised by Victoria over the retrospective Crimean awards was not possible during the Indian Mutiny when, as we have seen, Colin Campbell tried to exercise his provisional power to confer in ways unapproved by London. When General Hope was prosecuting the Third China War he recommended Ensign John Chaplin and Private Thomas Lane of the 67th Foot for raising the Queen's colour over a breach made in the wall of North Taku fort. Lane had also been instrumental in making the breach. Hope urged that although he had not exercised his authority to confer, his promise to recommend the men was 'almost tantamount to a provisional bestowal'.[3] Again, when Roberts led the Kabul Field Force into Afghanistan in 1879, enjoying all the authority of a general commanding on distinct and detached service, he did not exercise it. It was not for want of opportunity. On 14 December he was looking on through his telescope as Lance Corporal George Sellar led a storming party of Seaforth Highlanders up the Asmai heights north of Kabul. Sellar was severely wounded. Roberts visited him in hospital and promised to recommend him to the commander in chief. It would seem that after the mutiny provisional awards were no longer the done thing.

The practice of initiation at unit level and consideration up the chain of command, adopted for the Crimea issue, had become the norm.

Rule 7 was moribund but remained on the books for another sixty years, as did rule 8. Tardily, the general revision of the Warrant in 1920 eliminated provisional awards but was equivocal about self-nomination, the only way of getting one's name considered if officers had been looking elsewhere. The passive voice was employed.

> ... every recommendation for ... the Cross shall be made and reported through the usual channel to ... the Officer Commanding the Force, who shall call for such description, conclusive proof as far as the circumstances of the case will allow, and attestation of the act as he may think requisite.

The revisers, those who had also formally overturned Panmure's prohibition of posthumous awards, here weakened the self-nomination process by deleting reference to claimants. Using the same tortured logic of the posthumous awards debate, it could now be argued that as self-nomination was no longer mentioned it must be prohibited; conversely, if the wind changed it could be argued that because it was not expressly prohibited it could be permitted. Theoretically, claimants and their superiors had equal rights to recommend, but claimants had no responsibility for proof and attestation apart from their own evidence. In the circumstances self-nomination could only be a last resort when superiors were unconvinced about conformity with the Warrant or, as in the case of the six Crimean colonels, not disposed to stir themselves.

Few personal claims have succeeded. Of those that have, the most common were appeals along the lines of 'if him, why not me?'. The first of them was prompted by a late award of the VC to Surgeon James Mouat of the 6th Dragoons, who on the day after the Charge of the Light Brigade had brought in a wounded officer of the 17th Lancers left exposed on the battlefield. When Mouat was gazetted in 1858, four years after the event, Sergeant Major Charles Wooden of the 17th wrote to the surgeon pointing out that he had helped to dress the wound and bring Captain Morris in under fire. Mouat supported Wooden and his claim was allowed. Similarly, Lieutenant Frederick Miller of the Royal Artillery submitted that 'as the Victoria Cross has already been bestowed on an officer for a very similar act (viz. jumping over a wall in face of the enemy to encourage his comrades), I am induced to hope that His Royal Highness may recommend Her Majesty to confer the same distinction on myself'.[4] To its embarrassment, Horse Guards found that Miller had been recommended for Inkerman by the board that had initially considered all Crimean VC awards. It apologized to the War Office for mislaying the papers, pleading the volume of correspondence on the subject.

Miller got his Cross, but it was not for anything to do with a wall.[5] His citation referred instead to an incident when, a body of British infantry having retired through his battery, advancing Russians surrounded it. He personally attacked three Russians and with his gunners prevented any mischief being done to the guns.[6] These and other late claims, two years after the peace treaty had been signed, led the War Office to suggest that enough was enough.

It was the same with the Mutiny. On 30 June 1857, during the siege of Lucknow, Captain R.P. Anderson of the 25th Native Infantry had gone to the rescue of Mr Capper of the Bengal Civil Service, who had been buried under a verandah brought down by rebel artillery. Among the volunteers who came forward to assist Anderson was Corporal William Oxenham of the 32nd Foot. Under intense fire that kept the diggers flat to the ground, and while he was exposed supporting Capper's head, Anderson directed Oxenham to free Capper's legs, which required the corporal to stand. Oxenham was awarded the VC for saving the civilian. Eleven years later Capper recommended Anderson, writing that by word and example and contrary to the advice of his superior officer he had 'shamed the others to action'; if anyone had saved his life, it was Anderson. The recommendation was not accepted.[7] It was considerably more than two years after the end of hostilities and furthermore it reflected on Oxenham.

The gathering of evidence to support self-nomination was itself a hazardous process, as Surgeon Thomas Carey of the 64th Foot found in 1858 when he wrote to Horse Guards forwarding a petition from private soldiers of the regiment. The petitioners recommended him for services in the field and for saving the life of one of their number. Carey was informed that his letter did not establish his claim and furthermore

> The recommendation of an individual for the VC by the soldiers of a regiment without the sanction of the Commanding Officer is itself a great irregularity, and one

which it was your duty to have repressed instead of founding a claim upon it in direct opposition to your commanding officer's opinions.[8]

The commander's eye could not be all-seeing. In most actions he was dependent on his subordinates to produce witnesses. Should they fail to do so there was no information with which to proceed, which should have ruled out Billy Bishop. It also nearly ruled out Flying Officer Lloyd Trigg, a New Zealander serving with 200 Squadron. While patrolling the North Atlantic on 11 August 1943 he sighted *U-468* on the surface. He commenced a bombing run, but anti-aircraft fire heavily damaged his Liberator and set it on fire. Trigg could have aborted the attack but held his line, knowing that he would continue to present an easy target as he pulled up. The Liberator passed over the U-boat at 50 feet, taking more hits through the open bomb bay doors. The bombs bracketed and hit the submarine, whose crew watched as the aircraft plunged into the sea, killing all aboard. After his boat sank, Oberleutnant Schamong and a few of his crew took to a rubber dinghy that had broken free from the Liberator. Schamong told his British rescuers that its pilot deserved the Victoria Cross. The other survivors supported his account. This was the only Victoria Cross awarded solely on the eyewitness evidence of an enemy commander and his crew.

Chapter 25

One for All

Albert's anachronistic belief that a single individual could turn the course of a land battle was also at odds with his aim of rewarding collective success. The contradiction was felt more acutely in the navy given the confined and interdependent nature of service in ships. In action all were in the same boat, but by naval tradition the sole responsibility of the captain for his command also entitled him to the lion's share of any honours. The captain who went down with his ship had been accorded special respect long before there was a Victoria Cross to recognize his sacrifice, but what was to be done for the men that went down with him? Another difficulty was that in the navy the line between servicemen and civilians was not always as clear cut as in the army.

Frederick Parslow, a Merchant Navy master, was in command of the unarmed horse transport *Anglo-Californian* when a surfaced German submarine intercepted it near Queenstown, Ireland, on 4 July 1915. Parslow sent out an SOS and manoeuvred to keep the submarine astern. For ninety minutes the pursuer kept up a steady fire, scoring occasional hits, until it was close enough to signal that those aboard the ship should abandon her as soon as possible. To save life Parslow stopped engines and prepared to lower the boats. He then received a radio message that urged him to hold on until help arrived. When he restarted the engines the submarine directed its fire on the unprotected bridge, killing Parslow. The delay had been long enough for destroyers to come up and chase the U-boat away. Ship and cargo were saved. The citation described Parslow's devotion as a splendid example to the officers and men of the Mercantile Marine.[1]

SS *Otaki* was not completely unarmed when she was directed to stop by the German raider *Moewe* off Capetown on 10 March 1917. By then the Admiralty had armed many merchant ships for self-protection, but the *Otaki's* single 4.7-inch gun was no match for the seven guns, mostly of larger calibre, mounted on the raider. Archibald Bissett-Smith, master

HMS *Jervis Bay* (right) distracts the *Admiral Scheer* (far right) while the convoy scatters.

of the *Otaki*, nonetheless engaged at about 2,000 metres. For twenty minutes the ships pounded each other. Both ships were damaged and set on fire, but heavier armament told and Smith ordered the boats lowered. He remained on board and went down with his ship, colours still flying. A German account described the action as a duel as gallant as naval history can relate.[2]

The navy was keen to claim the Victoria Cross on behalf of both men, but they were merchant seamen and, as civilians, arguably ineligible. The Admiralty was up to the challenge. It gave them posthumous commissions as lieutenants in the Royal Naval Reserve, backdated to the day before death in action. The delayed announcement, by three and a half years in Parslow's case, can be seen as concern about consequences. In 1916 the Germans captured and executed a British merchant captain who had been presented with a gold watch by the Admiralty for attempting to ram a U-boat that had been attacking his ship. Had Parslow's VC been announced at the time it could have been used by the Germans to justify reprisals against other merchant seamen.

Unlike Parslow and Smith, acting Captain Edward Fegan was a career naval officer. His command in 1940 was the armed merchant cruiser *Jervis Bay*, mounting seven 6-inch guns. She was escorting convoy HX-84 when they encountered the pocket battleship *Admiral Scheer* south of Iceland. Hopelessly outranged by the 11-inch guns of the *Scheer*, Fegan dropped smoke floats and steered for the raider. For twenty-two minutes, unable to reply, the *Jervis Bay* held the German's fire. Crippled and ablaze she eventually succumbed, but by then the convoy was scattering as ordered. Fegan and 186 members of his crew perished with the ship.[3] Although darkness was falling *Scheer* began to overtake and sink the merchantmen. It appeared that many would still be lost.

Among them was SS *Beaverford*, commanded by Hugh Pettigrew. He reported by wireless each sinking as it occurred, using smoke and darkness to hide his own ship, but when he saw that *Scheer* was closing on SS *Kenbane Head* he turned towards the German and fired his 3-inch bow gun. The tiny shell did not even hit, but it succeeded in drawing the raider's attention. Pettigrew put out a last signal: 'It is our turn now. So long'. The frustrated raider, which had earlier counted 'target number 9' among the ships it had sunk, put two main salvos into redesignated target 11. Three of the rounds hit, as had sixteen from the secondary armament. With the *Beaverford* on fire, taking water and slowing it was just a matter of time. The torpedo with which *Scheer* ended the action detonated ammunition in the *Beaverford*'s hold, blowing the ship apart. She sank with all hands but subsequently the *Scheer* was able to find and sink only one more ship of the convoy.

That Fegan would be nominated for the VC was all but inevitable; that Pettigrew was not calls for an explanation. Merchant seamen 'who in the course of their duties may become subject to enemy action' had been eligible since revision of the Warrant in 1919. Two months before the epic of HX-84 the George Cross had made provision for seamen and others whose heroism was not in the presence of the enemy. Pettigrew was clearly eligible for a VC, but of the two awards the GC better suited the circumstances because it provided for collective recognition. The captain had lost his life helping to save the convoy, but so too had his entire crew. Malta is deservedly remembered as the George Cross island but, if an island, why not a ship? The question was not posed, much less answered, because it was not until 1944 that an eyewitness account of the *Beaverford*'s fight was published. By then the war had moved on.

After its experience in the Indian Mutiny, when thirty-one of the 182 VCs had been awarded by election, the army showed little enthusiasm for the process. It was 1900 before they tried again, polling the men who had saved the guns at Korn Spruit. The last straw seems to have been the muddled process that produced 'six VCs before breakfast' for officers and men of the Lancashire Fusiliers at Gallipoli. As for the Royal Navy, in the absence of a provision for collective awards it saw in election something nearly as well fitted to the circumstances of naval warfare. All share the risk; all should share the choice of recipients. The navy conducted a number of ballots late in the First World War. There were two polls taken of Q-ship crews in 1917 and others were held after the Zeebrugge raid of 22/23 April 1918.

At Zeebrugge on the Belgian coast the navy mounted a classic amphibious operation designed to block U-boat access to the North Sea. Marines and sailors were landed to cover the placing of block ships. Casualties were high, particularly among the marines, and separate ballots were held among marines and seamen to prevent the service with the highest number of survivors predominating. One officer and one NCO or ranker were elected by each service, which bore little relation to the rules laid down in rule 13 of the Warrant. Five individual VCs were also awarded to make nine altogether, the largest number ever for a single naval action. Curiously, among the individual awards were two posthumous VCs for naval officers. There was room for one of them to have been elected by their peers in the navy ballot, but neither was. The voted award went to the most senior officer present, Captain Alfred Carpenter of HMS *Vindictive*.

The marines were nearly as deferential, the officers voting for one of the company commanders, Captain Edward Bamford. More interesting was the election of Sergeant Norman Finch of the Royal Marine Artillery.[4] Most of those participating in the ballot were marine light infantry but Finch polled more than half of all votes cast. The decisive factor was probably his visibility during the action. Stationed with pom-pom and Lewis guns high in the foretop of *Vindictive*, he kept the guns in action suppressing enemy fire after all other members of their crews had been killed or wounded, including him. In his case it was the many eyes of his peers, not the eye of a commander, that counted. Finch was at pains to emphasize that in his view the award was strictly representative. 'This isn't really mine; I'm only selected to wear it on behalf of the regiment, and when I die it will have to be returned to the regiment'.[5] He was mistaken – if mistake it was – because there is no such requirement. The self-imposed obligation was nevertheless honoured: his Cross and other medals are in the Royal Marines Museum, Portsmouth.

Finch, however, had articulated a sentiment about selection with which the Admiralty could agree. The VC Warrant provided for awards to individuals, not units, but there was no restriction of what could be written about the awardee's unit in the gazette citation. In 1942 the navy was presented with an opportunity to reconsider the selection process it had adopted for the Zeebrugge raid; to that point not much had changed except the target. Britain was aiming to deny German capital ships access to the large French dry dock at St Nazaire. Army commandos landed on the night of 27/28 March. The destroyer HMS *Campbelltown*, bow packed with high explosive, was driven into the dock gates. The port was heavily defended and two commandos won individual VCs, as did Commander Robert Ryder, the senior naval officer. Thus far, much like Zeebrugge. So, would there be a ballot for representative VCs?

There was not. The committee that had reviewed the VC Warrant at the end of the First World War considered that the ballot of surviving Lancashire Fusiliers from the Gallipoli landing had been defective. The deputy military secretary, Colonel Graham, submitted that in the circumstances of modern war ballots were impractical.

> [The Fusiliers] landed and most of them got killed … I think it impossible that any large proportion of the survivors had a say in the matter at all … It was really that the survivors were asked to state their opinion, but the survivors were very few in number… in a forlorn hope in which you have elected VCs it is very seldom that there is any officer left to vote … We have used the elective principle in many cases in this war without its being done regularly. Practically every high distinction is given more or less on this elective principle, that is to say the Commanding Officer consults his officers, but it is not done on the terms laid down [in the Warrant].[6]

The new Warrant of 1920 left it to the officer directing a ballot to determine how it should be conducted, but there never was another. Instead, for St Nazaire the navy invented semi-representative awards, one for the *Campbelltown* and another for the small craft that evacuated the force. The final words of the citation for the commander of the *Campbelltown* read:

> This Victoria Cross is awarded to Lieutenant Commander Beattie in recognition not only of his own valour but also

that of the unnamed officers and men of a very gallant ship's company, many of whom have not returned.[7]

The corresponding award for the small boats was a posthumous one. Able Seaman William Savage of Motor Gun Boat 314 had been killed at his gun. His Cross was awarded for personal gallantry but also to recognize 'the valour shown by many others, unnamed …, who gallantly carried out their duty in entirely exposed positions against Enemy fire at very close range'.[8]

There have been no VCs awarded to naval personnel since the Second World War. The last naval citation of that conflict, gazetted in 1947, honoured a captain who had gone down with his ship and a crew that had fought until ordered to abandon it. On 14 February 1942 HMS *Li Wo*, formerly a passenger steamer on the Yangtze River, was proceeding from Singapore to Batavia carrying survivors from other ships and assorted service personnel. Two Japanese convoys were sighted, the larger being escorted by a heavy cruiser and destroyers. Temporary Lieutenant Thomas Wilkinson, Royal Naval Reserve, mustered the ship's company and told them that he intended to fight to the last in the hope of inflicting damage on the enemy. Although there were only practice rounds for the 4-inch gun, the volunteer crew that manned it nonetheless managed to set fire to a large freighter. Two machine guns were directed at any enemy personnel in sight and within range. After an hour the ammunition had been expended and the *Li Wo* was damaged and sinking. Wilkinson then tried to ram the freighter. Under heavy fire from the cruiser he finally gave the order to abandon ship but remained aboard himself, perishing with his command. The fate of captain and ship remained unknown until the few survivors of the sinking were released from captivity in 1945. The VC citation followed the navy's now-preferred template honouring both captain and crew.

> Lieutenant Wilkinson's valour was equalled only by the skill with which he fought his ship. The Victoria Cross is bestowed on him posthumously in recognition both of his own heroism and self-sacrifice, and that of all who fought and died with him.[9]

After the first war there were no more VC ballots and after the second war no more semi-representative awards either. In the absence of large numbers of claimants the army has since been content with individual awards, and yet a semi-representative citation could have spared it some awkwardness over the award to Colonel Herbert Jones; associating 2 Para's gallantry with that of its commander in his citation would have soothed ruffled feathers. His was a battalion action, but smaller units are growing in prominence in modern warfare. Formations like Special Air Service patrols take a disproportionate share both of risk and opportunity to distinguish themselves. In most circumstances it is difficult to see that the achievements of any one man would even be possible without total commitment from the others. Extension of the election principle to small formations would have avoided the controversy attendant on the Roberts-Smith award when his patrol leader was awarded the lesser Star of Gallantry for the same action.[10] Even though there is a risk that election would become a popularity contest and do less than justice to an individual, it is less likely to threaten unit morale than an unpopular award from on high.

Indeed, there is a case to be made for semi-representative awards to be the norm in circumstances other than those that honour a solitary, unsupported act of valour. The Royal Navy precedent demonstrates that such awards can be made without violating the principle of individual recognition. In the case of ballots, the navy also found a way of individually acknowledging those who had participated: the fact was noted on each man's certificate of service. The army did not follow suit, fearing that such a record could be interpreted as meaning that the man should have had a VC, which in its view might have tended to lessen regard for the decoration.[11]

The Royal Navy's approach could have been taken further and might have been had the idea of collective VC recognition not fallen into abeyance after 1947. Citations and individual service records are not the only media available. For example, although it is not strictly a decoration, Mention in Dispatches (MiD) currently entitles a person to wear a silver oak leaf pinned to the ribbon of the relevant campaign medal. A pin could similarly be used to acknowledge the personnel most closely cooperating with and supporting a Victoria Cross winner in the action that led to the award. There is a model for such a pin in the V-link that suspends a Victoria Cross from its ribbon, a symbolic design feature said to have been devised by Victoria herself.[12]

Chapter 26

A Preference for Victory

In Albert's scheme of things the Cross was an instrument of state, a reward for service. Averting disaster, as at Rorke's Drift, was one form of service; another was heroic failure, as in the Charge of the Light Brigade; but a service more important than either was implicit in the name of the decoration: the Cross privileged victory. General Sir Edward Lugard, who became permanent under-secretary at the War Office in 1861, emphasized that the VC should be for heroic and daring acts that produced 'important military results'.[1] He would only credit forlorn hopes like the Charge if, unlike the Charge, they resulted in victory.[2]

Technically Britain has been on the winning side of every formal war in which she has been engaged since 1854, although the path to victory has often been strewn with serious reverses, most notably during the world wars. The trajectory of VC awards in both of those wars is a Lugard line, upwards to victory. It is particularly pronounced for the First

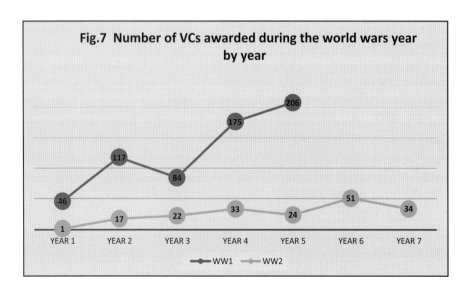

Fig.7 Number of VCs awarded during the world wars year by year

World War, when nearly one-third of its VCs were awarded for action in the last eight months of a fifty-one-month war. In August 1918, when the interdepartmental committee was considering general revision of the Warrant, Colonel Graham of the War Office asserted that there had been no reduction of standards. To the contrary, he told his colleagues, a VC of the current war could not be compared with that of any other 'because people are now getting the Military Medal for what would have won the VC in the South African War'.[3]

Preference for the victorious act was less evident in the second war, when the distribution was lower and more even across the years, although the rate of award still rose gradually as victory neared. The apparent downturn in year seven reflects the ending of hostilities early in the year (with Germany in May and with Japan in August 1945).

In ancient times victory was sometimes achieved by having champions engage in single combat, winner take all. It was an expedient that saved wear and tear on armies when a general engagement would have incurred costs disproportionate to a successful outcome for either side. The hereditary office of Champion of England exists to this day, although not since 1820 has the holder been asked to appear at a coronation to fight anyone who would challenge his liege lord's right to the throne. By then it was no longer possible to earn victory for the state through personal combat, although during the Indian Mutiny Lieutenant William McBean of the 93rd Highlanders did his best. At a narrow gate into the palace at Lucknow he encountered eleven mutineers. He slew ten with his sword, one after the other, until only a havildar was left. When other Highlanders came to his assistance he told them not to interfere. After a quick passage of swordplay the havildar was deceived by a feint and McBean accounted for him with a thrust to the chest. Complimented, he responded 'Tutts, it didna tak' me twenty minutes'.[4] But even a hundred such would not have quelled the Mutiny. The best that could be hoped for in modern times was victory on the cheap, a large success for a small outlay. Lugard would have been very pleased with Lieutenant Wallace Wright of the Queen's Royal West Surrey Regiment.

In 1903 Wright was sent with the West Africa Frontier Force to take the Fulani city of Kano in Nigeria. He found himself with one other officer and forty-four men facing an attacking force of 2,000 infantry and 1,000 cavalry. In two hours the British inflicted heavy losses on their opponents, who then began to withdraw in good order. With the odds still at more than sixty to one against him Wright ordered his little force to pursue the Fulani, forgoing the advantage of a defensive posture. Under pressure the enemy's attempt to disengage became a retreat. More than any other reverse, this one demonstrated to the emirs that they could not overcome British infantry firepower in open warfare, much less resist British artillery directed against the mud-brick walls of their cities. They surrendered. Wright's VC citation included a defence of his extremely hazardous proceeding:

> He in no way infringed his orders by his daring initiative, as, though warned of the possibility of meeting large bodies of the enemy, he had purposely been left a free hand.[5]

Wright had taken a great risk, as had all the men of his force, but his Victoria Cross was awarded for 'skillful leadership' and 'personal example'. There was no mention of valour in any of its linguistic guises. It might be expected that the more senior the officer, and therefore the more resources under command, the greater would be the victory dividend from VC-grade leadership. In the absence of any VCs awarded to officers above the rank of colonel before the First World War it is not possible to say one way or the other for the earlier period, but even the VCs awarded subsequently to brigadier general equivalents and above have been for individual acts of valour, with leadership mentioned as a secondary consideration if at all. In none of these cases could it be said that the exploit rewarded was militarily decisive, either in achieving victory or averting defeat, although it often contributed to the outcome.

There is, however, one VC exploit that, had it achieved the outcome sought, might well have turned a whole campaign. In 1941 Rommel was having success in North Africa quite disproportionate to the resources at his disposal. Allied commanders acknowledged his brilliance and regarded him as a force multiplier in his own right. British planning for an advance on Sidi Rezegh included disruptive raids behind enemy lines and a decapitation operation; among other tasks 11 Scottish Commando would attempt to capture or kill the German commander. On the night of 17/18 November Temporary Lieutenant Colonel Geoffrey Keyes attacked Rommel's supposed headquarters and residence at Beda Littoria on the Tobruk-Benghazi road. He had decided to lead this most

Geoffrey Keyes stormed Rommel's headquarters in North Africa.

hazardous of the raids in person, knowing that the chances of return were minimal even had the raid succeeded. Various setbacks disrupted the plan, with the result that it fell to Keyes, Captain Campbell and Sergeant Terry to make the final assault. They knocked on the door of the headquarters building and demanded entry in German, but the man who opened it seized the barrel of Keyes's revolver. Campbell shot him, perhaps wounding Keyes in the process. The two officers then stormed an occupied room with revolver and grenade, killing several Germans, but Keyes was shot. His companions dragged him outside where he died shortly afterwards. His commanding officer, Lieutenant Colonel Laycock, who had tried to talk Keyes out of what he regarded as a suicidal enterprise, wrote the VC recommendation. It was a model of its kind, summing up the considerations that had long exercised the thinkers referenced in these pages.

> Colonel Keyes' outstanding bravery was not that of the unimaginative bravado who may be capable of spectacular action in moments of excitement but that far more admirable calculated daring of one who knew all too well the odds against him.[6]

The citation writer reduced it to standard formulae. By his disregard of the dangers which he ran and of which he was aware, and by his magnificent leadership and outstanding gallantry, Keyes had 'set an example of supreme self-sacrifice and devotion to duty'.[7]

As both of his companions survived and neither received a VC, one might conclude that the factors that set Keyes apart were his leadership and self-sacrifice in the line of duty. Rommel was not in residence that night, but so admired the exploit that he sent his own chaplain to bury the British commando and the German dead with full military honours. The grave of Keyes was given pride of place on the right of the line.[8] If successful, the operation could have been a turning point for the Allied cause in the Western Desert. In the context of 1941, when both sides were bombing civilians, assassination seemed an acceptable if distasteful weapon, at least to the British. Given that even his intended victim praised Keyes's attempt, it would seem that few shared Victoria's concern that practices of dubious morality might sully her Cross. That valour could be acknowledged in such a context by friend and foe alike affirms Samuel Johnson's view that courage is a quality so necessary for maintaining virtue that it is always respected, even when it is associated with vice.[9] Furthermore, in Aristotelian terms it could be argued that the defeat of Hitler was a noble end, thereby justifying the means adopted.

Chapter 27

Rules and Exceptions

With amendment and consolidation the number of rules has been slightly reduced since the original formulation, but over the years a body of lore and practice has supplemented them. Moments before the Chief of the General Staff embraced Corporal Leakey in 2015 there had been another unmilitary occurrence: the general had saluted the corporal. Puzzled recruits thumbing through *Queen's Regulations* or their customs and traditions pamphlets would have found no authority for such an anomalous practice; to the contrary, they would have read that the corporal should have saluted the general, who would have been expected to reciprocate. On the face of it the general had been guilty of a breach of protocol, but had the puzzled ones inquired further they would have been told to forget about the book: everyone salutes a Victoria Cross winner irrespective of rank, yours or his.

The practice seems to have emerged during the First World War and might have acquired standing through a chance encounter on the streets of London in 1919. On 8 April Joseph Maxwell was strolling in the West End wearing the ribbon of his newly-presented VC when two smartly dressed young civilians came into view. As they drew abreast of Maxwell they raised their hats in salute. Edward Prince of Wales and his cousin Lord Louis Mountbatten were on their way to a society wedding and a photographer caught the moment.[1] The Prince had a profound respect for the decoration, best expressed in the speech he made at the 1929 reunion of Victoria Cross holders. He concluded by proposing a toast to 'the most democratic and at the same time the most exclusive of all orders of chivalry – the most enviable order of the Victoria Cross'.[2] Edward was well-tutored in exactly where and how the Victoria Cross fitted into the panoply of British honours. Even so, he could not resist the notion that Victoria Cross winners were the true knights of modern times who, commoners or not, constituted an order of chivalry, albeit one acknowledged in lower case letters.

A second reunion was held to celebrate the centenary of the decoration in 1956. John Smyth VC, now Sir John Smyth MP and former junior minister as well, took advantage of the occasion to promote the idea of an association of which all surviving recipients would be members, with George Cross holders admitted as associates. It was foreseen that GC awards were likely to be more common in future 'since warfare on the scale of the two world wars could not be visualised'.[3] The deaths of nineteen VCs between 1956 and 1958 without offsetting recruitment reinforced the point. In 1961 the association was renamed the Victoria Cross and George Cross Association and GC holders were admitted to full membership. Declining numbers notwithstanding, 145 VCs were able to attend the reunion of 1962. The oldest was General Lewis Halliday of the Royal Marine Light Infantry, who had won his at the siege of the Beijing legations during the Boxer Rebellion in 1900.

Contrary to Smyth's expectations, the number of George Cross holders has declined in parallel with VC numbers and the association today musters less than thirty members in total. Attrition continues to exceed recruitment to both groups. Paradoxically, while servicemen are in a majority the VC holders are not, partly because in Iraq and Afghanistan British soldiers have won more GCs than VCs. While it would be very antisocial to argue for more wars so that we can have more VCs, the fact is that the nine surviving holders are exemplars of military virtues which it is hard to believe the community will be able to dispense with completely until human nature takes a turn for the better. One way of spreading the message beyond their number without diluting standards would be to introduce an 'associated member of the unit' pin for the relevant campaign medal as suggested in the section One for All.

From time to time there are proposals to recruit from among the dead. Public campaigns are mounted to demand retrospective VCs for individuals whose claims, it is said, were overlooked at the time or defeated by prejudice, inefficiency or indifference. Such claims, if admitted, would cause difficulties far greater than those about which Edward VII had such reservations when he was asked to authorize retrospective posthumous awards. For historical claims the most serious difficulty, insuperable without a rule change, is the requirement for eyewitness evidence of a valiant act performed in the presence of the enemy. And under current British practice that evidence will be subjected to the most rigorous testing.

One of the strongest such campaigns has been mounted in Australia. It is a striking fact that while thirteen VCs were awarded for the Gallipoli landing on 25 April 1915 not one went to an Australian or a New Zealander. The anniversary of the landing is commemorated in Australia as if it were the national day, which perhaps explains the interest in gaining a VC for John Simpson Kirkpatrick of the 3rd Field Ambulance, Australian Imperial Force. He was a stretcher-bearer who shortly after the landing had found a stray donkey and on his own initiative began bringing wounded down to the beach. His self-imposed daily routine took him up aptly-named Shrapnel Gully, likewise notorious for machine-gun and sniper fire. Partnership with the donkey marked Kirkpatrick out from the crowd and the imperturbability of man and beast under fire was noted by many who saw them. Few thought that with the risks he took he could long survive, and twenty-five days after the landing he was killed by a machine-gun bullet.

Kirkpatrick's commanding officer, Lieutenant Colonel Sutton, hoped to obtain a Distinguished Conduct Medal for him, but came up against the reality that DCMs were reserved to the living. The only decoration for which the dead were eligible was the Victoria Cross, with its higher evidentiary requirements. In trying to put a case together for the higher award Sutton found that it was 'difficult to get evidence of any one act – the fact is he did so many'. Statements were gathered but they were insufficiently precise for the purpose. The other posthumous recognition that could be made was a Mention in Dispatches. Kirkpatrick's name went up the chain of command with several others. The officer who forwarded them to division, Colonel Neville Howse VC, emphasized that they were representative awards intended to acknowledge the work of all divisional medical personnel.

The most recent submissions seeking to have Kirkpatrick's MiD supplemented with a Victoria Cross were made to an enquiry commissioned by the Australian Government. In 2011 its Defence Honours and Awards Appeals Tribunal was asked to report on 'unresolved recognition' for past acts of gallantry and valour. The views put to it were divided. Some argued for special recognition beyond the rules, while others felt that exceptions would disrespect other worthy contributions that did not enjoy a public profile. The tribunal decided against recommending a Victoria Cross for Kirkpatrick or for any of the twelve other cases put before it. It noted that the official medallion issued to veterans of the Gallipoli campaign bore an image of Simpson (Kirkpatrick) and his donkey, and that he had been honoured by books, statues, paintings, stamps, coins and banknotes. One of the submissions against further recognition put him 'in a category of his own as a national icon, placing him beyond any award, retrospective or otherwise'.[4]

To a lesser extent the same is true of all historical candidates. The fact that their stories have lived on indicates that their fame requires no embellishment. By contrast, many Victoria Cross winners are remembered only locally if at all. Simpson/Kirkpatrick will be honoured for as long as there is an Australian left to remember him, but even immortals have to conform to the rules if the Cross is to retain its integrity. Loss of public confidence, whether caused by retrospective special pleading, dilution of standards or political expediency, would be disrespectful to all those awarded previously. The Cross has had to overcome internal contradictions, resistance, manipulation, poor administration and a host of other impediments. It is nonetheless respected like no other honour. Some awardees were unable to fathom why they had been chosen; others were aware of identical cases with different outcomes; many viewed the process with dismay; throughout, advocates for the disappointed were vocal. For all that, the parsimony that has prevailed after the first few years and the transparency afforded by gazettal has maintained confidence. There has never been the least doubt in the public's mind that those awarded the decoration must have done something uncommonly valiant to earn it; what that something was is less likely to have been remembered.

Appendix 1

The 1856 Victoria Cross Warrant

VICTORIA by the Grace of God of the United Kingdom of Great Britain and Ireland Queen Defender of the Faith &c. To all to whom these Presents shall come Greeting! Whereas We taking into Our Royal consideration that there exists no means of adequately rewarding the individual gallant services either of officers of the lower grades in Our Naval and Military Service, or of warrant and petty officers, seamen and marines in Our Navy, and non-commissioned officers in Our Army. And Whereas the third Class of Our Most Honourable Order of the Bath is limited, except in very rare cases, to the higher ranks of both services and the granting of Medals both in Our Navy and Army is only awarded for long service or meritorious conduct, rather than for bravery in Action or distinction before an enemy, such cases alone excepted while a general Medal is granted for a particular Action or Campaign, or a Clasp added to the Medal for some special engagement, in both of which cases all share equally in the boon and those who by their valour have particularly signalized themselves remain undistinguished from their comrades. Now for the purpose of attaining an end so desirable as that of rewarding individual instances of merit and valour We have instituted and created and by these Presents for Us Our Heirs and Successors, institute and create a new Naval and Military Decoration, which We are desirous should be highly prized and eagerly sought after by the Officers and Men of Our Naval and Military Services and are graciously pleased to make ordain and establish the following rules and ordinances for the government of the same which shall from henceforth be inviolably observed and kept.

Firstly It is ordained that the distinction shall be styled and designated the 'Victoria Cross', and shall consist of a Maltese Cross of Bronze, with Our Royal Crest in the centre and underneath which an escroll bearing this inscription 'For Valour'.

Secondly It is ordained that the Cross shall be suspended from the left breast by a Blue riband for the Navy, and by a Red riband for the Army.

Thirdly It is ordained that the names of those upon whom We may be pleased to confer the Decoration shall be published in the *London Gazette* and a registry thereof kept in the office of Our Secretary of State for War.

Fourthly It is ordained that anyone who, after having received the Cross, shall again perform an act of bravery which, if he had not received such Cross would have entitled him to it, such further act shall be recorded by a bar attached to the riband by which the Cross is suspended and for every additional act of bravery an additional bar may be added.

Fifthly It is ordained that the Cross shall only be awarded to those Officers and Men who have served Us in the presence of the enemy, and shall have then performed some signal act of valour or devotion to their Country.

Sixthly It is ordained with a view to placing all persons on a perfectly equal footing in relation to eligibility for the Decoration that neither rank nor long service nor wounds nor any other circumstance or condition whatsoever save the merit of conspicuous bravery shall be held to establish a sufficient claim to the honour.

Seventhly It is ordained that the Decoration may be conferred on the spot where the act to be rewarded by the grant of such Decoration has been performed, under the following circumstances:

I.   When the Fleet or Army in which such act has been performed is under the eye and command of an Admiral or General officer commanding the Forces.

II. Where the Naval or Military force is under the eye and command of an Admiral or Commodore Commanding a Squadron or detached Naval force or of a General Commanding a Corps or Division or Brigade on a distinct and detached Service when such Admiral or General Officer shall have the power of conferring the Decoration on the spot subject to confirmation by Us.

Eighthly It is ordained where such act shall not have been performed in sight of a Commanding Officer as aforesaid, then the claimant for the honour shall prove the act to the satisfaction of the Captain or Officer Commanding his ship or to the Officer Commanding the Regiment to which the claimant belongs, and such Captain or such Commanding Officer shall report the same through the usual channel to the Admiral or Commodore Commanding the Force employed on the Service or to the Officer Commanding the Forces in the Field who shall call for such description and attestation of the act as he may think requisite and on approval shall recommend the grant of the Decoration.

Ninthly It is ordained that every person selected for the Cross under rule seven shall be publicly decorated before the Naval or Military Force or body to which he belongs and with which the act of bravery for which he is to be rewarded shall have been performed, and his name shall be recorded in a General Order together with the cause of his especial distinction.

Tenthly It is ordained that every person selected under rule eight shall receive his Decoration as soon as possible, and his name shall likewise appear in a General Order as above required, such General Order to be issued by the Naval or Military commander of the Forces employed on the Service.

Eleventhly It is ordained that the general orders above referred to shall from time to time be transmitted to Our Secretary of State for War, to be laid before Us, and shall be by him registered.

Twelthly It is ordained that as cases may arise not falling within the rules above specified or in which a claim, though well founded, may not have been established on the spot We will on the joint submission of Our Secretary of State for War and of Our Commander-in-Chief of Our Army or on that of Our Lord High Admiral or Lords Commissioners of the Admiralty in the case of the Navy confer the Decoration but never without conclusive proof of the performance of the act of bravery for which the claim is made.

Thirteenthly It is ordained that in the event of a gallant and daring act having been performed by a Squadron Ship's Company a detached body of Seamen and Marines not under fifty in number, or by a Brigade Regiment Troop or Company in which the Admiral General or other Officer Commanding such Forces may deem that all are equally brave and distinguished and that no special selection can be made by them, Then in such case the Admiral General or other Officer Commanding may direct that for any such body of Seamen or Marines or for every Troop or Company of Soldiers, one Officer shall be selected by the Officers engaged for the Decoration; and in like manner one Petty Officer or Non-commissioned Officer shall be selected by the Petty officers and Non-commissioned Officers engaged; and two Seamen or Private Soldiers or Marines shall be selected by the Seamen or Private Soldiers or marines engaged respectively for the Decoration; and the names of those selected shall be transmitted by the Senior Officer in command of the Naval Force Brigade Regiment Troop or Company to the Admiral or General Officer Commanding who shall in due manner confer the Decoration as if the acts were done under his own eye.

Fourteenthly It is ordained that every Warrant Officer Petty Officer Seaman or Marine or Non-commissioned Officer or Soldier who shall have received the Cross shall from the date of the act by which the Decoration has been gained be entitled to a Special Pension of Ten Pounds a year: and each additional bar conferred under rule four on such Warrant or Petty Officers or Non-commissioned Officers or Men, shall carry with it an additional pension of Five Pounds per annum.

Fifteenthly In order to make such additional provision as shall effectually preserve pure this Most Honorable distinction it is ordained that if any person be convicted of Treason, Cowardice, Felony or of any infamous Crime, or if he be accused of any such offence, and doth not after a reasonable time surrender himself to be tried for the same his name shall forthwith be erased from the Registry of Individuals upon whom the said Decoration shall have been conferred by an especial Warrant under Our Royal Sign Manual, and the pension conferred under rule fourteen shall cease and determine from the date of such Warrant. It is hereby further declared that We Our Heirs and Successors shall be the sole judge of the circumstances demanding such expulsion; moreover We shall at all times have power to restore such persons as may at any time have been expelled, both to the enjoyment of the Decoration and Pension.

Given at Our Court at Buckingham Palace this twenty-ninth day of January in the Nineteenth Year of Our reign and in the Year of Our Lord One Thousand Eight Hundred and Fifty Six.

By Her Majesty's Command
Panmure

To Our Principal Secretary of State for War

Appendix 2

The Who, When, Where, What, Why and How of the Awards

This appendix lists awards of the Victoria Cross in date-of-incident order up to the present (2018). The primary source of information in each case is the citation published in the *London Gazette* and equivalents (e.g. *Commonwealth of Australia Gazette*) supplemented where possible from other published sources. The entries are structured to facilitate statistical analysis of the acts that gave rise to the awards.

Name is abbreviated to first given name and surname except for non-European names which are given in full. Otherwise they are as cited unless the citation was in error. Note that a number of awardees did not serve under their birth names and others subsequently changed their names.

Ranks are grouped. Senior officers are defined as those who command battalions, ships, aircraft squadrons and larger formations. Junior officers are their subordinates (up to major and equivalent, including midshipman in the Navy). Non-commissioned officers are taken to include warrant officers. The grouping 'other ranks' includes specialists like pipers. Medical personnel and chaplains are separately identified, as are civilians.

Service is categorized as army, navy, marines, air forces (the last comprising Britain's RFC, RNAS, RAF, Fleet Air Arm and their Empire equivalents) and police.

Date will be a multiple entry when a number dates have been mentioned in the citation. Position in the list is determined by the earliest date mentioned.

Place is generalized by geographical or geo-political location.

Personal Action is categorized by type of activity. When a number of acts were cited for a single award, the earliest was selected for summary unless a subsequent one was given more extended treatment in the citation.

Type of Personal Action is characterized as duty (obeying orders), exercise of choice (taking initiative or volunteering) or driven by necessity (self-preservation). In some cases the awardee's motivation is unknown.

Military Task of Unit is categorized by type of operation.

Relevance of Action to Task can be high, low, none or contrary. The relevance of the acts of non-combatant recipients such as doctors, chaplains and stretcher-bearers are assessed against their assigned functions rather than the unit's operational task except when the award is for acting as a combatant. Conversely, the entries for commanding officers reflect their overall responsibilities, which include ensuring the operational effectiveness of subordinates.

Casualty? Refers to any directly attributable physical consequence of the awarded act for the individual (categorized as a nil return, incapacity through exposure, wounded, captured or killed). The mortally wounded are listed as killed. Some of the wounded were also taken prisoner. The entries do not take account of death subsequent to and unrelated to the awarded action, although in some cases it might have been a factor in the deliberations of nominating and awarding authorities. Note that later untimely deaths, not recorded here, might also be war-related.

How Selected for Award The Warrants provide for selection through nomination by commanders or election by peers but there have been variations on the former involving acclamation, co-option and representative awards.

Although the summary format of the appendix precludes fine distinctions it facilitates analysis, and while the assessments of motivation and relevance are subjective, different interpretations in marginal cases are unlikely to disturb the broad conclusions. The earliest act for which a VC was awarded might serve as an example of a difficult assessment.

Boatswain's Mate Charles Lucas was serving on HMS *Hecla* during the bombardment of a Russian Baltic fort in 1854. A Russian shell, fuse burning, struck the deck near where he was standing. He picked it up and threw it overboard; it exploded as it hit the water. It was not part of Lucas's duty to jettison the shell, but by preventing damage and casualties he had ensured that it would not disrupt the bombardment, thereby making an indirect contribution to the operation. As the cry had been 'Down!' when the shell struck, Lucas might have been guilty of disobedience, but it was unclear if the word came from a superior and, if so, whether it was an order or a warning. The summary in the annex treats it as a warning, so there is no finding of acting contrary to orders, but as any operational benefit was indirect the relevance of the act has been assessed as low.

No.	Name	Rank	Service	Date	Place	Personal Action	Type of Personal Action	Military Task of Unit	Relevance of Action to Task	Casualty?	How Selected for Award
1	Charles LUCAS	NCO	Navy	21/06/1854	Baltic	Protect	Initiative	Bombard	Low	No	Nominated
2	John BYTHESEA	Junior Officer	Navy	9/08/1854 - 12/08/1854	Baltic	Ambush	Voluntary	Intercept	High	No	Nominated
3	William JOHNSTONE	OR	Navy	9/08/1854 - 12/08/1854	Baltic	Ambush	Voluntary	Intercept	High	No	Nominated
4	Edward BELL	Junior Officer	Army	20/09/1854	Crimea	Raid	Initiative	Attack	Low	No	Nominated
5	James McKECHNIE	NCO	Army	20/09/1854	Crimea	Rally	Duty	Attack	High	Wounded	Nominated
6	William REYNOLDS	OR	Army	20/09/1854	Crimea	Rally	Duty	Attack	High	No	Nominated
7	Robert LINDSAY	Junior Officer	Army	20/09/1854 5/11/1854	Crimea	Rally	Duty	Attack	High	No	Nominated
8	John PARK	NCO	Army	20/09/1854 5/11/1854 19/04/1855	Crimea	Combat	Duty	Attack	High	Wounded	Nominated
9	John KNOX	NCO	Army	20/09/1854 18/06/1855	Crimea	Combat	Initiative	Attack	High	Wounded	Nominated
10	Luke O'CONNOR	NCO	Army	20/09/1854 18/06/1855	Crimea	Rally	Duty	Attack	High	Wounded	Nominated
11	Francis WHEATLEY	OR	Army	12/10/1854	Crimea	Protect	Initiative	Defend	Low	No	Nominated
12	Collingwood DICKSON	Senior Officer	Army	17/10/1854	Crimea	Resupply	Duty	Bombard	High	No	Nominated
13	Thomas GRADY	OR	Army	18/10/1854 22/11/1854	Crimea	Repair	Duty	Defend	High	Wounded	Nominated
14	William PEEL	Senior Officer	Navy	18/10/1854 5/11/1854 18/06/1855	Crimea	Lead	Duty	Attack	High	Wounded	Nominated
15	Edward DANIEL	Junior Officer	Navy	18/10/1854 5/11/1854 18/06/1855	Crimea	Resupply	Initiative	Bombard	High	No	Nominated
16	William McWHEENEY	NCO	Army	20/10/1854 5/12/1854	Crimea	Rescue	Initiative	Withdraw	None	No	Nominated

No.	Name	Rank	Service	Date	Location	Action	Motivation	Type	Risk	Casualty	Status
17	Alexander DUNN	Junior Officer	Army	25/10/1854	Crimea	Rescue	Initiative	Attack	None	No	Nominated
18	John GRIEVE	NCO	Army	25/10/1854	Crimea	Rescue	Initiative	Attack	None	No	Nominated
19	John BERRYMAN	NCO	Army	25/10/1854	Crimea	Rescue	Initiative	Attack	None	No	Nominated
20	John FARRELL	NCO	Army	25/10/1854	Crimea	Rescue	Initiative	Attack	None	No	Nominated
21	Joseph MALONE	NCO	Army	25/10/1854	Crimea	Rescue	Initiative	Attack	None	No	Nominated
22	Samuel PARKES	OR	Army	25/10/1854	Crimea	Rescue	Initiative	Attack	None	POW	Nominated
23	James MOUAT	Medical Officer	Army	26/10/1854	Crimea	Rescue	Duty	Aid	High	No	Nominated
24	John CONOLLY	Junior Officer	Army	26/10/1854	Crimea	Lead	Duty	Defend	High	Wounded	Nominated
25	Ambrose MADDEN	NCO	Army	29/10/1854	Crimea	Sortie	Duty	Attack	High	No	Nominated
26	Henry RAMAGE	NCO	Army	26/10/1854	Crimea	Rescue	Initiative	Attack	None	No	Nominated
27	Charles WOODEN	NCO	Army	26/10/1854	Crimea	Rescue	Initiative	Attack	None	No	Claimed
28	William STANLACK	OR	Army	26/10/1854	Crimea	Recon	Initiative	Attack	High	No	Nominated
29	William HEWETT	Junior Officer	Navy	26/10/1854 5/11/1854	Crimea	Resist	Initiative	Withdraw	Contrary	No	Nominated
30	Gerald GOODLAKE	Junior Officer	Army	28/10/1854 Nov 1854	Crimea	Lead	Duty	Defend	High	No	Nominated
31	James OWENS	OR	Army	30/10/1854	Crimea	Rescue	Initiative	Defend	None	No	Nominated
32	Henry PERCY	Senior Officer	Army	5/11/1854	Crimea	Lead	Duty	Attack	High	Wounded	Nominated
33	Charles RUSSELL	Junior Officer	Army	5/11/1854	Crimea	Lead	Duty	Attack	High	No	Nominated
34	Hugh ROWLANDS	Junior Officer	Army	5/11/1854	Crimea	Rescue	Initiative	Defend	None	No	Nominated
35	Henry CLIFFORD	Junior Officer	Army	5/11/1854	Crimea	Lead	Duty	Attack	High	No	Nominated
36	Frederick MILLER	Junior Officer	Army	5/11/1854	Crimea	Lead	Duty	Attack	High	No	Nominated
37	Mark WALKER	Junior Officer	Army	5/11/1854	Crimea	Lead	Duty	Attack	High	No	Nominated
38	Andrew HENRY	NCO	Army	5/11/1854	Crimea	Combat	Duty	Defend	High	Wounded	Nominated
39	George WALTERS	NCO	Army	5/11/1854	Crimea	Rescue	Initiative	Defend	None	No	Nominated
40	John PRETTYJOHN	NCO	Marines	5/11/1854	Crimea	Lead	Duty	Defend	High	No	Nominated
41	Thomas REEVES	OR	Navy	5/11/1854	Crimea	Repulse	Duty	Defend	High	No	Nominated

185

No.	Name	Rank	Service	Date	Place	Personal Action	Type of Personal Action	Military Task of Unit	Relevance of Action to Task	Casualty?	How Selected for Award
42	Thomas BEACH	OR	Army	5/11/1854	Crimea	Protect	Initiative	Defend	None	No	Nominated
43	John McDERMOND	OR	Army	5/11/1854	Crimea	Rescue	Initiative	Defend	None	No	Nominated
44	Anthony PALMER	OR	Army	5/11/1854	Crimea	Rescue	Voluntary	Attack	Low	No	Nominated
45	Mark SCHOLEFIELD	OR	Navy	5/11/1854	Crimea	Repulse	Duty	Defend	High	No	Nominated
46	James GORMAN	OR	Navy	5/11/1854	Crimea	Repulse	Duty	Defend	High	No	Nominated
47	John BYRNE	OR	Army	5/11/1854 11/05/1855	Crimea	Rescue	Initiative	Withdraw	None	No	Nominated
48	Claud BOURCHIER	Junior Officer	Army	20/11/1854	Crimea	Lead	Duty	Attack	High	No	Nominated
49	William CUNNINGHAME	Junior Officer	Army	20/11/1854	Crimea	Lead	Duty	Attack	High	No	Nominated
50	Wilbraham LENNOX	Junior Officer	Army	20/11/1854	Crimea	Entrench	Duty	Defend	High	No	Nominated
51	William NORMAN	OR	Army	19/12/1854	Crimea	Capture	Duty	Defend	High	No	Nominated
52	William LENDRIM	NCO	Army	14/02/1855 11/03/1855 20/04/1855	Crimea	Repair	Voluntary	Beseige	High	No	Nominated
53	Alexander WRIGHT	OR	Army	22/03/1855 19/04/1855	Crimea	Repulse	Duty	Defend	High	Wounded	Nominated
54	George GARDINER	NCO	Army	22/03/1855 18/06/1855	Crimea	Rally	Duty	Attack	High	No	Nominated
55	William COFFEY	OR	Army	29/03/1855	Crimea	Protect	Initiative	Defend	Low	No	Nominated
56	Frederick ELTON	Junior Officer	Army	29/03/1855 7/06/1855 4/08/1855	Crimea	Lead	Duty	Beseige	High	No	Nominated
57	John SULLIVAN	NCO	Navy	10/04/1855	Crimea	Erect	Voluntary	Beseige	High	No	Nominated
58	Samuel EVANS	OR	Army	13/04/1855	Crimea	Repair	Initiative	Beseige	High	No	Nominated
59	Matthew DIXON	Junior Officer	Army	17/04/1855	Crimea	Lead	Duty	Defend	High	No	Nominated
60	Henry MacDONALD	NCO	Army	19/04/1855	Crimea	Lead	Duty	Attack	High	No	Nominated
61	Joseph BRADSHAW	OR	Army	22/04/1855	Crimea	Capture	Initiative	Beseige	High	No	Nominated

No.	Name	Rank	Service	Date	Location	Action	Initiative	Response	Level	Wounded	Status
62	Robert HUMPSTON	OR	Army	22/04/1855	Crimea	Capture	Initiative	Beseige	High	No	Nominated
63	Roderick McGREGOR	OR	Army	22/04/1855 July 1855	Crimea	Capture	Initiative	Beseige	High	No	Nominated
64	Thomas HAMILTON	Junior Officer	Army	11/05/1855	Crimea	Lead	Duty	Beseige	High	No	Nominated
65	Hugh BURGOYNE	Junior Officer	Navy	29/05/1855	Sea of Azov	Raid	Voluntary	Attack	High	No	Nominated
66	John ROBARTS	NCO	Navy	29/05/1855	Sea of Azov	Raid	Voluntary	Attack	High	No	Nominated
67	Cecil BUCKLEY	Junior Officer	Navy	29/05/1855 3/06/1855	Sea of Azov	Raid	Voluntary	Attack	High	No	Nominated
68	Henry COOPER	NCO	Navy	3/06/1855	Sea of Azov	Raid	Voluntary	Attack	High	No	Nominated
69	George SYMONS	NCO	Army	6/06/1855	Crimea	Unmask	Voluntary	Attack	High	Wounded	Nominated
70	Henry JONES	Junior Officer	Army	7/06/1855	Crimea	Repulse	Duty	Defend	High	Wounded	Nominated
71	Thomas WILKINSON	NCO	Marines	7/06/1855	Crimea	Repair	Duty	Defend	High	No	Nominated
72	Thomas ARTHUR	OR	Army	7/06/1855 18/06/1855	Crimea	Resupply	Voluntary	Withdraw	Contrary	No	Nominated
73	Matthew HUGHES	OR	Army	7/06/1855 18/06/1855	Crimea	Rescue	Voluntary	Attack	None	Wounded	Nominated
74	John LYONS	OR	Army	10/06/1855	Crimea	Protect	Initiative	Defend	Low	No	Nominated
75	Joseph PROSSER	OR	Army	16/06/1855 11/08/1855	Crimea	Capture	Duty	Hold	High	No	Nominated
76	Howard ELPHINSTONE	Junior Officer	Army	18/06/1855	Crimea	Search	Voluntary	Recover	High	No	Nominated
77	William HOPE	Junior Officer	Army	18/06/1855	Crimea	Rescue	Initiative	Withdraw	None	No	Nominated
78	Gerald GRAHAM	Junior Officer	Army	18/06/1855	Crimea	Combat	Duty	Attack	High	No	Nominated
79	Henry RABY	Junior Officer	Navy	18/06/1855	Crimea	Rescue	Initiative	Withdraw	None	No	Nominated
80	Peter LEITCH	NCO	Army	18/06/1855	Crimea	Bridge	Duty	Attack	High	Wounded	Nominated
81	Felix SMITH	NCO	Army	18/06/1855	Crimea	Rescue	Initiative	Withdraw	None	No	Nominated
82	Henry CURTIS	NCO	Navy	18/06/1855	Crimea	Rescue	Initiative	Withdraw	None	No	Nominated
83	John TAYLOR	NCO	Navy	18/06/1855	Crimea	Rescue	Initiative	Withdraw	None	No	Nominated
84	John SIMS	OR	Army	18/06/1855	Crimea	Rescue	Initiative	Withdraw	None	No	Nominated
85	John PERIE	OR	Army	18/06/1855	Crimea	Search	Voluntary	Recover	High	Wounded	Nominated

No.	Name	Rank	Service	Date	Place	Personal Action	Type of Personal Action	Military Task of Unit	Relevance of Action to Task	Casualty?	How Selected for Award
86	Thomas ESMONDE	Junior Officer	Army	18/06/1855 20/06/1855	Crimea	Protect	Initiative	Attack	None	No	Nominated
87	John ALEXANDER	OR	Army	18/06/1855 6/09/1855	Crimea	Rescue	Initiative	Withdraw	None	No	Nominated
88	Charles McCORRIE	OR	Army	23/06/1855	Crimea	Protect	Initiative	Defend	None	No	Nominated
89	Joseph TREWAVAS	OR	Navy	3/07/1855	Sea of Azov	Raid	Duty	Attack	High	Wounded	Nominated
90	George DOWELL	Junior Officer	Marines	13/07/1855	Baltic	Rescue	Initiative	Attack	None	No	Nominated
91	George INGOUVILLE	NCO	Navy	13/07/1855	Baltic	Rescue	Initiative	Attack	None	Wounded	Nominated
92	John SHEPPARD	NCO	Navy	15/07/1855 16/08/1855	Crimea	Raid	Duty	Attack	High	No	Nominated
93	John ROSS	NCO	Army	21/07/1855 23/08/1855 8/09/1855	Crimea	Sap	Duty	Attack	High	No	Nominated
94	John COLEMAN	NCO	Army	30/08/1855	Crimea	Sap	Duty	Defend	High	No	Nominated
95	Joseph KELLAWAY	NCO	Navy	31/08/1855	Sea of Azov	Raid	Duty	Attack	High	POW	Nominated
96	Alfred ABLETT	OR	Army	2/09/1855	Crimea	Protect	Initiative	Defend	None	No	Nominated
97	James CRAIG	NCO	Army	6/09/1855	Crimea	Rescue	Voluntary	Defend	None	Wounded	Nominated
98	Frederick MAUDE	Senior Officer	Army	8/09/1855	Crimea	Cover	Duty	Defend	High	Wounded	Nominated
99	Thomas HALE	Medical Officer	Army	8/09/1855	Crimea	Rescue	Duty	Aid	High	No	Nominated
100	Gronow DAVIS	Junior Officer	Army	8/09/1855	Crimea	Spike	Duty	Attack	High	No	Nominated
101	Charles LUMLEY	Junior Officer	Army	8/09/1855	Crimea	Lead	Duty	Attack	High	Wounded	Nominated
102	Andrew MOYNIHAN	NCO	Army	8/09/1855	Crimea	Storm	Duty	Attack	High	No	Nominated
103	Robert SHIELDS	NCO	Army	8/09/1855	Crimea	Rescue	Voluntary	Attack	None	No	Nominated
104	Daniel CAMBRIDGE	NCO	Army	8/09/1855	Crimea	Spike	Voluntary	Attack	High	Wounded	Nominated
105	John CONNORS	NCO	Army	8/09/1855	Crimea	Combat	Duty	Attack	High	No	Nominated
106	William SYLVESTER	Medical Officer	Army	8/09/1855 18/09/1855	Crimea	Rescue	Duty	Aid	High	No	Nominated

						Recon	Duty	Attack	High	Exposure	Nominated
107	George DAY	Junior Officer	Navy	17/09/1855 21/09/1855	Sea of Azov	Recon	Initiative	Defend	High	No	Nominated
108	George STRONG	OR	Army	Sept 1855	Crimea	Protect	Initiative	Defend	Low	No	Nominated
109	Christopher TEESDALE	Junior Officer	Army	29/09/1855	Turkey	Lead	Voluntary	Defend	High	No	Nominated
110	John COMMERELL	Senior Officer	Navy	11/10/1855	Sea of Azov	Raid	Duty	Attack	High	No	Nominated
111	William RICKARD	NCO	Navy	11/10/1855	Sea of Azov	Raid	Duty	Attack	High	No	Nominated
112	John WOOD	Junior Officer	Army	9/12/1856	Persia	Storm	Duty	Attack	High	Wounded	Nominated
113	John MALCOLMSON	Junior Officer	Army	8/02/1857	Persia	Rescue	Initiative	Attack	Low	No	Nominated
114	Arthur MOORE	Junior Officer	Army	8/02/1857	Persia	Charge	Duty	Attack	High	No	Nominated
115	Dighton PROBYN	Junior Officer	Army	1857–1858	India	Capture	Duty	Attack	Low	Wounded	Nominated
116	John BUCKLEY	Junior Officer	Army	11/05/1857	India	Deny	Duty	Defend	High	POW	Nominated
117	George FORREST	Junior Officer	Army	11/05/1857	India	Deny	Duty	Defend	High	No	Nominated
118	William RAYNOR	Junior Officer	Army	11/05/1857	India	Deny	Duty	Defend	High	No	Nominated
119	Everard LISLE-PHILLIPPS	Junior Officer	Army	30/05/1857 18/09/1857	India	Proclaim	Duty	Control	High	Wounded	Nominated
120	Alfred HEATHCOTE	Junior Officer	Army	Jun–Sept 1857	India	Combat	Voluntary	Attack	High	Wounded	Elected
121	Peter GILL	NCO	Army	4/06/1857	India	Rescue	Voluntary	Defend	None	No	Nominated
122	Matthew ROSAMUND	NCO	Army	4/06/1857	India	Rescue	Voluntary	Defend	None	No	Nominated
123	John KIRK	OR	Army	4/06/1857	India	Rescue	Voluntary	Defend	None	No	Nominated
124	Cornelius COGHLAN	NCO	Army	8/06/1857 18/07/1857	India	Lead	Duty	Attack	High	No	Nominated
125	Alfred JONES	Junior Officer	Army	8/06/1857 10/10/1857	India	Charge	Duty	Attack	High	Wounded	Nominated
126	Henry HARTIGAN	NCO	Army	8/06/1857 10/10/1857	India	Rescue	Initiative	Defend	None	No	Nominated
127	Thomas CADELL	Junior Officer	Army	12/06/1857	India	Rescue	Initiative	Defend	None	No	Nominated
128	Thomas HANCOCK	OR	Army	19/06/1857	India	Rescue	Initiative	Defend	None	No	Nominated
129	John PURCELL	OR	Army	19/06/1857	India	Rescue	Initiative	Defend	None	No	Nominated
130	Samuel TURNER	OR	Army	19/06/1857	India	Rescue	Initiative	Attack	None	Wounded	Nominated

189

No.	Name	Rank	Service	Date	Place	Personal Action	Type of Personal Action	Military Task of Unit	Relevance of Action to Task	Casualty?	How Selected for Award
131	Stephen GARVIN	NCO	Army	23/06/1857	India	Lead	Voluntary	Attack	None	No	Nominated
132	John McGOVERN	OR	Army	23/06/1957	India	Rescue	Initiative	Attack	None	No	Nominated
133	William CUBITT	Junior Officer	Army	30/06/1857	India	Rescue	Initiative	Withdraw	None	No	Nominated
134	William OXENHAM	NCO	Army	30/06/1857	India	Rescue	Initiative	Defend	None	No	Nominated
135	Robert AITKEN	Junior Officer	Army	30/06/1857 - 22/11/1857	India	Combat	Duty	Attack	None	No	Nominated
136	James TRAVERS	NCO	Army	1/07/1857	India	Charge	Duty	Defend	None	No	Nominated
137	William DOWLING	OR	Army	4/07/1857 9/07/1857 27/09/1857	India	Sortie	Duty	Attack	None	No	Nominated
138	William CONNOLLY	OR	Army	7/07/1957	India	Combat	Duty	Withdraw	High	Wounded	Nominated
139	Samuel LAWRENCE	Junior Officer	Army	7/07/1857 26/09/1857	India	Charge	Duty	Attack	High	No	Nominated
140	Henry TOMBS	Junior Officer	Army	9/07/1857	India	Combat	Duty	Defend	High	Wounded	Nominated
141	James HILLS	Junior Officer	Army	9/07/1857	India	Charge	Duty	Defend	High	No	Nominated
142	James THOMPSON	OR	Army	9/07/1857	India	Rescue	Initiative	Defend	None	No	Elected
143	William KERR	Junior Officer	Army	10/07/1857	India	Sortie	Duty	Attack	High	No	Nominated
144	Abraham BOULGER	NCO	Army	12/07/1857- 25/09/1857	India	Combat	Duty	Attack	High	Wounded	Nominated
145	Patrick MYLOTT	OR	Army	12/07/1857- 25/09/1857	India	Capture	Duty	Attack	High	No	Elected
146	Henry HAVELOCK	Junior Officer	Army	16/07/1857	India	Lead	Voluntary	Attack	Low	No	Nominated
147	Richard WADESON	Junior Officer	Army	18/07/1857	India	Rescue	Initiative	Defend	Low	No	Nominated
148	Andrew BOGLE	Junior Officer	Army	29/07/1857	India	Storm	Duty	Attack	High	Wounded	Nominated
149	George LAMBERT	NCO	Army	29/07/1857 16/08/1857 25/09/1857	India	Combat	Duty	Attack	High	No	Nominated
150	Ross MANGLES	Civilian	Army	30/07/1857	India	Rescue	Voluntary	Retreat	Low	Wounded	Nominated
151	William McDONELL	Civilian	Army	30/07/1857	India	Rescue	Voluntary	Retreat	Low	Wounded	Nominated

190

152	William SUTTON	OR	Army	2/08/1857 13/09/1857	India		Voluntary	Attack	High	No	Elected
153	Joseph CROWE	Junior Officer	Army	12/08/1857	India	Storm	Duty	Attack	High	No	Nominated
154	James BLAIR	Junior Officer	Army	12/08/1857 23/10/1857	India	Arrest	Voluntary	Attack	High	Wounded	Nominated
155	Denis DEMPSEY	OR	Army	12/08/1857 14/03/1857	India	Demolish	Voluntary	Attack	High	No	Nominated
156	Charles GOUGH	Junior Officer	Army	15/08/1857 18/08/1857 27/01/1858 23/02/1858	India	Charge	Duty	Attack	High	No	Nominated
157	Henry GORE-BROWN	Junior Officer	Army	21/08/1857	India	Sortie	Duty	Attack	High	No	Nominated
158	John DIVANE	OR	Army	10/09/1857	India	Charge	Duty	Attack	High	Wounded	Elected
159	Patrick GREEN	OR	Army	11/09/1857	India	Rescue	Initiative	Defend	None	No	Nominated
160	Duncan HOME	Junior Officer	Army	14/09/1857	India	Demolish	Duty	Attack	High	No	Nominated
161	Philip SALKELD	Junior Officer	Army	14/09/1857	India	Demolish	Duty	Attack	High	Wounded	Nominated
162	Robert SHEBBEARE	Junior Officer	Army	14/09/1857	India	Charge	Duty	Attack	High	Wounded	Nominated
163	James McGUIRE	NCO	Army	14/09/1857	India	Protect	Duty	Guard	High	No	Nominated
164	John SMITH	NCO	Army	14/09/1857	India	Demolish	Duty	Attack	High	No	Nominated
165	Henry SMITH	NCO	Army	14/09/1857	India	Rescue	Initiative	Retreat	None	No	Nominated
166	Robert HAWTHORNE	OR	Army	14/09/1857	India	Demolish	Duty	Attack	High	No	Nominated
167	Miles RYAN	OR	Army	14/09/1857	India	Protect	Duty	Guard	High	No	Nominated
168	Herbert READE	Medical Officer	Army	14/09/1857 16/09/1857	India	Lead	Initiative	Aid	Low	No	Nominated
169	George WALLER	NCO	Army	14/09/1857 18/09/1857	India	Charge	Duty	Attack	High	No	Elected
170	George RENNY	Junior Officer	Army	16/09/1857	India	Repulse	Duty	Defend	High	No	Nominated
171	Edward THACKERAY	Junior Officer	Army	16/09/1857	India	Protect	Duty	Defend	High	No	Nominated
172	Patrick MAHONEY	NCO	Army	21/09/1857	India	Capture	Voluntary	Attack	High	No	Nominated

No.	Name	Rank	Service	Date	Place	Personal Action	Type of Personal Action	Military Task of Unit	Relevance of Action to Task	Casualty?	How Selected for Award
173	William RENNIE	Junior Officer	Army	21/09/1857 25/09/1857	India	Charge	Duty	Attack	High	No	Nominated
174	Robert GRANT	NCO	Army	24/09/1857	India	Rescue	Initiative	Advance	None	No	Nominated
175	Joseph JEE	Medical Officer	Army	25/09/1857	India	Rescue	Duty	Aid	High	No	Nominated
176	Valentine McMASTER	Medical Officer	Army	25/09/1857	India	Rescue	Duty	Aid	High	No	Nominated
177	Francis MAUDE	Junior Officer	Army	25/09/1857	India	Lead	Duty	Attack	High	No	Elected
178	William OLPHERTS	Junior Officer	Army	25/09/1857	India	Charge	Duty	Attack	High	No	Elected
179	Herbert MacPHERSON	Junior Officer	Army	25/09/1857	India	Charge	Duty	Attack	High	No	Nominated
180	Joel HOLMES	OR	Army	25/09/1857	India	Replace	Voluntary	Attack	High	No	Nominated
181	Henry WARD	OR	Army	25/09/1857 - 26/09/1857	India	Escort	Duty	Rescue	High	No	Nominated
182	Anthony HOME	Medical Officer	Army	26/09/1857	India	Combat	Necessity	Aid	Low	No	Nominated
183	William BRADSHAW	Medical Officer	Army	26/09/1857	India	Rescue	Duty	Aid	High	No	Nominated
184	Stewart McPHERSON	NCO	Army	26/09/1857	India	Rescue	Initiative	Relieve	None	No	Nominated
185	Thomas DUFFY	OR	Army	26/09/1857	India	Recover	Duty	Recover	High	No	Nominated
186	James HOLLOWELL	OR	Army	26/09/1857	India	Escort	Duty	Defend	High	No	Nominated
187	Peter McMANUS	OR	Army	26/09/1857	India	Escort	Duty	Defend	High	Wounded	Nominated
188	John RYAN	OR	Army	26/09/1857	India	Escort	Duty	Defend	High	No	Nominated
189	Jacob THOMAS	NCO	Army	27/09/1857	India	Rescue	Initiative	Defend	None	No	Nominated
190	Robert BLAIR	Junior Officer	Army	28/09/1857	India	Lead	Duty	Recover	High	Wounded	Nominated
191	Bernard DIAMOND	NCO	Army	28/09/1857	India	Combat	Duty	Bombard	High	No	Nominated
192	Robert KELLS	NCO	Army	28/09/1857	India	Rescue	Initiative	Attack	None	No	Nominated
193	Patrick DONOHUE	OR	Army	28/09/1857	India	Rescue	Initiative	Attack	None	No	Nominated
194	Richard FITZGERALD	OR	Army	28/09/1857	India	Combat	Duty	Bombard	High	No	Nominated

192

No	Name	Rank	Service	Date	Country						
195	James ROBERTS	OR	Army	28/09/1857	India	Rescue	Initiative	Attack	None	Wounded	Nominated
196	Augustus ANSON	Junior Officer	Army	28/09/1857 16/11/1857	India	Charge	Duty	Attack	High	Wounded	Nominated
197	Denis DYNON	NCO	Army	2/10/1857	India	Charge	Duty	Attack	High	No	Nominated
198	John DAUNT	Junior Officer	Army	2/10/1857 2/11/1857	India	Charge	Duty	Attack	High	Wounded	Nominated
199	Patrick McHALE	OR	Army	2/10/1857 22/12/1857	India	Capture	Duty	Attack	High	No	Nominated
200	John SINNOTT	NCO	Army	6/10/1857	India	Rescue	Initiative	Defend	None	Wounded	Elected
201	John FREEMAN	OR	Army	10/10/1857	India	Rescue	Initiative	Attack	None	No	Nominated
202	James MILLER	NCO	Army	28/10/1857	India	Rescue	Initiative	Attack	None	Wounded	Nominated
203	Thomas KAVANAGH	Civilian	Army	9/11/1857	India	Guide	Voluntary	Relieve	High	No	Nominated
204	Hugh GOUGH	Junior Officer	Army	12/11/1857 25/02/1858	India	Charge	Duty	Attack	High	Wounded	Nominated
205	John WATSON	Junior Officer	Army	14/11/1857	India	Combat	Duty	Relieve	High	Wounded	Nominated
206	Hastings HARINGTON	Junior Officer	Army	14/11/1857 - 22/11/1857	India	Combat	Duty	Relieve	High	Wounded	Elected
207	Edward JENNINGS	OR	Army	14/11/1857 - 22/11/1857	India	Combat	Duty	Relieve	High	No	Elected
208	Thomas LAUGHNAN	OR	Army	14/11/1857 - 22/11/1857	India	Combat	Duty	Relieve	High	No	Elected
209	Hugh McINNES	OR	Army	14/11/1857 - 22/11/1857	India	Combat	Duty	Relieve	High	No	Elected
210	James PARK	OR	Army	14/11/1857 - 22/11/1857	India	Combat	Duty	Relieve	High	No	Elected
211	William STEUART	Junior Officer	Army	16/11/1857	India	Lead	Duty	Attack	High	No	Elected
212	Francis BROWN	Junior Officer	Army	16/11/1857	India	Rescue	Initiative	Attack	None	No	Nominated
213	Alfred FFRENCH	Junior Officer	Army	16/11/1857	India	Lead	Duty	Attack	High	No	Elected
214	Nowell SALMON	Junior Officer	Navy	16/11/1857	India	Dislodge	Voluntary	Attack	High	Wounded	Nominated
215	Thomas YOUNG	Junior Officer	Navy	16/11/1857	India	Lead	Duty	Attack	High	Wounded	Nominated

No.	Name	Rank	Service	Date	Place	Personal Action	Type of Personal Action	Military Task of Unit	Relevance of Action to Task	Casualty?	How Selected for Award
216	James MUNRO	NCO	Army	16/11/1857	India	Rescue	Initiative	Attack	None	Wounded	Elected
217	John PATON	NCO	Army	16/11/1857	India	Recon	Duty	Attack	High	No	Elected
218	John DUNLEY	NCO	Army	16/11/1857	India	Combat	Initiative	Attack	High	Wounded	Elected
219	Peter GRANT	OR	Army	16/11/1857	India	Combat	Duty	Attack	High	No	Elected
220	Charles IRWIN	OR	Army	16/11/1857	India	Combat	Duty	Attack	High	Wounded	Elected
221	James KENNY	OR	Army	16/11/1857	India	Resupply	Voluntary	Attack	High	No	Elected
222	David McKAY	OR	Army	16/11/1857	India	Capture	Duty	Attack	None	Wounded	Elected
223	John SMITH	OR	Army	16/11/1857	India	Combat	Duty	Attack	High	Wounded	Elected
224	John HARRISON	NCO	Navy	16/11/1857	India	Dislodge	Voluntary	Attack	High	No	Nominated
225	William HALL	OR	Navy	16/11/1857	India	Combat	Voluntary	Bombard	High	No	Nominated
226	John GUISE	Junior Officer	Army	16/11/1857 - 17/11/1857	India	Rescue	Initiative	Attack	None	No	Elected
227	Samuel HILL	NCO	Army	16/11/1857 - 17/11/1857	India	Rescue	Initiative	Attack	None	No	Elected
228	Charles PYE	NCO	Army	17/11/1857	India	Resupply	Duty	Attack	High	No	Elected
229	Patrick GRAHAM	OR	Army	17/11/1857	India	Rescue	Initiative	Attack	None	No	Elected
230	Thomas HACKETT	Junior Officer	Army	18/11/1857	India	Rescue	Initiative	Attack	None	No	Nominated
231	George MONGER	OR	Army	18/11/1857	India	Rescue	Initiative	Attack	None	No	Nominated
232	Harry PRENDERGAST	Junior Officer	Army	21/11/1857	India	Warn	Duty	Attack	Low	Wounded	Nominated
233	Arthur MAYO	Junior Officer	Navy	22/11/1857	India	Charge	Duty	Attack	High	No	Nominated
234	Thomas FLINN	OR	Army	28/11/1857	India	Charge	Duty	Attack	High	Wounded	Nominated
235	Frederick ROBERTS	Junior Officer	Army	2/01/1858	India	Capture	Initiative	Attack	Low	No	Nominated
236	Bernard McQUIRT	OR	Army	6/01/1858	India	Combat	Duty	Attack	High	Wounded	Nominated
237	David SPENCE	NCO	Army	17/01/1858	India	Rescue	Initiative	Attack	None	No	Nominated
238	John TYTLER	Junior Officer	Army	10/02/1858	India	Charge	Duty	Attack	High	Wounded	Nominated
239	James INNES	Junior Officer	Army	23/02/1858	India	Skirmish	Duty	Attack	High	No	Nominated
240	Frederick AIKMAN	Junior Officer	Army	1/03/1858	India	Lead	Duty	Attack	High	Wounded	Nominated

194

241	William GOAT	NCO	Army	6/03/1858	India	Rescue	Initiative	Relieve	None	No	Nominated
242	Thomas BUTLER	Junior Officer	Army	9/03/1858	India	Raid	Voluntary	Attack	High	No	Nominated
243	Francis FARQUHARSON	Junior Officer	Army	9/03/1858	India	Spike	Duty	Storm	High	No	Nominated
244	Henry WILMOT	Junior Officer	Army	11/03/1858	India	Cover	Duty	Withdraw	High	No	Nominated
245	William McBEAN	Junior Officer	Army	11/03/1858	India	Combat	Duty	Attack	High	No	Nominated
246	William NASH	NCO	Army	11/03/1858	India	Rescue	Duty	Withdraw	Low	No	Nominated
247	David HAWKE	OR	Army	11/03/1858	India	Rescue	Duty	Withdraw	Low	Wounded	Nominated
248	Edward ROBINSON	OR	Navy	13/03/1858	India	Repair	Duty	Defend	High	Wounded	Nominated
249	Richard KEATINGE	Junior Officer	Army	17/03/1858	India	Lead	Voluntary	Attack	High	Wounded	Nominated
250	David RUSHE	NCO	Army	19/03/1858	India	Combat	Duty	Attack	High	No	Nominated
251	William BANKES	Junior Officer	Army	19/03/1858	India	Charge	Duty	Attack	High	Killed	Nominated
252	Robert NEWELL	OR	Army	19/03/1858	India	Rescue	Initiative	Attack	None	No	Nominated
253	Aylmer CAMERON	Junior Officer	Army	30/03/1858	India	Storm	Duty	Attack	High	Wounded	Nominated
254	Hugh COCHRANE	Junior Officer	Army	1/04/1858	India	Capture	Duty	Attack	High	No	Nominated
255	James LEITH	Junior Officer	Army	1/04/1858	India	Rescue	Initiative	Attack	None	No	Nominated
256	Michael SLEAVON	NCO	Army	3/04/1858	India	Sap	Duty	Attack	High	No	Nominated
257	Joseph BRENNAN	NCO	Army	3/04/1858	India	Direct	Duty	Attack	High	No	Nominated
258	James BYRNE	OR	Army	3/04/1858	India	Rescue	Initiative	Attack	None	Wounded	Nominated
259	James PEARSON	OR	Army	3/04/1858	India	Combat	Duty	Attack	High	Wounded	Nominated
260	Frederick WHIRLPOOL	OR	Army	3/04/1858 6/05/1858	India	Rescue	Voluntary	Attack	None	Wounded	Nominated
261	Henry JEROME	Junior Officer	Army	3/04/1858 28/05/1858	India	Rescue	Initiative	Attack	None	Wounded	Nominated
262	William NAPIER	NCO	Army	6/04/1858	India	Rescue	Initiative	Defend	None	No	Nominated
263	Patrick CARLIN	OR	Army	6/04/1858	India	Rescue	Initiative	Attack	None	No	Nominated
264	William CAFE	Junior Officer	Army	15/04/1858	India	Rescue	Initiative	Attack	None	Wounded	Nominated
265	John SIMPSON	NCO	Army	15/04/1858	India	Rescue	Voluntary	Attack	None	No	Nominated
266	Alexander THOMPSON	NCO	Army	15/04/1858	India	Rescue	Voluntary	Attack	None	No	Nominated

No.	Name	Service	Rank	Date	Place	Personal Action	Type of Personal Action	Military Task of Unit	Relevance of Action to Task	Casualty?	How Selected for Award
267	James DAVIS	Army	OR	15/04/1858	India	Rescue	Voluntary	Attack	None	No	Nominated
268	Samuel MORLEY	Army	OR	15/04/1858	India	Rescue	Initiative	Attack	None	No	Nominated
269	Michael MURPHY	Army	OR	15/04/1858	India	Rescue	Initiative	Attack	None	No	Nominated
270	Edward SPENCE	Army	OR	15/04/1858	India	Rescue	Voluntary	Attack	Low	Wounded	Nominated
271	William GARDNER	Army	NCO	5/05/1858	India	Rescue	Initiative	Attack	None	No	Nominated
272	Valentine BAMBRICK	Army	OR	6/05/1858	India	Resist	Necessity	Attack	Low	Wounded	Nominated
273	Henry LYSTER	Army	Junior Officer	23/05/1858	India	Charge	Initiative	Attack	High	No	Nominated
274	Samuel SHAW	Army	OR	13/06/1858	India	Combat	Duty	Attack	High	Wounded	Nominated
275	George RODGERS	Army	OR	16/06/1858	India	Combat	Duty	Attack	High	No	Nominated
276	Clement HENEAGE-WALKER	Army	Junior Officer	17/06/1858	India	Charge	Duty	Attack	High	No	Elected
277	Joseph WARD	Army	NCO	17/06/1858	India	Charge	Duty	Attack	High	No	Elected
278	George HOLLIS	Army	OR	17/06/1858	India	Charge	Duty	Attack	High	No	Elected
279	John PEARSON	Army	OR	17/06/1858	India	Charge	Duty	Attack	High	No	Elected
280	William WALLER	Army	Junior Officer	20/06/1858	India	Storm	Duty	Attack	High	No	Nominated
281	Samuel BROWNE	Army	Junior Officer	31/08/1858	India	Charge	Duty	Attack	High	Wounded	Nominated
282	James CHAMPION	Police	NCO	03/09/1858	India	Pursuit	Duty	Attack	High	Wounded	Nominated
283	Charles BAKER	Army	Junior Officer	27/09/1858	India	Charge	Duty	Attack	High	No	Nominated
284	Patrick RODDY	Army	Junior Officer	27/09/1858	India	Charge	Duty	Attack	High	No	Nominated
285	George CHICKEN	Navy	Civilian	27/09/1858	India	Charge	Duty	Attack	High	Wounded	Nominated
286	Thomas MONAGHAN	Army	OR	8/10/1858	India	Rescue	Initiative	Attack	High	No	Nominated
287	Charles ANDERSON	Army	OR	8/10/1858	India	Rescue	Initiative	Attack	Low	No	Nominated
288	Hanson JARRETT	Army	Junior Officer	14/10/1858	India	Storm	Duty	Attack	High	No	Nominated
289	Evelyn WOOD	Army	Junior Officer	19/10/1858 29/12/1858	India	Rescue	Duty	Attack	High	No	Nominated
290	Charles FRASER	Army	Junior Officer	31/12/1858	India	Rescue	Voluntary	Pursue	Low	Wounded	Nominated
291	Henry ADDISON	Army	OR	2/01/1859	India	Rescue	Initiative	Defend	Low	Wounded	Nominated

196

No.	Name	Rank	Service	Date	Place	Charge	Duty	Attack		Wounded	
292	Herbert CLOGSTOUN	Junior Officer	Army	15/01/1859	India	Lead	Initiative	Attack	High	No	Nominated
293	Walter COOK	OR	Army	15/01/1859	India	Lead	Initiative	Skirmish	High	No	Nominated
294	Duncan MILLAR	OR	Army	15/01/1859	India	Lead	Initiative	Skirmish	High	Wounded	Nominated
295	George RICHARDSON	OR	Army	27/04/1859	India	Capture	Duty	Attack	High	No	Nominated
296	Charles GOODFELLOW	Junior Officer	Army	06/10/1859	India	Rescue	Initiative	Attack	None	No	Nominated
297	William ODGERS	NCO	Navy	28/03/1860	New Zealand	Storm	Duty	Attack	High	Wounded	Nominated
298	Nathaniel BURSLEM	Junior Officer	Army	21/08/1860	China	Sortie	Duty	Storm	High	No	Nominated
299	Edmund LENON	Junior Officer	Army	21/08/1860	China	Sortie	Duty	Storm	High	Wounded	Nominated
300	Robert ROGERS	Junior Officer	Army	21/08/1860	China	Sortie	Duty	Storm	High	Wounded	Nominated
301	John CHAPLIN	Junior Officer	Army	21/08/1860	China	Sortie	Duty	Storm	Low	Wounded	Nominated
302	Thomas LANE	OR	Army	21/08/1860	China	Sortie	Duty	Storm	High	Wounded	Nominated
303	John McDOUGALL	OR	Army	21/08/1860	China	Sortie	Duty	Storm	High	Wounded	Nominated
304	Andrew FITZGIBBON	Medical OR	Army	21/08/1860	China	Rescue	Duty	Advance	High	Wounded	Nominated
305	John LUCAS	NCO	Army	18/03/1861	New Zealand	Resist	Duty	Skirmish	High	No	Nominated
306	George HINCKLEY	OR	Navy	9/10/1862	China	Rescue	Voluntary	Attack	None	No	Nominated
307	Edward McKENNA	NCO	Army	7/09/1863	New Zealand	Charge	Duty	Withdraw	High	No	Nominated
308	John RYAN	NCO	Army	7/09/1863	New Zealand	Rescue	Initiative	Attack	None	No	Nominated
309	John DOWN	Junior Officer	Army	2/10/1863	New Zealand	Rescue	Voluntary	Attack	None	No	Nominated
310	Dudley STAGPOOLE	OR	Army	2/10/1863	New Zealand	Rescue	Voluntary	Attack	None	No	Nominated
311	George FOSBERY	Junior Officer	Army	30/10/1863	India	Lead	Duty	Retake	High	No	Nominated
312	Henry PITCHER	Junior Officer	Army	30/10/1863 16/11/1863	India	Lead	Duty	Retake	High	Wounded	Nominated
313	William TEMPLE	Medical Officer	Army	20/11/1863	New Zealand	Rescue	Duty	Aid	High	No	Nominated
314	Arthur PICKARD	Junior Officer	Army	20/11/1863	New Zealand	Rescue	Initiative	Attack	None	No	Nominated
315	Charles HEAPHY	Junior Officer	Army	11/02/1864	New Zealand	Rescue	Initiative	Skirmish	None	Wounded	Nominated
316	John McNEILL	Junior Officer	Army	30/03/1864	New Zealand	Rescue	Initiative	Withdraw	Low	No	Nominated
317	William MANLEY	Medical Officer	Army	29/04/1864	New Zealand	Rescue	Voluntary	Aid	High	No	Nominated

No.	Name	Service	Date	Place	Personal Action	Type of Personal Action	Military Task of Unit	Relevance of Action to Task	Casualty?	How Selected for Award
318	Samuel MITCHELL	NCO	Navy	29/04/1864	New Zealand	Rescue	Initiative	Attack	Contrary	No	Nominated
319	Frederick SMITH	Junior Officer	Army	21/06/1864	New Zealand	Lead	Duty	Attack	High	Wounded	Nominated
320	John MURRAY	NCO	Army	21/06/1864	New Zealand	Lead	Duty	Attack	High	Wounded	Nominated
321	Duncan BOYES	Junior Officer	Navy	6/09/1864	Japan	Rally	Initiative	Attack	High	No	Nominated
322	Thomas PRIDE	NCO	Navy	6/09/1864	Japan	Rally	Initiative	Attack	High	Wounded	Nominated
323	William SEELEY	OR	Navy	6/09/1864	Japan	Recon	Duty	Attack	High	Wounded	Nominated
324	Hugh SHAW	Junior Officer	Army	24/01/1865	New Zealand	Rescue	Initiative	Skirmish	None	No	Nominated
325	William TREVOR	Junior Officer	Army	30/04/1865	Bhutan	Guide	Duty	Attack	High	Wounded	Nominated
326	James DUNDAS	Junior Officer	Army	30/04/1865	Bhutan	Guide	Duty	Attack	High	Wounded	Nominated
327	Timothy O'HEA	OR	Army	9/06/1866	Canada	Protect	Initiative	N/A	N/A	No	Nominated
328	Samuel HODGE	OR	Army	30/06/1866	Gambia	Demolish	Duty	Attack	High	Wounded	Acclaimed
329	Campbell DOUGLAS	Medical Officer	Army	07/05/1867	Andaman Islands	Rescue	Duty	Aid	High	No	Nominated
330	David BELL	OR	Army	07/06/1867	Andaman Islands	Rescue	Unknown	Aid	High	No	Nominated
331	James COOPER	OR	Army	07/06/1867	Andaman Islands	Rescue	Unknown	Aid	High	No	Nominated
332	William GRIFFITHS	OR	Army	07/06/1867	Andaman Islands	Rescue	Unknown	Aid	High	No	Nominated
333	Thomas MURPHY	OR	Army	07/06/1867	Andaman Islands	Rescue	Unknown	Aid	High	No	Nominated
334	James BERGIN	OR	Army	13/04/1868	Abyssinia	Scout	Duty	Attack	High	No	Nominated
335	Michael MAGNER	OR	Army	13/04/1868	Abyssinia	Scout	Duty	Attack	High	No	Nominated
336	Donald MacINTYRE	Junior Officer	Army	04/01/1872	India	Storm	Duty	Attack	High	No	Nominated
337	Edric GIFFORD	Junior Officer	Army	1873-74	Ghana	Scout	Duty	Scout	High	No	Nominated
338	Reginald SARTORIUS	Junior Officer	Army	17/01/1874	Ghana	Rescue	Initiative	Attack	None	No	Nominated
339	Samuel McGAW	NCO	Army	21/01/1874	Ghana	Lead	Duty	Attack	High	Wounded	Nominated
340	Mark BELL	Junior Officer	Army	04/02/1874	Ghana	Lead	Duty	Attack	High	No	Nominated

198

#	Name	Rank	Service	Date	Location	Action	Duty	Manoeuvre	Risk	Outcome	Status
341	George CHANNER	Junior Officer	Army	20/12/1875	Malaya	Rescue	Initiative	Attack	High	No	Nominated
342	Andrew SCOTT	Junior Officer	Army	26/07/1877	Baluchistan	Rescue	Initiative	N/A	N/A	No	Nominated
343	Hans MOORE	Junior Officer	Army	29/12/1877	South Africa	Rescue	Initiative	Retreat	None	Wounded	Nominated
344	John COOK	Junior Officer	Army	02/12/1878	Afghanistan	Rescue	Initiative	Attack	None	Wounded	Nominated
345	Teignmouth MELVILL	Junior Officer	Army	22/01/1879	South Africa	Protect	Initiative	Defend	None	Killed	Nominated
346	Nevill COGHILL	Junior Officer	Army	22/01/1879	South Africa	Protect	Initiative	Defend	None	Killed	Nominated
347	Samuel WASSALL	OR	Army	22/01/1879	South Africa	Rescue	Initiative	Defend	None	No	Nominated
348	John CHARD	Junior Officer	Army	22/01/1879 - 23/01/1879	South Africa	Lead	Necessity	Defend	High	No	Nominated
349	Gonville BROMHEAD	Junior Officer	Army	22/01/1879 - 23/01/1879	South Africa	Lead	Necessity	Defend	High	No	Nominated
350	James REYNOLDS	Medical Officer	Army	22/01/1879 - 23/01/1879	South Africa	Attend	Duty	Aid	High	No	Nominated
351	James DALTON	Junior Officer	Army	22/01/1879 - 23/01/1879	South Africa	Combat	Necessity	Defend	High	Wounded	Nominated
352	William ALLEN	NCO	Army	22/01/1879 - 23/01/1879	South Africa	Combat	Necessity	Defend	High	Wounded	Nominated
353	Ferdinand SCHEISS	NCO	Army	22/01/1879 - 23/01/1879	South Africa	Combat	Necessity	Defend	High	No	Nominated
354	Alfred HOOK	OR	Army	22/01/1879 - 23/01/1879	South Africa	Combat	Necessity	Defend	High	No	Nominated
355	William JONES	OR	Army	22/01/1879 - 23/01/1879	South Africa	Combat	Necessity	Defend	High	No	Nominated
356	Robert JONES	OR	Army	22/01/1879 -23/10/1879	South Africa	Combat	Necessity	Defend	High	No	Nominated
357	John WILLIAMS	OR	Army	22/01/1879 - 23/01/1879	South Africa	Combat	Necessity	Defend	High	No	Nominated
358	Frederick HITCH	OR	Army	22/01/1879 - 23/01/1879	South Africa	Combat	Necessity	Defend	High	Wounded	Nominated
359	Reginald HART	Junior Officer	Army	31/01/1879	Afghanistan	Rescue	Initiative	Convoy	None	No	Nominated
360	Anthony BOOTH	NCO	Army	12/03/1879	South Africa	Lead	Duty	Retreat	High	No	Nominated

No.	Name	Rank	Service	Date	Place	Personal Action	Type of Personal Action	Military Task of Unit	Relevance of Action to Task	Casualty?	How Selected for Award
361	Edward LEACH	Junior Officer	Army	17/03/1879	Afghanistan	Cover	Duty	Retreat	High	Wounded	Nominated
362	Redvers BULLER	Junior Officer	Army	28/03/1879	South Africa	Cover	Duty	Retreat	High	No	Nominated
363	William LEET	Junior Officer	Army	28/03/1879	South Africa	Rescue	Initiative	Retreat	None	No	Nominated
364	Henry LYSONS	Junior Officer	Army	28/03/1879	South Africa	Combat	Duty	Attack	High	No	Nominated
365	Edmund FOWLER	OR	Army	28/03/1879	South Africa	Combat	Duty	Attack	High	No	Nominated
366	Edward BROWNE	Junior Officer	Army	29/03/1879	South Africa	Rescue	Initiative	Withdraw	None	No	Nominated
367	Walter HAMILTON	Junior Officer	Army	2/04/1879	Afghanistan	Charge	Duty	Attack	None	No	Nominated
368	Robert SCOTT	NCO	Army	8/04/1879	South Africa	Bomb	Voluntary	Attack	High	Wounded	Nominated
369	Peter BROWN	OR	Army	8/04/1879	South Africa	Attend	Initiative	Attack	None	Wounded	Nominated
370	O'Moore CREAGH	Junior Officer	Army	21/04/1879	Afghanistan	Lead	Duty	Protect	High	No	Nominated
371	Edmund HARTLEY	Medical Officer	Army	5/06/1879	South Africa	Rescue	Duty	Aid	High	No	Nominated
372	William BERESFORD	Junior Officer	Army	3/07/1879	South Africa	Rescue	Initiative	Retire	None	No	Nominated
373	Henry D'ARCY	Junior Officer	Army	3/07/1879	South Africa	Rescue	Initiative	Retire	None	No	Nominated
374	Edmund O'TOOLE	NCO	Army	3/07/1879	South Africa	Rescue	Duty	Retire	None	No	Co-opted
375	George WHITE	Junior Officer	Army	6/10/1879	Afghanistan	Lead	Duty	Attack	High	No	Nominated
376	Euston SARTORIUS	Junior Officer	Army	24/10/1879	Afghanistan	Lead	Duty	Attack	High	Wounded	Nominated
377	Richard RIDGEWAY	Junior Officer	Army	22/11/1879	India	Charge	Initiative	Attack	High	Wounded	Nominated
378	Francis FITZPATRICK	OR	Army	28/11/1879	South Africa	Rescue	Initiative	Attack	None	No	Nominated
379	Thomas FLAWN	OR	Army	28/11/1879	South Africa	Rescue	Initiative	Attack	None	No	Nominated
380	James ADAMS	Chaplain	Army	11/12/1879	Afghanistan	Rescue	Duty	Aid	High	No	Nominated
381	William DICK-CUNYNGHAM	Junior Officer	Army	13/12/1879	Afghanistan	Charge	Duty	Attack	High	No	Nominated
382	Arthur HAMMOND	Junior Officer	Army	14/12/1879	Afghanistan	Resist	Duty	Retire	High	No	Nominated
383	William VOUSDEN	Junior Officer	Army	14/12/1879	Afghanistan	Charge	Duty	Attack	High	No	Nominated
384	George SELLAR	NCO	Army	14/12/1879	Afghanistan	Charge	Duty	Attack	High	Wounded	Nominated
385	Patrick MULLANE	NCO	Army	27/07/1880	Afghanistan	Rescue	Initiative	Retreat	None	No	Nominated

No.	Name	Rank	Service	Date	Location	Action	Duty	Manoeuvre	Risk	Casualty	Status
386	James COLLIS	OR	Army	28/07/1880	Afghanistan	Resist	Duty	Retreat	High	No	Nominated
387	William CHASE	Junior Officer	Army	16/08/1880	Afghanistan	Rescue	Initiative	Retreat	None	No	Nominated
388	Thomas ASHFORD	OR	Army	16/08/1880	Afghanistan	Rescue	Initiative	Retreat	None	No	Nominated
389	John McCREA	Medical Officer	Army	14/01/1881	South Africa	Rescue	Duty	Aid	High	Wounded	Nominated
390	James MURRAY	NCO	Army	16/01/1881	South Africa	Rescue	Initiative	Engage	None	Wounded	Nominated
391	John DANAHER	OR	Army	16/01/1881	South Africa	Rescue	Initiative	Engage	None	POW	Nominated
392	Alan HILL	Junior Officer	Army	16/01/1881	South Africa	Rescue	Initiative	Retreat	None	No	Nominated
393	John DOOGAN	OR	Army	28/01/1881	South Africa	Rescue	Initiative	Attack	None	Wounded	Nominated
394	James OSBORNE	OR	Army	22/02/1881	South Africa	Rescue	Initiative	Defend	None	No	Nominated
395	Joseph FARMER	NCO	Army	27/02/1881	South Africa	Rescue	Initiative	Relieve	None	POW	Nominated
396	Israel HARDING	NCO	Navy	11/07/1882	Egypt	Protect	Initiative	Bombard	Low	No	Nominated
397	Frederick CORBETT	OR	Army	5/08/1882	Egypt	Rescue	Voluntary	Retreat	Low	No	Nominated
398	William EDWARDS	Junior Officer	Army	13/09/1882	Egypt	Storm	Duty	Attack	High	No	Nominated
399	Arthur WILSON	Senior Officer	Navy	29/02/1884	Sudan	Repel	Voluntary	Defend	High	No	Nominated
400	William MARSHALL	NCO	Army	29/02/1884	Sudan	Rescue	Initiative	Attack	None	No	Nominated
401	Percival MARLING	Junior Officer	Army	13/03/1884	Sudan	Rescue	Initiative	Defend	None	No	Nominated
402	Thomas EDWARDS	OR	Army	13/03/1884	Sudan	Combat	Duty	Defend	High	Wounded	Nominated
403	Alfred SMITH	OR	Army	17/01/1885	Sudan	Combat	Duty	Defend	High	No	Nominated
404	John CRIMMIN	Medical Officer	Army	1/01/1889	Burma	Combat	Initiative	Skirmish	High	No	Nominated
405	Ferdinand LE QUESNE	Medical Officer	Army	4/05/1889	Burma	Rescue	Duty	Aid	High	Wounded	Nominated
406	Charles GRANT	Junior Officer	Army	21/03/1891 - 9/04/1891	India	Lead	Voluntary	Relieve	High	Wounded	Nominated
407	Fenton AYLMER	Junior Officer	Army	2/12/1891	India	Combat	Duty	Attack	High	Wounded	Nominated
408	Guy BOISRAGON	Junior Officer	Army	2/12/1891	India	Lead	Duty	Attack	High	No	Nominated
409	John MANNERS-SMITH	Junior Officer	Army	20/12/1891	India	Lead	Duty	Attack	High	No	Nominated
410	William GORDON	NCO	Army	13/03/1892	Gambia	Protect	Initiative	Attack	Low	Wounded	Nominated

No.	Name	Rank	Service	Date	Place	Personal Action	Type of Personal Action	Military Task of Unit	Relevance of Action to Task	Casualty?	How Selected for Award
411	Owen LLOYD	Medical Officer	Army	6/01/1893	Burma	Rescue	Duty	Aid	High	Wounded	Nominated
412	Harry WHITCHURCH	Medical Officer	Army	3/03/1895	India	Rescue	Duty	Aid	High	No	Nominated
413	Herbert HENDERSON	OR	Army	30/03/1896	Rhodesia	Rescue	Initiative	Defend	Low	No	Nominated
414	Frank BAXTER	OR	Army	22/04/1896	Rhodesia	Rescue	Initiative	Retire	None	Killed	Nominated
415	Randolph NESBITT	Junior Officer	Police	19/06/1896	Rhodesia	Lead	Duty	Rescue	High	No	Nominated
416	Edmond COSTELLO	Junior Officer	Army	26/07/1897	India	Rescue	Initiative	Defend	None	No	Nominated
417	Robert ADAMS	Junior Officer	Army	17/08/1897	India	Rescue	Initiative	Pursuit	None	No	Nominated
418	Hector MacLEAN	Junior Officer	Army	17/08/1897	India	Rescue	Initiative	Pursuit	None	Killed	Nominated
419	Alexander FINCASTLE	Junior Officer	Army	17/08/1897	India	Rescue	Initiative	Pursuit	None	No	Nominated
420	James COLVIN	Junior Officer	Army	16/09/1897 - 17/09/1897	India	Combat	Voluntary	Attack	High	No	Nominated
421	Thomas WATSON	Junior Officer	Army	16/09/1897 - 17/09/1897	India	Lead	Duty	Attack	High	Wounded	Nominated
422	James SMITH	NCO	Army	16/09/1897 - 17/90/1897	India	Combat	Voluntary	Attack	High	Wounded	Nominated
423	Henry PENNELL	Junior Officer	Army	20/10/1897	India	Rescue	Initiative	Attack	None	No	Nominated
424	George FINDLATER	OR	Army	20/10/1897	India	Encourage	Duty	Attack	High	Wounded	Nominated
425	Edward LAWSON	OR	Army	20/10/1897	India	Rescue	Initiative	Attack	None	Wounded	Nominated
426	Samuel VICKERY	OR	Army	20/10/1897 16/11/1897	India	Rescue	Initiative	Attack	None	No	Nominated
427	Paul KENNA	Junior Officer	Army	2/09/1898	Sudan	Rescue	Initiative	Attack	None	No	Nominated
428	Nevill SMYTH	Junior Officer	Army	2/09/1898	Sudan	Rescue	Initiative	Attack	Low	Wounded	Nominated
429	Raymond De MONTMORENCY	Junior Officer	Army	2/09/1898	Sudan	Rescue	Initiative	Attack	Low	No	Nominated
430	Thomas BYRNE	OR	Army	2/09/1898	Sudan	Rescue	Initiative	Attack	Low	Wounded	Nominated
431	William MAILLARD	Medical Officer	Navy	6/09/1898	Crete	Rescue	Duty	Aid	None	No	Nominated

202

No.	Name	Rank	Service	Date	Location	Action	Motivation	Type	Risk	Casualty	Status
432	Alexander HORE-RUTHVEN	Junior Officer	Army	22/09/1898	Sudan	Rescue	Initiative	Attack	None	No	Nominated
433	Charles FITZCLARENCE	Junior Officer	Army	14/10/1899 27/10/1899 26/12/1899	South Africa	Lead	Duty	Attack	High	Wounded	Nominated
434	Robert JOHNSTON	Junior Officer	Army	21/10/1899	South Africa	Rally	Duty	Attack	High	No	Nominated
435	Matthew MEIKLEJOHN	Junior Officer	Army	21/10/1899	South Africa	Rally	Duty	Attack	High	Wounded	Nominated
436	Charles MULLINS	Junior Officer	Army	21/10/1899	South Africa	Rally	Duty	Attack	High	Wounded	Nominated
437	William ROBERTSON	NCO	Army	21/10/1899	South Africa	Lead	Duty	Attack	High	Wounded	Nominated
438	John NORWOOD	Junior Officer	Army	30/10/1899	South Africa	Rescue	Initiative	Patrol	None	No	Nominated
439	Henry DOUGLAS	Medical Officer	Army	11/12/1899	South Africa	Rescue	Duty	Aid	High	No	Nominated
440	John SHAUL	Medical NCO	Army	11/12/1899	South Africa	Rescue	Duty	Aid	High	No	Nominated
441	Ernest TOWSE	Junior Officer	Army	11/12/1899 30/04/1900	South Africa	Charge	Duty	Attack	High	Wounded	Nominated
442	William BABTIE	Medical Officer	Army	15/12/1899	South Africa	Rescue	Duty	Aid	High	No	Nominated
443	Walter CONGREVE	Junior Officer	Army	15/12/1899	South Africa	Recover	Duty	Recover	High	No	Nominated
444	Hamilton REED	Junior Officer	Army	15/12/1899	South Africa	Recover	Duty	Recover	High	No	Nominated
445	Harry SCHOFIELD	Junior Officer	Army	15/12/1899	South Africa	Recover	Duty	Recover	High	Wounded	Nominated
446	Frederick ROBERTS	Junior Officer	Army	15/12/1899	South Africa	Recover	Duty	Recover	High	Killed	Nominated
447	George NURSE	NCO	Army	15/12/1899	South Africa	Recover	Duty	Recover	High	No	Nominated
448	George RAVENHILL	OR	Army	15/12/1899	South Africa	Recover	Duty	Recover	High	No	Nominated
449	Horace MARTINEAU	NCO	Army	26/12/1899	South Africa	Rescue	Initiative	Retreat	None	Wounded	Nominated
450	Horace RAMSDEN	OR	Army	26/12/1899	South Africa	Rescue	Initiative	Retreat	None	No	Nominated
451	John MILBANKE	Junior Officer	Army	5/01/1900	South Africa	Rescue	Initiative	Recon	None	No	Nominated
452	Robert DIGBY-JONES	Junior Officer	Army	6/01/1900	South Africa	Capture	Duty	Attack	High	Killed	Nominated
453	James MASTERSON	Junior Officer	Army	6/01/1900	South Africa	Lead	Duty	Attack	High	Wounded	Nominated
454	Herman ALBRECHT	OR	Army	6/01/1900	South Africa	Capture	Duty	Attack	High	Killed	Nominated
455	James PITTS	OR	Army	6/01/1900	South Africa	Resist	Duty	Defend	High	No	Nominated

No.	Name	Rank	Service	Date	Place	Personal Action	Type of Personal Action	Military Task of Unit	Relevance of Action to Task	Casualty?	How Selected for Award
456	Robert SCOTT	OR	Army	6/01/1900	South Africa	Combat	Duty	Defend	High	No	Nominated
457	Francis PARSONS	Junior Officer	Army	18/02/1900	South Africa	Rescue	Initiative	Attack	None	No	Nominated
458	Alfred ATKINSON	NCO	Army	18/02/1900	South Africa	Rescue	Initiative	Attack	None	Killed	Nominated
459	Albert CURTIS	OR	Army	23/02/1900	South Africa	Rescue	Initiative	Attack	None	No	Nominated
460	Edgar INKSTON	Medical Officer	Army	24/02/1900	South Africa	Rescue	Duty	Aid	High	No	Nominated
461	James FIRTH	NCO	Army	24/02/1900	South Africa	Rescue	Initiative	Defend	None	Wounded	Nominated
462	Conwyn MANSEL-JONES	Junior Officer	Army	27/02/1900	South Africa	Rally	Duty	Attack	High	Wounded	Nominated
463	Henry ENGLEHEART	NCO	Army	13/03/1900	South Africa	Rescue	Initiative	Return	None	No	Nominated
464	Edmund PHIPPS-HORNBY	Junior Officer	Army	31/03/1900	South Africa	Lead	Duty	Retire	High	No	Elected
465	Francis MAXWELL	Junior Officer	Army	31/03/1900	South Africa	Save	Initiative	Retire	High	No	Nominated
466	Charles PARKER	NCO	Army	31/03/1900	South Africa	Save	Duty	Retire	High	No	Elected
467	Isaac LODGE	OR	Army	31/03/1900	South Africa	Save	Duty	Retire	High	No	Elected
468	Horace GLASOCK	OR	Army	31/03/1900	South Africa	Save	Duty	Retire	High	No	Elected
469	William NICKERSON	Medical Officer	Army	20/04/1900	South Africa	Rescue	Duty	Aid	High	No	Nominated
470	Harry BEET	NCO	Army	22/04/1900	South Africa	Rescue	Initiative	Retreat	None	No	Nominated
471	John MacKAY	NCO	Army	20/05/1900	South Africa	Rescue	Initiative	Pursue	None	No	Nominated
472	Frank KIRBY	NCO	Army	2/06/1900	South Africa	Rescue	Initiative	Retreat	None	No	Nominated
473	John MacKENZIE	NCO	Army	6/06/1900	Ghana	Charge	Voluntary	Attack	High	Wounded	Nominated
474	Lewis HALLIDAY	Junior Officer	Marines	24/06/1900	China	Lead	Duty	Defend	High	Wounded	Nominated
475	Charles WARD	OR	Army	26/06/1900	South Africa	Reinforce	Voluntary	Defend	High	Wounded	Nominated
476	Arthur RICHARDSON	NCO	Army	5/07/1900	South Africa	Rescue	Initiative	Retire	None	No	Nominated
477	William GORDON	Junior Officer	Army	11/07/1900	South Africa	Save	Duty	Defend	High	No	Nominated
478	David YOUNGER	Junior Officer	Army	11/07/1900	South Africa	Save	Duty	Defend	High	Killed	Nominated
479	Basil GUY	Junior Officer	Navy	13/07/1900	South Africa	Rescue	Initiative	Attack	None	No	Nominated

204

	Name	Medical Officer	Army	24/07/1900	South Africa	Rescue	Duty	Aid	High	No	Nominated
480	Neville HOWSE	Medical Officer	Army	24/07/1900	South Africa	Rescue	Duty	Aid	High	No	Nominated
481	William HOUSE	OR	Army	2/08/1900	South Africa	Rescue	Initiative	Attack	None	Wounded	Nominated
482	Brian LAWRENCE	NCO	Army	7/08/1900	South Africa	Rescue	Initiative	Patrol	None	No	Nominated
483	Harry HAMPTON	NCO	Army	21/08/1900	South Africa	Lead	Duty	Retire	High	Wounded	Nominated
484	Henry KNIGHT	NCO	Army	21/08/1900	South Africa	Lead	Duty	Retire	High	No	Nominated
486	Alfred DURRANT	OR	Army	27/08/1900	South Africa	Rescue	Initiative	Pursue	None	No	Nominated
487	Guy WYLLY	Junior Officer	Army	1/09/1900	South Africa	Rescue	Initiative	Scout	Low	Wounded	Nominated
488	John BISDEE	OR	Army	1/09/1900	South Africa	Rescue	Initiative	Scout	Low	No	Nominated
489	Charles MELLIS	Junior Officer	Army	30/09/1900	Ghana	Charge	Duty	Attack	High	Wounded	Nominated
490	Edward BROWN	Junior Officer	Army	13/10/1900	South Africa	Rescue	Initiative	Retire	None	No	Nominated
491	Alexis DOXAT	Junior Officer	Army	20/10/1900	South Africa	Rescue	Initiative	Recon	None	No	Nominated
492	Hampden COCKBURN	Junior Officer	Army	7/11/1900	South Africa	Repel	Duty	Defend	High	Wounded	Nominated
493	Richard TURNER	Junior Officer	Army	7/11/1900	South Africa	Repel	Duty	Defend	High	Wounded	Nominated
494	Edward HOLLAND	NCO	Army	7/11/1900	South Africa	Repel	Duty	Defend	High	No	Nominated
495	Charles KENNEDY	OR	Army	22/11/1900	South Africa	Rescue	Initiative	Pursue	None	No	Nominated
496	Donald FARMER	NCO	Army	13/12/1900	South Africa	Rescue	Initiative	Relieve	None	POW	Nominated
497	John BARRY	OR	Army	7/01/1901 - 8/01/1901	South Africa	Deny	Duty	Defend	High	Killed	Nominated
498	William HARDHAM	NCO	Army	28/01/1901	South Africa	Rescue	Initiative	Retire	None	No	Nominated
499	William TRAYNOR	NCO	Army	6/02/1901	South Africa	Rescue	Initiative	Defend	None	Wounded	Nominated
500	John CLEMENTS	NCO	Army	24/02/1901	South Africa	Capture	Duty	Defend	High	Wounded	Nominated
501	Frederic DUGDALE	Junior Officer	Army	3/03/1901	South Africa	Rescue	Duty	Retire	Low	No	Nominated
502	Frederick BELL	Junior Officer	Army	16/05/1901	South Africa	Rescue	Duty	Retire	Low	No	Nominated
503	Gustavus COULSON	Junior Officer	Army	18/05/1901	South Africa	Rescue	Initiative	Rearguard	None	Killed	Nominated
504	James ROGERS	NCO	Police	15/06/1901	South Africa	Rescue	Initiative	Rearguard	None	No	Nominated
505	William ENGLISH	Junior Officer	Army	3/07/1901	South Africa	Resupply	Duty	Defend	High	No	Nominated
506	Harry CRANDON	OR	Army	4/07/1901	South Africa	Rescue	Initiative	Scout	None	No	Nominated
507	Alexander YOUNG	NCO	Police	13/08/1901	South Africa	Capture	Duty	Attack	High	No	Nominated

No.	Name	Rank	Service	Date	Place	Personal Action	Type of Personal Action	Military Task of Unit	Relevance of Action to Task	Casualty?	How Selected for Award
508	Llewellyn PRICE-DAVIES	Junior Officer	Army	17/09/1901	South Africa	Deny	Duty	Defend	High	Wounded	Nominated
509	Frederick BRADLEY	OR	Army	29/09/1901	South Africa	Resupply	Voluntary	Defend	High	No	Nominated
510	William BEES	OR	Army	30/09/1901	South Africa	Rescue	Initiative	Attack	None	No	Nominated
511	Leslie MAYGAR	Junior Officer	Army	23/11/1901	South Africa	Rescue	Duty	Retire	Low	No	Nominated
512	Thomas CREAN	Medical Officer	Army	18/12/1901	South Africa	Rescue	Duty	Aid	High	Wounded	Nominated
513	Alfred IND	OR	Army	20/12/1901	South Africa	Resist	Duty	Defend	High	No	Nominated
514	Arthur MARTIN-LEAKE	Medical Officer	Police	8/02/1902	South Africa	Rescue	Duty	Aid	High	No	Nominated
515	Alexander COBB	Junior Officer	Army	6/10/1902	Somaliland	Resist	Duty	Retire	High	No	Nominated
516	Wallace WRIGHT	Junior Officer	Army	26/02/1903	Nigeria	Lead	Duty	Attack	High	No	Nominated
517	John GOUGH	Junior Officer	Army	22/04/1903	Somaliland	Rescue	Initiative	Retreat	None	No	Nominated
518	George ROLLAND	Junior Officer	Army	22/04/1903	Somaliland	Rescue	Initiative	Retreat	None	No	Nominated
519	William WALKER	Junior Officer	Army	22/04/1903	Somaliland	Rescue	Initiative	Retreat	None	No	Nominated
520	Herbert CARTER	Junior Officer	Army	19/12/1903	Somaliland	Rescue	Initiative	Retire	None	No	Nominated
521	Clement SMITH	Junior Officer	Army	10/01/1904	Somaliland	Rescue	Initiative	Defend	None	No	Nominated
522	John GRANT	Junior Officer	Army	6/07/1904	Tibet	Lead	Duty	Storm	High	Wounded	Nominated
523	Maurice DEASE	Junior Officer	Army	23/08/1914	Belgium	Lead	Duty	Delay	High	Killed	Nominated
524	Sydney GODLEY	OR	Army	23/08/1914	Belgium	Cover	Voluntary	Retreat	High	POW	Nominated
525	Charles JARVIS	NCO	Army	23/08/1914	Belgium	Demolish	Duty	Delay	High	No	Nominated
526	Charles GARFORTH	NCO	Army	23/08/1914 3/09/1914	France	Demolish	Voluntary	Rearguard	High	No	Nominated
527	Theodore WRIGHT	Junior Officer	Army	23/08/1914 14/09/1914	Belgium	Repair	Duty	Bridge	High	Killed	Nominated
528	Ernest ALEXANDER	Junior Officer	Army	24/08/1914	Belgium	Lead	Duty	Withdraw	High	No	Nominated
529	Francis GRENFELL	Junior Officer	Army	24/08/1914	Belgium	Lead	Duty	Withdraw	High	Wounded	Nominated

#	Name	Rank	Army	Date	Country	Extinguish	Duty	Engage	High	Wounded	Nominated
530	George WYATT	NCO	Army	25/08/1914 - 26/08/1914	France	Lead	Duty	Defend	High	Wounded	Nominated
531	Charles YATE	Junior Officer	Army	26/08/1914	France	Rescue	Initiative	Defend	High	Wounded	Nominated
532	Frederick HOLMES	NCO	Army	26/08/1914	France	Save	Voluntary	Retire	None	No	Nominated
533	Job DRAIN	OR	Army	26/08/1914	France	Save	Voluntary	Retire	High	No	Nominated
534	Frederick LUKE	OR	Army	26/08/1914	France	Save	Voluntary	Retire	High	No	Nominated
535	Douglas REYNOLDS	Junior Officer	Army	26/08/1914 9/09/1914	France	Lead	Duty	Retire	High	No	Nominated
536	Edward BRADBURY	Junior Officer	Army	1/09/1914	France	Lead	Duty	Defend	High	Killed	Nominated
537	George DORRELL	NCO	Army	1/09/1914	France	Lead	Duty	Defend	High	No	Nominated
538	David NELSON	NCO	Army	1/09/1914	France	Resist	Duty	Defend	High	No	Nominated
539	William JOHNSTON	Junior Officer	Army	14/09/1914	France	Resupply	Duty	Sustain	High	No	Nominated
540	William FULLER	NCO	Army	14/09/1914	France	Rescue	Initiative	Attack	None	No	Nominated
541	Ross TOLLERTON	OR	Army	14/09/1914	France	Rescue	Initiative	Attack	None	Wounded	Nominated
542	George WILSON	OR	Army	14/09/1914	France	Capture	Initiative	Attack	High	No	Nominated
543	Ernest HORLOCK	NCO	Army	15/09/1914	France	Rejoin	Initiative	Evacuate	Contrary	Wounded	Nominated
544	Harry RANKEN	Medical Officer	Army	19/09/1914 - 20/09/1914	France	Rescue	Duty	Aid	High	Killed	Nominated
545	Frederick DOBSON	OR	Army	28/09/1914	France	Rescue	Voluntary	Recon	None	No	Nominated
546	Henry MAY	OR	Army	22/10/1914	France	Rescue	Initiative	Retire	None	No	Nominated
547	William KENNY	OR	Army	23/10/1914	Belgium	Rescue	Initiative	Defend	None	No	Nominated
548	James BROOKE	Junior Officer	Army	29/10/1914	Belgium	Charge	Duty	Regain	High	Killed	Nominated
549	James LEACH	Junior Officer	Army	29/10/1914	France	Capture	Voluntary	Retake	High	No	Nominated
550	John HOGAN	NCO	Army	29/10/1914	France	Capture	Voluntary	Retake	High	No	Nominated
551	Arthur MARTIN-LEAKE	Medical Officer	Army	29/10/1914- 8/11/1914	Belgium	Rescue	Duty	Aid	High	No	Nominated
552	KHUDADAD KAHN	OR	Army	1/10/1914	Belgium	Resist	Duty	Hold	High	Wounded	Nominated
553	Spencer BENT	OR	Army	1/11/1914 - 3/11/1914	Belgium	Lead	Initiative	Hold	High	No	Nominated
554	John VALLENTIN	Junior Officer	Army	7/11/1914	Belgium	Lead	Duty	Attack	High	Killed	Nominated

No.	Name	Rank	Service	Date	Place	Personal Action	Type of Personal Action	Military Task of Unit	Relevance of Action to Task	Casualty?	How Selected for Award
555	Walter BRODIE	Junior Officer	Army	11/11/1914	Belgium	Charge	Duty	Regain	High	No	Nominated
556	John DIMMER	Junior Officer	Army	12/11/1914	Belgium	Resist	Duty	Defend	High	Wounded	Nominated
557	John BUTLER	Junior Officer	Army	17/11/1914 - 27/12/1914	Cameroons	Lead	Duty	Attack	High	No	Nominated
558	Thomas RENDLE	Medical OR	Army	20/11/1914	Belgium	Rescue	Duty	Aid	High	No	Nominated
559	DARWAN SING NEGI	NCO	Army	23/11/1914 - 24/11/1914	Belgium	Retake	Duty	Attack	High	Wounded	Nominated
560	Frank de PASS	Junior Officer	Army	24/11/1914	France	Sortie	Duty	Attack	High	No	Nominated
561	Henry RITCHIE	Junior Officer	Navy	28/11/1914	East Africa	Raid	Duty	Attack	High	Wounded	Nominated
562	Norman HOLBROOK	Junior Officer	Navy	13/12/1914	Dardanelles	Sinking	Duty	Attack	High	No	Nominated
563	Henry ROBSON	OR	Army	14/12/1914	Belgium	Rescue	Initiative	Defend	None	Wounded	Nominated
564	William BRUCE	Junior Officer	Army	19/12/1914	France	Capture	Duty	Attack	High	Killed	Nominated
565	Philip NEAME	Junior Officer	Army	19/12/1914	France	Bomb	Duty	Hold	High	No	Nominated
566	James MacKENZIE	OR	Army	19/12/1914	France	Rescue	Unknown	Attack	None	No	Nominated
567	Abraham ACTON	OR	Army	21/12/1914	France	Rescue	Voluntary	Attack	None	No	Nominated
568	James SMITH	OR	Army	21/12/1914	France	Rescue	Voluntary	Attack	None	No	Nominated
569	Eustace JOTHAM	Junior Officer	Army	7/01/1915	India	Rescue	Duty	Retire	Low	Killed	Nominated
570	Michael O'LEARY	NCO	Army	1/02/1915	France	Storm	Duty	Attack	High	No	Nominated
571	Eric ROBINSON	Junior Officer	Navy	26/02/1915	Dardanelles	Raid	Duty	Attack	High	No	Nominated
572	GOBAR SING NEGI	OR	Army	10/03/1915	France	Bomb	Duty	Attack	High	Killed	Nominated
573	William BUCKINGHAM	Medical OR	Army	10/03/1915 - 12/03/1915	France	Rescue	Duty	Attack	High	Wounded	Nominated
574	Charles FOSS	Junior Officer	Army	12/03/1915	France	Retake	Initiative	Regain	High	No	Nominated
575	Cyril MARTIN	Junior Officer	Army	12/03/1915	Belgium	Bomb	Voluntary	Attack	High	Wounded	Nominated
576	Harry DANIELS	NCO	Army	12/03/1915	France	Cut wire	Voluntary	Attack	High	Wounded	Nominated
577	Wilfred FULLER	NCO	Army	12/03/1915	France	Bomb	Duty	Attack	High	No	Nominated
578	William ANDERSON	NCO	Army	12/03/1915	France	Bomb	Duty	Attack	High	No	Nominated

208

No.	Name	Rank	Service	Date	Location	Action	Voluntary	Type	Risk	Outcome	Award
579	Cecil NOBLE	NCO	Army	12/03/1915	France	Cut wire	Voluntary	Attack	High	Killed	Nominated
580	Edward BARBER	OR	Army	12/03/1915	France	Bomb	Duty	Attack	High	No	Nominated
581	Robert MORROW	OR	Army	12/03/1915	Belgium	Rescue	Initiative	Attack	None	No	Nominated
582	Jacob RIVERS	OR	Army	12/03/1915	France	Bomb	Initiative	Attack	High	Killed	Nominated
583	George WHEELER	Junior Officer	Army	12/04/1915 13/04/1915	Iraq	Charge	Duty	Attack	High	Killed	Nominated
584	George ROUPELL	Junior Officer	Army	20/04/1915	Belgium	Reinforce	Duty	Defend	High	Wounded	Nominated
585	Edward DWYER	OR	Army	20/04/1915	Belgium	Bomb	Duty	Defend	High	No	Nominated
586	Benjamin GEARY	Junior Officer	Army	20/04/1915	Belgium	Reinforce	Duty	Defend	High	No	Nominated
587	Geoffrey WOOLLEY	Junior Officer	Army	20/04/1915	Belgium	Bomb	Duty	Defend	High	No	Nominated
588	Frederick FISHER	NCO	Army	23/04/1915	Belgium	Combat	Duty	Defend	High	Killed	Nominated
589	Frederick HALL	NCO	Army	23/04/1915 - 24/04/1915	Belgium	Rescue	Initiative	Relieve	None	Killed	Nominated
590	Edward BELLEW	Junior Officer	Army	24/04/1915	Belgium	Resist	Duty	Defend	High	Wounded POW	Nominated
591	Cuthbert BROMLEY	Junior Officer	Army	25/04/1915	Gallipoli	Lead	Duty	Land	High	No	Elected
592	Francis SCRIMGER	Medical Officer	Army	25/04/1915	Belgium	Rescue	Duty	Aid	High	No	Nominated
593	Edward UNWIN	Junior Officer	Navy	25/04/1915	Gallipoli	Secure	Duty	Land	High	Wounded	Nominated
594	Richard WILLIS	Junior Officer	Army	25/04/1915	Gallipoli	Lead	Duty	Land	High	No	Elected
595	Arthur TISDALL	Junior Officer	Navy	25/04/1915	Gallipoli	Rescue	Initiative	Land	None	No	Nominated
596	Alfred RICHARDS	NCO	Army	25/04/1915	Gallipoli	Combat	Duty	Land	High	Wounded	Elected
597	Frank STUBBS	NCO	Army	25/04/1915	Gallipoli	Combat	Duty	Land	High	No	Elected
598	John GRIMSHAW	NCO	Army	25/04/1915	Gallipoli	Combat	Duty	Land	High	No	Elected
599	George DREWRY	Junior Officer	Navy	25/04/1915	Gallipoli	Secure	Duty	Land	High	Wounded	Nominated
600	Wilfred MALLESON	Junior Officer	Navy	25/04/1915	Gallipoli	Secure	Duty	Land	High	No	Nominated
601	William KENEALLY	OR	Army	25/04/1915	Gallipoli	Combat	Duty	Land	High	No	Elected
602	William WILLIAMS	OR	Navy	25/04/1915	Gallipoli	Secure	Duty	Land	High	Wounded	Nominated
603	George SAMSON	OR	Navy	25/04/1915	Gallipoli	Secure	Duty	Land	High	Wounded	Nominated
604	Charles DOUGHTY-WYLIE	Senior Officer	Army	25/04/1915	Gallipoli	Lead	Duty	Attack	High	Killed	Nominated

No.	Name	Rank	Service	Date	Place	Personal Action	Type of Personal Action	Military Task of Unit	Relevance of Action to Task	Casualty?	How Selected for Award
605	Garth WALFORD	Senior Officer	Army	26/04/1915	Gallipoli	Lead	Duty	Attack	High	Killed	Nominated
606	William RHODES-MOORHOUSE	Junior Officer	RFC	26/04/1915	Belgium	Bomb	Duty	Attack	High	Killed	Nominated
607	MIR DAST	Junior Officer	Army	26/04/1915	Belgium	Rally	Duty	Attack	High	No	Nominated
608	William COSGROVE	NCO	Army	26/04/1915	Gallipoli	Cut wire	Duty	Attack	High	No	Nominated
609	Issy SMITH	NCO	Army	26/04/1915	Belgium	Rescue	Initiative	Defend	None	No	Nominated
610	Edward BOYLE	Junior Officer	Navy	27/04/1915-18/05/1915	Dardanelles	Sinking	Duty	Attack	High	No	Nominated
611	Walter PARKER	Medical NCO	Marines	30/04/1915 - 1/05/1915	Gallipoli	Rescue	Voluntary	Aid	High	Wounded	Nominated
612	Edward WARNER	OR	Army	1/05/1915	Belgium	Recover	Initiative	Hold	High	Killed	Nominated
613	John LYNN	OR	Army	2/05/1915	Belgium	Combat	Duty	Defend	High	Killed	Nominated
614	John RIPLEY	NCO	Army	9/05/1915	France	Lead	Duty	Attack	High	Wounded	Nominated
615	James UPTON	NCO	Army	9/05/1915	France	Rescue	Initiative	Attack	None	No	Nominated
616	Charles SHARPE	NCO	Army	9/05/1915	France	Bomb	Duty	Attack	High	No	Nominated
617	David FINLAY	NCO	Army	9/05/1915	France	Lead	Duty	Attack	High	No	Nominated
618	Douglas BELCHER	NCO	Army	13/05/1915	Belgium	Remain	Duty	Defend	High	No	Nominated
619	Frederick BARTER	NCO	Army	16/05/1915	France	Lead	Duty	Attack	High	No	Nominated
620	John SMYTH	Junior Officer	Army	18/05/1915	France	Resupply	Duty	Hold	High	No	Nominated
621	Albert JACKA	NCO	Army	19/05/1915	Gallipoli	Charge	Duty	Attack	High	No	Nominated
622	Martin NASMITH	Junior Officer	Navy	20/05/1915-8/06/1915	Dardanelles	Sinking	Duty	Attack	High	No	Nominated
623	William MARINER	OR	Army	22/05/1915	France	Sortie	Voluntary	Attack	High	No	Nominated
624	Leonard KEYWORTH	NCO	Army	25/05/1915	France	Bomb	Duty	Attack	High	No	Nominated
625	George MOOR	Junior Officer	Army	5/06/1915	Gallipoli	Rally	Duty	Attack	High	No	Nominated
626	Reginald WARNEFORD	Junior Officer	RNAS	7/06/1915	Belgium	Downing	Duty	Patrol	High	No	Nominated
627	William ANGUS	NCO	Army	12/06/1915	France	Rescue	Voluntary	Attack	None	Wounded	Nominated

						Lead	Duty	Attack	High	Killed	Nominated
628	Frederick CAMPBELL	Junior Officer	Army	15/06/1915	France	Rescue	Initiative	Attack	High	No	Nominated
629	Joseph TOMBS	NCO	Army	16/06/1915	France	Rally	Initiative	Attack	None	No	Nominated
630	Herbert JAMES	Junior Officer	Army	28/06/1915 - 3/07/1915	Gallipoli		Initiative	Attack	High	No	Nominated
631	Gerald O'SULLIVAN	Junior Officer	Army	1/07/1915	Gallipoli	Bomb	Voluntary	Recapture	High	Wounded	Nominated
632	James SOMERS	NCO	Army	1/07/1915	Gallipoli	Bomb	Duty	Recapture	High	No	Nominated
633	Frederick PARSLOW	Junior Officer	Navy	4/07/1915	Atlantic	Evade	Duty	Escape	High	Killed	Nominated
634	Lanoe HAWKER	Junior Officer	RFC	26/07/1915	Belgium	Downing	Duty	Patrol	High	No	Nominated
635	Sidney WOODROFFE	Junior Officer	Army	30/07/1915	Belgium	Lead	Duty	Attack	High	Killed	Nominated
636	John LIDDELL	Junior Officer	RFC	31/07/1915	Belgium	Save	Duty	Recon	Low	Killed	Nominated
637	George BOYD-ROCHFORT	Junior Officer	Army	3/08/1915	France	Protect	Duty	Defend	Low	No	Nominated
638	Cyril BASSETT	NCO	Army	7/08/1915	Gallipoli	Repair	Duty	Hold	High	No	Nominated
639	Leonard KEYSOR	OR	Army	7/08/1915 - 8/08/1915	Gallipoli	Bomb	Voluntary	Defend	High	Wounded	Nominated
640	William FORSHAW	Junior Officer	Army	7/08/1915 - 9/08/1915	Gallipoli	Bomb	Voluntary	Defend	High	No	Nominated
641	William SYMONS	Junior Officer	Army	8/08/1915	Gallipoli	Retake	Duty	Defend	High	No	Nominated
642	Percy HANSEN	Junior Officer	Army	9/08/1915	Gallipoli	Rescue	Initiative	Retire	None	No	Nominated
643	Alfred SHOUT	Junior Officer	Army	9/08/1915	Gallipoli	Capture	Duty	Attack	High	Killed	Nominated
644	Frederick TUBB	Junior Officer	Army	9/08/1915	Gallipoli	Repulse	Duty	Defend	High	Wounded	Nominated
645	Alexander BURTON	NCO	Army	9/08/1915	Gallipoli	Repulse	Duty	Defend	High	Killed	Nominated
646	William DUNSTAN	NCO	Army	9/08/1915	Gallipoli	Repulse	Duty	Defend	High	No	Nominated
647	John HAMILTON	OR	Army	9/08/1915	Gallipoli	Repulse	Duty	Defend	High	No	Nominated
648	David LAUDER	OR	Army	13/08/1915	Gallipoli	Protect	Initiative	Attack	None	Wounded	Nominated
649	Frederick POTTS	OR	Army	21/08/1915	Gallipoli	Rescue	Initiative	Attack	None	Wounded	Nominated
650	Hugo THROSSELL	Junior Officer	Army	29/08/1915	Gallipoli	Repulse	Duty	Defend	High	Wounded	Nominated
651	Wilbur DARTNELL	Junior Officer	Army	3/09/1915	East Africa	Rescue	Duty	Withdraw	Low	Killed	Nominated
652	Charles HULL	OR	Army	5/09/1915	India	Rescue	Initiative	Withdraw	None	No	Nominated

211

No.	Name	Rank	Service	Date	Place	Personal Action	Type of Personal Action	Military Task of Unit	Relevance of Action to Task	Casualty?	How Selected for Award
653	Arthur KILBY	Junior Officer	Army	25/09/1915	France	Lead	Voluntary	Attack	High	Killed	Nominated
654	Anketell READ	Junior Officer	Army	25/09/1915	France	Rally	Duty	Attack	High	Killed	Nominated
655	George MALING	Medical Officer	Army	25/09/1915	France	Rescue	Duty	Aid	High	No	Nominated
656	Frederick JOHNSON	Junior Officer	Army	25/09/1915	France	Rally	Duty	Attack	High	Wounded	Nominated
657	Harry WELLS	NCO	Army	25/09/1915	France	Rally	Duty	Attack	High	Killed	Nominated
658	Henry KENNY	OR	Army	25/09/1915	France	Rescue	Initiative	Attack	None	Wounded	Nominated
659	George PEACHMENT	OR	Army	25/09/1915	France	Rescue	Initiative	Retire	None	Killed	Nominated
660	KULBIR THAPA	OR	Army	25/09/1915	France	Rescue	Initiative	Attack	None	Wounded	Nominated
661	Daniel LAIDLAW	OR	Army	25/09/1915	France	Rally	Duty	Attack	High	Wounded	Nominated
662	Arthur VICKERS	OR	Army	25/09/1915	France	Cut wire	Initiative	Attack	High	No	Nominated
663	Angus DOUGLAS-HAMILTON	Senior Officer	Army	25/09/1915 - 26/09/1915	France	Rally	Duty	Attack	High	Killed	Nominated
664	Rupert HALLOWES	Junior Officer	Army	25/09/1915 - 30/09/1915	France	Lead	Duty	Hold	High	Killed	Nominated
665	Arthur SAUNDERS	NCO	Army	26/09/1915	France	Cover	Duty	Retreat	High	Wounded	Nominated
666	Robert DUNSIRE	OR	Army	26/09/1915	France	Rescue	Initiative	Attack	None	No	Nominated
667	Alfred BURT	NCO	Army	27/09/1915	France	Protect	Initiative	Attack	Low	No	Nominated
668	James POLLOCK	NCO	Army	27/09/1915	France	Bomb	Voluntary	Defend	High	Wounded	Nominated
669	Edgar COOKSON	Junior Officer	Navy	28/09/1915	Iraq	Destroy	Duty	Attack	High	Killed	Nominated
670	Alexander TURNER	Junior Officer	Army	28/09/1915	France	Bomb	Voluntary	Attack	High	Killed	Nominated
671	Arthur FLEMING-SANDES	Junior Officer	Army	29/09/1915	France	Rally	Duty	Attack	High	Wounded	Nominated
672	Samuel HARVEY	OR	Army	29/09/1915	France	Resupply	Voluntary	Defend	High	Wounded	Nominated
673	Oliver BROOKS	NCO	Army	8/10/1915	France	Bomb	Duty	Retake	High	No	Nominated
674	John RAYNES	NCO	Army	11/10/1915	France	Rescue	Initiative	Bombard	None	Wounded	Nominated
675	James DAWSON	NCO	Army	13/10/1915	France	Protect	Duty	Defend	High	No	Nominated

212

676	Charles VICKERS	Junior Officer	Army	14/10/1915	France	Bomb	Duty	Defend	High	Wounded	Nominated
677	Harry CHRISTIAN	OR	Army	18/10/1915	France	Rescue	Initiative	Defend	None	No	Nominated
678	Thomas KENNY	OR	Army	4/11/1915	France	Rescue	Initiative	Patrol	None	No	Nominated
679	Gilbert INSALL	Junior Officer	RFC	7/11/1915	France	Combat	Initiative	Patrol	High	No	Nominated
680	John CAFFREY	OR	Army	16/11/1915	France	Rescue	Unknown	Hold	None	No	Nominated
681	Richard DAVIES	Junior Officer	RNAS	19/11/1915	Bulgaria	Rescue	Initiative	Patrol	None	No	Nominated
682	Samuel MEEKOSHA	NCO	Army	19/11/1915	France	Rescue	Initiative	Hold	None	No	Nominated
683	Alfred DRAKE	NCO	Army	23/11/1915	France	Rescue	Initiative	Patrol	None	Killed	Nominated
684	William YOUNG	OR	Army	22/12/1915	France	Rescue	Initiative	Hold	None	Wounded	Nominated
685	Alfred SMITH	Junior Officer	Army	23/12/1915	Gallipoli	Protect	Initiative	Bombard	None	Killed	Nominated
686	CHATTA SINGH	OR	Army	13/01/1916	Iraq	Rescue	Initiative	Attack	None	No	Nominated
687	John SINTON	Medical Officer	Army	21/01/1916	Iraq	Rescue	Duty	Aid	High	Wounded	Nominated
688	LALA	NCO	Army	21/01/1916	Iraq	Rescue	Initiative	Attack	None	No	Nominated
689	Eric McNAIR	Junior Officer	Army	14/02/1916	Belgium	Reinforce	Duty	Defend	High	No	Nominated
690	William COTTER	NCO	Army	6/03/1916	France	Lead	Duty	Hold	High	Wounded	Nominated
691	George STRINGER	OR	Army	8/03/1916	Iraq	Guard	Duty	Withdraw	High	No	Nominated
692	Edward MELLISH	Chaplain	Army	27/03/1916 - 29/03/1916	Belgium	Rescue	Duty	Aid	High	No	Nominated
693	Angus BUCHANAN	Junior Officer	Army	5/04/1916	Iraq	Rescue	Initiative	Attack	None	No	Nominated
694	Sidney WARE	NCO	Army	6/04/1916	Iraq	Rescue	Initiative	Retire	None	No	Nominated
695	William ADDISON	Chaplain	Army	9/04/1916	Iraq	Rescue	Duty	Aid	High	No	Nominated
696	Edgar MYLES	Junior Officer	Army	9/04/1916	Iraq	Rescue	Initiative	Attack	None	No	Nominated
697	James FYNN	OR	Army	9/04/1916	Iraq	Rescue	Initiative	Attack	None	No	Nominated
698	SHAHAMAD KHAN	NCO	Army	12/04/1916 - 13/04/1916	Iraq	Cover	Duty	Defend	High	No	Nominated
699	Edward BAXTER	Junior Officer	Army	17/04/1916 - 18/04/1916	France	Protect	Initiative	Raid	High	No	Nominated
700	Charles COWLEY	Junior Officer	Navy	24/04/1916 - 25/04/1916	Iraq	Resupply	Voluntary	Relieve	High	Killed	Nominated

No.	Name	Rank	Service	Date	Place	Personal Action	Type of Personal Action	Military Task of Unit	Relevance of Action to Task	Casualty?	How Selected for Award
701	Humphrey FIRMAN	Junior Officer	Navy	24/04/1916 - 25/04/1916	Iraq	Resupply	Voluntary	Relieve	High	Killed	Nominated
702	Richard JONES	Junior Officer	Army	21/05/1916	France	Lead	Duty	Hold	High	Killed	Nominated
703	Francis HARVEY	Junior Officer	Marines	31/05/1916	Jutland	Protect	Duty	Attack	Low	Killed	Nominated
704	Edward BINGHAM	Senior Officer	Navy	31/05/1916	Jutland	Combat	Duty	Attack	High	POW	Nominated
705	Loftus JONES	Senior Officer	Navy	31/05/1916	Jutland	Combat	Duty	Attack	High	Killed	Nominated
706	John CORNWELL	OR	Navy	31/05/1916	Jutland	Standfast	Duty	Bombard	High	Killed	Nominated
707	George CHAFER	OR	Army	3/06/1916 - 4/06/1916	France	Deliver	Initiative	Hold	High	Wounded	Nominated
708	Arthur PROCTOR	OR	Army	4/06/1916	France	Rescue	Initiative	Hold	None	No	Nominated
709	John ERSKINE	NCO	Army	22/06/1916	France	Rescue	Initiative	Hold	None	No	Nominated
710	William HACKETT	OR	Army	22/06/1916 - 23/06/1916	France	Protect	Initiative	Tunnel	None	Killed	Nominated
711	Arthur BATTEN-POOLL	Junior Officer	Army	25/06/1916	France	Lead	Duty	Raid	High	Wounded	Nominated
712	William JACKSON	OR	Army	25/06/1916 - 26/06/1916	France	Rescue	Initiative	Raid	None	Wounded	Nominated
713	James HUTCHINSON	OR	Army	28/06/1916	France	Cover	Initiative	Retire	High	No	Nominated
714	Nelson CARTER	NCO	Army	30/06/1916	France	Lead	Duty	Attack	High	Killed	Nominated
715	William McFADZEAN	OR	Army	1/07/1916	France	Protect	Initiative	Attack	Low	Killed	Nominated
716	Stewart LOUDOUN-SHAND	Junior Officer	Army	1/07/1916	France	Lead	Duty	Attack	High	Killed	Nominated
717	Lionel REES	Junior Officer	RFC	1/07/1916	France	Sortie	Duty	Patrol	High	Wounded	Nominated
718	John GREEN	Medical Officer	Army	1/07/1916	France	Rescue	Duty	Aid	High	Killed	Nominated
719	Eric BELL	Junior Officer	Army	1/07/1916	France	Rally	Initiative	Attack	High	Killed	Nominated
720	Geoffrey CATHER	Junior Officer	Army	1/07/1916	France	Rescue	Initiative	Attack	None	Killed	Nominated
721	James TURNBULL	NCO	Army	1/07/1916	France	Combat	Duty	Hold	High	Killed	Nominated

No.	Name	Rank	Service	Date	Country	Combat	Duty	Action	Intensity	Casualty	Outcome
722	George SANDERS	NCO	Army	1/07/1916	France	Rescue	Voluntary	Hold	High	No	Nominated
723	Robert QUIGG	OR	Army	1/07/1916	France	Rally	Duty	Attack	None	No	Nominated
724	Walter RITCHIE	OR	Army	1/07/1916	France	Rally	Duty	Attack	High	No	Nominated
725	Adrian CARTON de WIART	Junior Officer	Army	2/07/1916 - 3/07/1916	France	Lead	Duty	Hold	High	No	Nominated
726	Thomas TURRAL	OR	Army	3/07/1916	France	Rescue	Initiative	Retire	None	No	Nominated
727	Thomas WILKINSON	Junior Officer	Army	5/07/1916	France	Lead	Duty	Attack	High	Killed	Nominated
728	Donald BELL	Junior Officer	Army	5/07/1916	France	Sortie	Initiative	Attack	High	No	Nominated
729	William CONGREVE	Junior Officer	Army	6/07/1916 - 20/07/1916	France	Lead	Initiative	Attack	High	Killed	Nominated
730	William BOULTER	NCO	Army	14/07/1916	France	Bomb	Duty	Attack	High	Wounded	Nominated
731	William FAULDS	OR	Army	18/07/1916	France	Rescue	Initiative	Attack	None	No	Nominated
732	Joseph DAVIES	NCO	Army	20/07/1916	France	Combat	Duty	Attack	High	No	Nominated
733	Albert HILL	OR	Army	20/07/1916	France	Combat	Duty	Attack	High	No	Nominated
734	Theodore VEALE	OR	Army	20/07/1916	France	Rescue	Initiative	Attack	None	No	Nominated
735	Arthur BLACKBURN	Junior Officer	Army	23/07/1916	France	Lead	Duty	Attack	High	No	Nominated
736	John LEAK	OR	Army	23/07/1916	France	Bomb	Duty	Attack	High	No	Nominated
737	Thomas COOKE	OR	Army	24/07/1916 - 25/07/1916	France	Combat	Duty	Defend	High	Killed	Nominated
738	Albert GILL	NCO	Army	27/07/1916	France	Rally	Duty	Defend	High	Killed	Nominated
739	Claude CASTLETON	NCO	Army	28/07/1916 - 29/07/1916	France	Rescue	Initiative	Attack	None	Killed	Nominated
740	George EVANS	NCO	Army	30/07/1916	France	Deliver	Voluntary	Attack	High	Wounded	Nominated
741	James MILLER	OR	Army	30/07/1916 - 1/08/1916	France	Deliver	Duty	Hold	High	Killed	Nominated
742	William SHORT	OR	Army	6/08/1916	France	Bomb	Duty	Attack	High	Killed	Nominated
743	Gabriel COURY	Junior Officer	Army	8/08/1916	France	Lead	Duty	Attack	High	No	Nominated
744	Noel CHAVASSE	Medical Officer	Army	9/08/1916 - 10/08/1916	France	Rescue	Duty	Aid	High	Wounded	Nominated

215

No.	Name	Rank	Service	Date	Place	Personal Action	Type of Personal Action	Military Task of Unit	Relevance of Action to Task	Casualty?	How Selected for Award
745	Martin O'MEARA	OR	Army	9/08/1916 - 12/08/1916	France	Rescue	Initiative	Attack	None	No	Nominated
746	William BLOOMFIELD	Junior Officer	Army	24/08/1916	East Africa	Rescue	Initiative	Withdraw	None	No	Nominated
747	William ROBINSON	Junior Officer	RFC	2/09/1916 - 3/09/1916	England	Combat	Duty	Defend	High	No	Nominated
748	William ALLEN	Medical Officer	Army	3/09/1916	France	Rescue	Duty	Aid	High	Wounded	Nominated
749	John HOLLAND	Junior Officer	Army	3/09/1916	France	Bomb	Duty	Attack	High	No	Nominated
750	David JONES	NCO	Army	3/09/1916	France	Combat	Duty	Hold	High	No	Nominated
751	Thomas HUGHES	OR	Army	3/09/1916	France	Combat	Duty	Attack	High	Wounded	Nominated
752	Leo CLARKE	NCO	Army	3/09/1916	France	Combat	Duty	Attack	High	Killed	Nominated
753	John CAMPBELL	Senior Officer	Army	15/09/1916	France	Rally	Duty	Attack	High	No	Nominated
754	Donald BROWN	NCO	Army	15/09/1916	France	Combat	Duty	Attack	High	No	Nominated
755	Frederick McNESS	NCO	Army	15/09/1916	France	Combat	Duty	Attack	High	Wounded	Nominated
756	John KERR	OR	Army	16/09/1916	France	Bomb	Duty	Attack	High	Wounded	Nominated
757	Thomas JONES	OR	Army	25/09/1916	France	Combat	Initiative	Hold	High	No	Nominated
758	Frederick EDWARDS	OR	Army	26/09/1916	France	Bomb	Initiative	Attack	High	No	Nominated
759	Robert RYDER	OR	Army	26/09/1916	France	Combat	Duty	Attack	High	No	Nominated
760	Tom ADLAM	Junior Officer	Army	27/09/1916 - 28/09/1916	France	Lead	Duty	Attack	High	Wounded	Nominated
761	Archie WHITE	Junior Officer	Army	27/09/1916 - 1/10/1916	France	Lead	Duty	Hold	High	No	Nominated
762	Roland BRADFORD	Senior Officer	Army	1/10/1916	France	Lead	Duty	Attack	High	No	Nominated
763	Henry KELLY	Junior Officer	Army	4/10/1916	France	Rally	Duty	Attack	High	No	Nominated
764	James RICHARDSON	OR	Army	8/10/1916 - 9/10/1916	France	Rally	Voluntary	Attack	High	No	Nominated
765	Hubert LEWIS	OR	Army	22/10/1916 - 23/10/1916	Salonika	Combat	Duty	Raid	High	Wounded	Nominated

No.	Name	Rank	Service	Date	Location	Action	Motivation	Type	Risk	Outcome	Status
766	Robert DOWNIE	NCO	Army	23/10/1916	France	Lead	Duty	Attack	High	Wounded	Nominated
767	Eugene BENNETT	Junior Officer	Army	5/11/1916	France	Lead	Duty	Attack	High	Wounded	Nominated
768	Bernard FREYBERG	Senior Officer	Army	13/11/1916	France	Lead	Duty	Attack	High	Wounded	Nominated
769	John CUNNINGHAM	OR	Army	13/11/1916	France	Bomb	Duty	Attack	High	No	Nominated
770	Thomas MOTTERSHEAD	NCO	RFC	7/01/1917	France	Protect	Necessity	Scout	None	Killed	Nominated
771	Edward HENDERSON	Senior Officer	Army	25/01/1917	Iraq	Lead	Duty	Attack	High	Killed	Nominated
772	Robert PHILLIPS	Junior Officer	Army	25/01/1917	Iraq	Rescue	Initiative	Attack	None	No	Nominated
773	Edward MOTT	NCO	Army	27/01/1917	France	Combat	Duty	Attack	High	Wounded	Nominated
774	Henry MURRAY	Junior Officer	Army	4/02/1917 - 5/02/1917	France	Combat	Duty	Attack	High	No	Nominated
775	Frederick BOOTH	NCO	Police	12/02/1917	East Africa	Rally	Duty	Attack	High	No	Nominated
776	Frederick PALMER	NCO	Army	16/02/1917 - 17/02/1917	France	Lead	Duty	Attack	High	No	Nominated
777	Gordon CAMPBELL	Senior Officer	Navy	17/02/1917	Atlantic	Decoy	Duty	Attack	High	No	Nominated
778	Thomas STEELE	NCO	Army	22/02/1917	Iraq	Rally	Duty	Defend	High	Wounded	Nominated
779	George WHEELER	Junior Officer	Army	23/02/1917	Iraq	Lead	Duty	Attack	High	Wounded	Nominated
780	John READITT	OR	Army	25/02/1917	Iraq	Lead	Initiative	Attack	High	No	Nominated
781	Jack WHITE	OR	Army	7/03/1917 - 8/03/1917	Iraq	Rescue	Initiative	Attack	Low	No	Nominated
782	George CATES	Junior Officer	Army	8/03/1917	France	Protect	Initiative	Hold	Low	Killed	Nominated
783	Oswald REID	Junior Officer	Army	8/03/1917 - 10/03/1917	Iraq	Lead	Duty	Hold	High	Wounded	Nominated
784	Archibald BISSETT-SMITH	Junior Officer	Navy	10/03/1917	Atlantic	Combat	Duty	Resist	High	Killed	Nominated
785	Christopher COX	Medical OR	Army	13/03/1917 - 17/03/1917	France	Rescue	Duty	Aid	High	No	Nominated
786	Frank McNAMARA	Junior Officer	RFC	20/03/1917	Egypt	Rescue	Initiative	Sortie	None	No	Nominated
787	Percy CHERRY	Junior Officer	Army	26/03/1917	France	Lead	Duty	Storm	High	Killed	Nominated
788	Frederick HARVEY	Junior Officer	Army	27/03/1917	France	Lead	Duty	Attack	High	No	Nominated

No.	Name	Rank	Service	Date	Place	Personal Action	Type of Personal Action	Military Task of Unit	Relevance of Action to Task	Casualty?	How Selected for Award
789	Jorgan JENSEN	OR	Army	2/04/1917	France	Capture	Duty	Attack	High	No	Nominated
790	Frederick LUMSDEN	Junior Officer	Marines	3/04/1917 - 4/04/1917	France	Lead	Duty	Recover	High	No	Nominated
791	William GOSLING	NCO	Army	5/04/1917	France	Protect	Initiative	Bombard	Low	No	Nominated
792	James NEWLAND	Junior Officer	Army	7/04/1917 - 9/04/1917 15/04/1917	France	Lead	Duty	Attack	High	No	Nominated
793	Thain MacDOWELL	Junior Officer	Army	9/04/1917	France	Capture	Initiative	Attack	High	Wounded	Nominated
794	Harry CATOR	NCO	Army	9/04/1917	France	Combat	Duty	Hold	High	No	Nominated
795	John WHITTLE	NCO	Army	9/04/1917	France	Lead	Duty	Hold	High	No	Nominated
796	Ellis SIFTON	NCO	Army	9/04/1917	France	Combat	Duty	Attack	High	Killed	Nominated
797	Thomas BRYAN	NCO	Army	9/04/1917	France	Combat	Duty	Attack	High	Wounded	Nominated
798	Thomas KENNY	OR	Army	9/04/1917	France	Combat	Duty	Attack	High	No	Nominated
799	William MILNE	OR	Army	9/04/1917	France	Combat	Duty	Attack	High	Killed	Nominated
800	John PATTISON	OR	Army	10/04/1917	France	Combat	Duty	Attack	High	No	Nominated
801	Horace WALLER	OR	Army	10/04/1917	France	Combat	Duty	Defend	High	Killed	Nominated
802	Donald MacKINTOSH	Junior Officer	Army	11/04/1917	France	Lead	Duty	Attack	High	Killed	Nominated
803	Harold MUGFORD	NCO	Army	11/04/1917	France	Combat	Duty	Defend	High	Wounded	Nominated
804	John CUNNINGHAM	NCO	Army	12/04/1917	France	Combat	Duty	Attack	High	Killed	Nominated
805	John ORMSBY	NCO	Army	14/04/1917	France	Lead	Duty	Attack	High	No	Nominated
806	Charles POPE	Junior Officer	Army	15/04/1917	France	Lead	Duty	Hold	High	Killed	Nominated
807	Ernest SYKES	Medical OR	Army	19/04/1917	France	Rescue	Duty	Aid	High	No	Nominated
808	Charles MELVIN	OR	Army	21/04/1917	Iraq	Combat	Duty	Attack	High	No	Nominated
809	John GRAHAM	Junior Officer	Army	22/04/1917	Iraq	Combat	Duty	Attack	High	Wounded	Nominated
810	Arthur HENDERSON	Junior Officer	Army	23/04/1917	France	Lead	Duty	Attack	High	Wounded	Nominated
811	David HIRSCH	Junior Officer	Army	23/04/1917	France	Lead	Duty	Attack	High	Killed	Nominated
812	Edward FOSTER	NCO	Army	24/04/1917	France	Combat	Duty	Attack	High	No	Nominated

813	Albert BALL	Junior Officer	RFC	25/04/1917 - 6/07/1917	France	Destroy	Duty	Scout	High	Killed	Nominated
814	Edward BROOKS	NCO	Army	28/04/1917	France	Combat	Initiative	Raid	High	No	Nominated
815	Reginald HAINE	Junior Officer	Army	28/04/1917- 29/04/1917	France	Lead	Duty	Hold	High	No	Nominated
816	Alfred POLLARD	Junior Officer	Army	29/04/1917	France	Lead	Duty	Regain	High	No	Nominated
817	James WELCH	NCO	Army	29/04/1917	France	Combat	Initiative	Attack	High	Wounded	Nominated
818	William SANDERS	Junior Officer	Navy	30/04/1917	Atlantic	Destroy	Duty	Decoy	High	No	Nominated
819	Robert COMBE	Junior Officer	Army	3/05/1917	France	Lead	Duty	Attack	High	Killed	Nominated
820	John HARRISON	Junior Officer	Army	3/05/1917	France	Lead	Duty	Attack	High	Killed	Nominated
821	George JARRATT	NCO	Army	3/05/1917	France	Protect	Initiative	N/A	N/A	Killed	Nominated
822	George HOWELL	NCO	Army	6/05/1917	France	Bomb	Initiative	Defend	High	Wounded	Nominated
823	Michael HEAVISIDE	Medical OR	Army	6/05/1917	France	Rescue	Voluntary	Aid	High	No	Nominated
824	Rupert MOON	Junior Officer	Army	12/05/1917	France	Lead	Duty	Attack	High	Wounded	Nominated
825	Tom DRESSER	OR	Army	12/05/1917	France	Deliver	Duty	Attack	High	Wounded	Nominated
826	Joseph WATT	Junior Officer	Navy	15/05/1917	Italy	Combat	Initiative	Blockade	High	No	Nominated
827	Albert WHITE	NCO	Army	19/05/1917	France	Combat	Duty	Attack	High	Killed	Nominated
828	William BISHOP	Junior Officer	RFC	2/06/1917	France	Combat	Initiative	Sortie	High	No	Nominated
829	Thomas MAUFE	Junior Officer	Army	4/06/1917	France	Repair	Initiative	Bombard	High	No	Nominated
830	John CRAIG	Junior Officer	Army	5/06/1917	Egypt	Rescue	Duty	Retake	Low	Wounded	Nominated
831	Robert GRIEVE	Junior Officer	Army	7/06/1917	Belgium	Lead	Duty	Attack	High	Wounded	Nominated
832	Samuel FRICKLETON	NCO	Army	7/06/1917	Belgium	Bomb	Duty	Attack	High	Wounded	Nominated
833	Ronald STUART	Junior Officer	Navy	7/06/1917	Atlantic	Decoy	Duty	Destroy	High	No	Elected
834	William WILLIAMS	OR	Navy	7/06/1917	Atlantic	Decoy	Duty	Destroy	High	No	Elected
835	John CARROLL	OR	Army	7/06/1917 - 12/06/1917	Belgium	Combat	Duty	Attack	High	No	Nominated
836	William RATCLIFFE	OR	Army	14/06/1917	Belgium	Combat	Initiative	Attack	High	No	Nominated
837	John DUNVILLE	Junior Officer	Army	24/06/1917 - 25/06/1917	France	Cut wire	Duty	Raid	High	Killed	Nominated
838	Frank WEARNE	Junior Officer	Army	28/06/1917	France	Lead	Duty	Raid	High	Killed	Nominated

No.	Name	Rank	Service	Date	Place	Personal Action	Type of Personal Action	Military Task of Unit	Relevance of Action to Task	Casualty?	How Selected for Award
839	Frederick YOUENS	Junior Officer	Army	7/07/1917	Belgium	Protect	Initiative	Defend	Low	Killed	Nominated
840	Thomas BARRATT	OR	Army	27/07/1917	Belgium	Cover	Voluntary	Withdraw	High	No	Nominated
841	Clifford COFFIN	Senior Officer	Army	31/07/1917	Belgium	Lead	Duty	Attack	High	No	Nominated
842	Bertram BEST-DUNKLEY	Senior Officer	Army	31/07/1917	Belgium	Lead	Duty	Attack	High	Killed	Nominated
843	Thomas COLYER-FERGUSSON	Junior Officer	Army	31/07/1917	Belgium	Lead	Duty	Attack	High	Killed	Nominated
844	Dennis HEWITT	Junior Officer	Army	31/07/1917	Belgium	Lead	Duty	Attack	High	Killed	Nominated
845	Robert BYE	NCO	Army	31/07/1917	Belgium	Clear	Voluntary	Attack	High	No	Nominated
846	Alexander EDWARDS	NCO	Army	31/07/1917	Belgium	Lead	Duty	Attack	High	Wounded	Nominated
847	Ivor REES	NCO	Army	31/07/1917	Belgium	Lead	Duty	Attack	High	No	Nominated
848	Tom MAYSON	NCO	Army	31/07/1917	Belgium	Bomb	Initiative	Attack	High	No	Nominated
849	Leslie ANDREW	NCO	Army	31/07/1917	France	Lead	Initiative	Attack	High	No	Nominated
850	James DAVIES	NCO	Army	31/07/1917	Belgium	Combat	Duty	Attack	High	Killed	Nominated
851	George McINTOSH	OR	Army	31/07/1917	Belgium	Bomb	Duty	Hold	High	No	Nominated
852	Thomas WHITHAM	OR	Army	31/07/1917	Belgium	Capture	Initiative	Attack	High	No	Nominated
853	Harold ACKROYD	Medical Officer	Army	31/07/1917 - 1/08/1917	Belgium	Rescue	Duty	Aid	High	No	Nominated
854	Noel CHAVASSE	Medical Officer	Army	31/07/1917 - 2/08/1917	Belgium	Rescue	Duty	Aid	High	Killed	Nominated
855	William BUTLER	OR	Army	6/08/1917	France	Protect	Initiative	Unknown	N/A	No	Nominated
856	Charles BONNER	Junior Officer	Navy	8/08/1917	Bay of Biscay	Decoy	Duty	Destroy	High	No	Nominated
857	Ernest PITCHER	NCO	Navy	8/08/1917	Bay of Biscay	Decoy	Duty	Destroy	High	No	Elected
858	Arnold LOOSEMORE	OR	Army	11/08/1917	Belgium	Combat	Initiative	Attack	High	No	Nominated
859	Thomas CRISP	Junior Officer	Navy	15/08/1917	North Sea	Combat	Duty	Attack	High	Killed	Nominated
860	Michael O'ROURKE	Medical OR	Army	15/08/1917 - 17/08/1917	France	Rescue	Duty	Aid	High	No	Nominated

220

No.	Name	Rank	Service	Date	Country	Combat	Duty	Action	Level	Wounded	Status
861	William GRIMBALDESTON	NCO	Army	16/08/1917	Belgium	Combat	Initiative	Attack	High	No	Nominated
862	Edward COOPER	NCO	Army	16/08/1917	Belgium	Rescue	Duty	Aid	High	No	Nominated
863	Frederick ROOM	Medical NCO	Army	16/08/1917	Belgium	Deliver	Duty	Defend	High	Killed	Nominated
864	Harry BROWN	OR	Army	16/08/1917	France	Lead	Initiative	Attack	High	No	Nominated
865	Wilfred EDWARDS	OR	Army	16/08/1917	Belgium	Charge	Duty	Defend	High	Killed	Nominated
866	Okill LEARMONTH	Junior Officer	Army	18/08/1917	France	Lead	Duty	Attack	High	Wounded	Nominated
867	John SKINNER	NCO	Army	18/08/1917	Belgium	Combat	Duty	Defend	High	Killed	Nominated
868	Frederick HOBSON	NCO	Army	18/08/1917	France	Combat	Voluntary	Attack	High	No	Nominated
869	Montague MOORE	Junior Officer	Army	20/08/1917	Belgium	Remain	Duty	Defend	High	Killed	Nominated
870	Hardy PARSONS	Junior Officer	Army	20/08/1917 - 21/08/1917	France	Lead	Duty	Attack	High	No	Nominated
871	Robert HANNA	NCO	Army	21/08/1917	France	Lead	Duty	Attack	High	Wounded	Nominated
872	Filip KONOWAL	NCO	Army	22/08/1917 - 24/08/1917	France	Bomb	Duty	Clear	High	No	Nominated
873	Sidney DAY	NCO	Army	26/08/1917	France	Protect	Initiative	Entrench	Low	Wounded	Nominated
874	John CARMICHAEL	NCO	Army	8/09/1917	Belgium	Lead	Duty	Withdraw	High	No	Nominated
875	John MOYNEY	NCO	Army	12/09/1917 - 13/09/1917	Belgium	Rescue	Initiative	Withdraw	None	No	Nominated
876	Thomas WOODCOCK	OR	Army	12/08/1917 - 13/09/1917	Belgium	Combat	Voluntary	Attack	High	No	Nominated
877	Reginald INWOOD	OR	Army	19/09/1917 - 22/09/1917	Belgium	Capture	Duty	Attack	High	Wounded	Nominated
878	Henry REYNOLDS	Junior Officer	Army	20/09/1917	Belgium	Combat	Duty	Attack	High	No	Nominated
879	Frederick BIRKS	Junior Officer	Army	20/09/1917	Belgium	Lead	Duty	Attack	High	No	Nominated
880	Hugh COLVIN	Junior Officer	Army	20/09/1917	Belgium	Combat	Duty	Attack	High	No	Nominated
881	William BURMAN	NCO	Army	20/09/1917	Belgium	Combat	Initiative	Attack	High	No	Nominated
882	Alfred KNIGHT	NCO	Army	20/09/1917	Belgium	Combat	Duty	Attack	High	Wounded	Nominated
883	William HEWITT	NCO	Army	20/09/1917	Belgium	Combat	Duty	Attack	High	No	Nominated
884	Walter PEELER	NCO	Army	20/09/1917	Belgium						Nominated

No.	Name	Rank	Service	Date	Place	Personal Action	Type of Personal Action	Military Task of Unit	Relevance of Action to Task	Casualty?	How Selected for Award
885	Ernest EGERTON	NCO	Army	20/09/1917	Belgium	Combat	Initiative	Attack	High	No	Nominated
886	John HAMILTON	NCO	Army	25/09/1917 - 26/09/1917	Belgium	Resupply	Initiative	Defend	High	No	Nominated
887	John DWYER	NCO	Army	26/09/1917	Belgium	Combat	Duty	Attack	High	No	Nominated
888	Patrick BUGDEN	OR	Army	26/09/1917 - 28/09/1917	Belgium	Capture	Voluntary	Attack	High	Killed	Nominated
889	Philip BENT	Senior Officer	Army	1/10/1917	Belgium	Lead	Duty	Defend	High	Killed	Nominated
890	Lewis EVANS	Senior Officer	Army	4/10/1917	Belgium	Lead	Duty	Attack	High	Wounded	Nominated
891	Clement ROBERTSON	Junior Officer	Army	4/10/1917	Belgium	Lead	Duty	Attack	High	Killed	Nominated
892	Charles COVERDALE	NCO	Army	4/10/1917	Belgium	Combat	Duty	Attack	High	No	Nominated
893	Lewis McGEE	NCO	Army	4/10/1917	Belgium	Combat	Duty	Attack	High	No	Nominated
894	James OCKENDON	NCO	Army	4/10/1917	Belgium	Capture	Duty	Attack	High	No	Nominated
895	Fred GREAVES	NCO	Army	4/10/1917	Belgium	Lead	Initiative	Attack	High	No	Nominated
896	Arthur HUTT	OR	Army	4/10/1917	Belgium	Lead	Initiative	Attack	High	No	Nominated
897	Thomas SAGE	OR	Army	4/10/1917	Belgium	Protect	Initiative	Attack	Low	Wounded	Nominated
898	Joseph LISTER	NCO	Army	9/10/1917	Belgium	Capture	Duty	Attack	High	No	Nominated
899	John MOLYNEUX	NCO	Army	9/10/1917	Belgium	Capture	Initiative	Attack	High	No	Nominated
900	John RHODES	NCO	Army	9/10/1917	Belgium	Capture	Duty	Attack	High	No	Nominated
901	William CLAMP	NCO	Army	9/10/1917	Belgium	Capture	Duty	Attack	High	Killed	Nominated
902	Frederick DANCOX	OR	Army	9/10/1917	Belgium	Capture	Duty	Mop-up	High	No	Nominated
903	Clarence JEFFRIES	Junior Officer	Army	12/10/1917	Belgium	Capture	Initiative	Attack	High	Killed	Nominated
904	Albert HALTON	OR	Army	12/10/1917	Belgium	Capture	Duty	Attack	High	No	Nominated
905	Christopher O'KELLY	Junior Officer	Army	26/10/1917	Belgium	Lead	Duty	Attack	High	No	Nominated
906	Robert SHANKLAND	Junior Officer	Army	26/10/1917	Belgium	Lead	Duty	Hold	High	No	Nominated
907	Thomas HOLMES	OR	Army	26/10/1917	Belgium	Capture	Initiative	Attack	High	No	Nominated
908	Alexander LAFONE	Junior Officer	Army	27/10/1917	Palestine	Lead	Duty	Hold	High	Killed	Nominated
909	Hugh McKENZIE	Junior Officer	Army	30/10/1917	Belgium	Lead	Duty	Attack	High	Killed	Nominated

No.	Name	Rank	Service	Date	Location	Action	Duty	Type	Grade	Outcome	Status
910	George MULLIN	NCO	Army	30/10/1917	Belgium	Capture	Duty	Attack	High	No	Nominated
911	Cecil KINROSS	OR	Army	30/10/1917	Belgium	Combat	Duty	Attack	High	Wounded	Nominated
912	George PEARKES	Junior Officer	Army	30/10/1917 - 1/11/1917	Belgium	Lead	Duty	Attack	High	Wounded	Nominated
913	John COLLINS	NCO	Army	31/10/1917	Palestine	Combat	Initiative	Attack	High	No	Nominated
914	John RUSSELL	Medical Officer	Army	6/11/1917	Palestine	Rescue	Duty	Aid	High	Killed	Nominated
915	Colin BARRON	NCO	Army	6/11/1917	Belgium	Combat	Initiative	Attack	High	No	Nominated
916	James ROBERTSON	OR	Army	6/11/1917	Belgium	Combat	Duty	Attack	High	Killed	Nominated
917	Arthur BORTON	Senior Officer	Army	7/11/1917	Palestine	Lead	Duty	Attack	High	No	Nominated
918	John CARLESS	OR	Navy	17/11/1917	North Sea	Combat	Duty	Attack	High	Killed	Nominated
919	John SHERWOOD-KELLY	Senior Officer	Army	20/11/1917	France	Lead	Duty	Attack	High	No	Nominated
920	Richard WAIN	Junior Officer	Army	20/11/1917	France	Combat	Duty	Attack	High	Killed	Nominated
921	Harcus STRACHAN	Junior Officer	Army	20/11/1917	France	Lead	Duty	Attack	High	No	Nominated
922	Charles SPACKMAN	NCO	Army	20/11/1917	France	Combat	Duty	Attack	High	No	Nominated
923	Robert McBEATH	NCO	Army	20/11/1917	France	Combat	Voluntary	Attack	High	No	Nominated
924	Albert SHEPHERD	OR	Army	20/11/1917	France	Combat	Voluntary	Attack	Contrary	No	Nominated
925	John McAULEY	NCO	Army	27/11/1917	France	Lead	Initiative	Attack	High	No	Nominated
926	George CLARE	Medical OR	Army	28/11/1917 - 28/11/1917	France	Rescue	Duty	Aid	High	Killed	Nominated
927	Neville ELLIOTT-COOPER	Senior Officer	Army	30/11/1917	France	Lead	Duty	Defend	High	Killed	Nominated
928	Robert GEE	Junior Officer	Army	30/11/1917	France	Lead	Duty	Defend	High	Wounded	Nominated
929	Walter STONE	Junior Officer	Army	30/11/1917	France	Lead	Duty	Defend	High	Killed	Nominated
930	Samuel WALLACE	Junior Officer	Army	30/11/1917	France	Lead	Duty	Defend	High	No	Nominated
931	Cyril GOURLEY	NCO	Army	30/11/1917	France	Lead	Duty	Defend	High	No	Nominated
932	John THOMAS	NCO	Army	30/11/1917	France	Snipe	Initiative	Defend	High	No	Nominated
933	Allastair McREADY-DIARMID	Junior Officer	Army	30/11/1917 - 1/12/1917	France	Lead	Duty	Defend	High	Killed	Nominated

No.	Name	Rank	Service	Date	Place	Personal Action	Type of Personal Action	Military Task of Unit	Relevance of Action to Task	Casualty?	How Selected for Award
934	George PATON	Junior Officer	Army	1/12/1917	France	Lead	Duty	Defend	High	Killed	Nominated
935	Stanley BOUGHEY	Junior Officer	Army	1/12/1917	Palestine	Combat	Duty	Defend	High	Killed	Nominated
936	GOBIND SINGH	NCO	Army	1/12/1917	France	Deliver	Voluntary	Hold	High	No	Nominated
937	Arthur LASCELLES	Junior Officer	Army	3/12/1917	France	Lead	Initiative	Defend	High	Wounded	Nominated
938	Henry NICHOLAS	OR	Army	3/12/1917	Belgium	Combat	Duty	Attack	High	No	Nominated
939	James EMERSON	Junior Officer	Army	6/12/1917	France	Lead	Duty	Defend	High	Killed	Nominated
940	Charles TRAIN	NCO	Army	8/12/1917	Palestine	Combat	Initiative	Attack	High	No	Nominated
941	Walter MILLS	OR	Army	10/12/1917 - 11/12/1917	France	Combat	Duty	Defend	High	Killed	Nominated
942	John CHRISTIE	NCO	Army	21/12/1917 - 22/12/1917	Palestine	Bomb	Duty	Attack	High	No	Nominated
943	James McCUDDEN	Junior Officer	RFC	23/12/1917 - 2/02/1918	France	Destroy	Duty	Patrol	High	No	Nominated
944	James DUFFY	Medical OR	Army	27/12/1917	Palestine	Rescue	Duty	Aid	High	No	Nominated
945	Geoffrey SAXTON-WHITE	Junior Officer	Navy	28/01/1918	Dardanelles	Protect	Initiative	Attack	None	Killed	Nominated
946	Charles ROBERTSON	NCO	Army	8/03/1918 - 9/03/1918	Belgium	Repel	Initiative	Defend	High	Wounded	Nominated
947	Harold WHITFIELD	OR	Army	10/03/1918	Egypt	Repel	Initiative	Hold	High	No	Nominated
948	Wilfrith ELSTOB	Senior Officer	Army	21/03/1918	France	Lead	Duty	Defend	High	Killed	Nominated
949	Manley JAMES	Junior Officer	Army	21/03/1918	France	Lead	Duty	Defend	High	Wounded	Nominated
950	Allan KER	Junior Officer	Army	21/03/1918	France	Combat	Duty	Defend	High	POW	Nominated
951	John BUCHAN	Junior Officer	Army	21/03/1918	France	Lead	Duty	Defend	High	Killed	Nominated
952	Edmund de WIND	Junior Officer	Army	21/03/1918	France	Lead	Duty	Defend	High	Killed	Nominated
953	John SAYER	NCO	Army	21/03/1918	France	Combat	Initiative	Defend	High	Killed	Nominated
954	Charles STONE	OR	Army	21/03/1918	France	Combat	Initiative	Defend	High	No	Nominated
955	Reginald HAYWARD	Junior Officer	Army	21/03/1918 - 22/03/1918	France	Lead	Duty	Defend	High	Wounded	Nominated

956	Ernest BEAL	Junior Officer	Army	21/03/1918 - 22/03/1918	France	Lead	Duty	Clear	High	Killed	Nominated
957	Cecil KNOX	Junior Officer	Army	22/03/1918	France	Demolish	Duty	Delay	High	No	Nominated
958	Harold JACKSON	NCO	Army	22/03/1918	France	Lead	Voluntary	Attack	High	No	Nominated
959	Herbert COLUMBINE	OR	Army	22/03/1918	France	Resist	Duty	Defend	High	Killed	Nominated
960	John COLLINGS-WELLS	Senior Officer	Army	22/03/1918 - 27/03/1918	France	Lead	Duty	Attack	High	Killed	Nominated
961	Frank ROBERTS	Senior Officer	Army	22/03/1918 - 2/04/1918	France	Lead	Duty	Defend	High	No	Nominated
962	Christopher BUSHELL	Senior Officer	Army	23/03/1918	France	Lead	Duty	Attack	High	Wounded	Nominated
963	Julian GRIBBLE	Junior Officer	Army	23/03/1918	France	Lead	Duty	Hold	High	Killed	Nominated
964	Alfred HERRING	Junior Officer	Army	23/03/1918 - 24/03/1918	France	Lead	Initiative	Defend	High	POW	Nominated
965	John DAVIES	NCO	Army	24/03/1918	France	Cover	Duty	Withdraw	High	POW	Nominated
966	William ANDERSON	Senior Officer	Army	25/03/1918	France	Lead	Duty	Defend	High	Killed	Nominated
967	Alfred TOYE	Junior Officer	Army	25/03/1918	France	Lead	Duty	Defend	High	No	Nominated
968	Arthur CROSS	NCO	Army	25/03/1918	France	Recon	Voluntary	Recapture	High	No	Nominated
969	Thomas YOUNG	Medical OR	Army	25/03/1918 - 31/03/1918	France	Rescue	Duty	Aid	High	No	Nominated
970	Albert MOUNTAIN	NCO	Army	26/03/1918	France	Combat	Voluntary	Defend	High	No	Nominated
971	Basil HORSFALL	Junior Officer	Army	27/03/1918	France	Combat	Duty	Defend	High	Killed	Nominated
972	Alan McLEOD	Junior Officer	RFC	27/03/1918	France	Combat	Duty	Attack	High	Wounded	Nominated
973	Oliver WATSON	Senior Officer	Army	28/03/1918	France	Lead	Duty	Counter-attack	High	Killed	Nominated
974	Bernard CASSIDY	Junior Officer	Army	28/03/1918	France	Rally	Duty	Hold	High	Killed	Nominated
975	Stanley McDOUGALL	NCO	Army	28/03/1918	France	Combat	Duty	Defend	High	No	Nominated
976	Gordon FLOWERDEW	Junior Officer	Army	30/03/1918	France	Charge	Duty	Attack	High	Killed	Nominated
977	Alan JERRARD	Junior Officer	RFC	30/03/1918	Italy	Combat	Duty	Patrol	High	POW	Nominated
978	Theodore HARDY	Chaplain	Army	5/04/1918 25/04/1918 27/04/1918	France	Rescue	Duty	Aid	High	No	Nominated

No.	Name	Rank	Service	Date	Place	Personal Action	Type of Personal Action	Military Task of Unit	Relevance of Action to Task	Casualty?	How Selected for Award
979	Percy STORKEY	Junior Officer	Army	7/04/1918	France	Lead	Duty	Attack	High	No	Nominated
980	Joseph COLLIN	Junior Officer	Army	9/04/1918	France	Cover	Duty	Withdraw	High	Killed	Nominated
981	John SCHOFIELD	Junior Officer	Army	9/04/1918	France	Lead	Duty	Attack	High	Killed	Nominated
982	Richard MASTERS	Medical OR	Army	9/04/1918	France	Rescue	Duty	Aid	High	No	Nominated
983	Eric DOUGALL	Junior Officer	Army	10/04/1918	France	Lead	Duty	Defend	High	No	Nominated
984	KARANBAHADUR RANA	OR	Army	10/04/1918	Egypt	Combat	Duty	Defend	High	No	Nominated
985	Arthur POULTER	Medical OR	Army	10/04/1918	France	Rescue	Duty	Aid	High	Wounded	Nominated
986	Thomas PRYCE	Junior Officer	Army	11/04/1918	France	Combat	Duty	Defend	High	Killed	Nominated
987	James FORBES-ROBERTSON	Senior Officer	Army	11/04/1918 - 12/04/1918	France	Lead	Duty	Defend	High	No	Nominated
988	John CROWE	Junior Officer	Army	14/04/1918	Belgium	Combat	Duty	Defend	High	No	Nominated
989	Jack COUNTER	OR	Army	16/04/1918	France	Deliver	Voluntary	Defend	High	No	Nominated
990	Joseph WOODALL	NCO	Army	22/04/1918	France	Lead	Initiative	Attack	High	No	Nominated
991	Edward BAMFORD	Junior Officer	Marines	22/04/1918 - 23/04/1918	Belgium	Lead	Initiative	Storm	High	No	Elected
992	Alfred CARPENTER	Senior Officer	Navy	22/04/1918 - 23/04/1918	Belgium	Lead	Duty	Blockade	High	No	Elected
993	George BRADFORD	Junior Officer	Navy	22/04/1918 - 23/04/1918	Belgium	Land	Initiative	Blockade	High	Killed	Nominated
994	Arthur HARRISON	Junior Officer	Navy	22/04/1918 - 23/04/1918	Belgium	Lead	Duty	Storm	High	Killed	Nominated
995	Percy DEAN	Junior Officer	Navy	22/04/1918 - 23/04/1918	Belgium	Lead	Duty	Evacuate	High	No	Nominated
996	Richard SANDFORD	Junior Officer	Navy	22/04/1918 - 23/04/1918	Belgium	Lead	Duty	Blockade	High	No	Nominated
997	Norman FINCH	NCO	Marines	22/04/1918 - 23/04/1918	Belgium	Combat	Duty	Support	High	Wounded	Elected

226

		OR		Date		Combat	Duty	Storm	High	Wounded	Elected
998	Albert McKENZIE	OR	Navy	22/04/1918 - 23/04/1918	Belgium						
999	Victor CRUTCHLEY	Junior Officer	Navy	22/04/1918 - 23/04/1918 9/05/1918 - 10/04/1918	Belgium	Lead	Voluntary	Blockade	High	No	Nominated
1000	Clifford SADLIER	Junior Officer	Army	24/04/1918 - 25/04/1918	France	Capture	Duty	Counter-attack	High	Wounded	Nominated
1001	James HEWITSON	NCO	Army	26/04/1918	France	Lead	Initiative	Attack	High	No	Nominated
1002	George McKEAN	Junior Officer	Army	27/04/1918 - 28/04/1918	France	Lead	Duty	Raid	High	No	Nominated
1003	Robert CRUIKSHANK	OR	Army	1/05/1918	Palestine	Deliver	Voluntary	Attack	High	Wounded	Nominated
1004	William GREGG	NCO	Army	6/05/1918	France	Lead	Duty	Attack	High	No	Nominated
1005	William BEESLEY	OR	Army	8/05/1918	France	Lead	Initiative	Raid	High	No	Nominated
1006	Rowland BOURKE	Junior Officer	Navy	9/05/1918 - 10/05/1918	Belgium	Rescue	Voluntary	Evacuate	High	No	Nominated
1007	Geoffrey DRUMMOND	Junior Officer	Navy	9/05/1918 - 10/05/1918	Belgium	Rescue	Voluntary	Evacuate	High	Wounded	Nominated
1008	William RUTHVEN	NCO	Army	19/05/1918	France	Lead	Initiative	Attack	High	No	Nominated
1009	George GROGAN	Senior Officer	Army	27/05/1918	France	Lead	Duty	Defend	High	No	Nominated
1010	Joel HALLIWELL	NCO	Army	27/05/1918	France	Rescue	Initiative	Withdraw	None	No	Nominated
1011	Joseph KAEBLE	NCO	Army	8-9/06/1918	France	Combat	Duty	Defend	High	Killed	Nominated
1012	Charles HUDSON	Senior Officer	Army	15/06/1918	Italy	Lead	Duty	Defend	High	Wounded	Nominated
1013	John YOULL	Junior Officer	Army	15/06/1918	Italy	Lead	Duty	Defend	High	No	Nominated
1014	Edward MANNOCK	Junior Officer	RFC	17/06/1918 - 22/07/1918	France Flanders	Combat	Duty	Scout	High	Killed	Nominated
1015	Philip DAVEY	NCO	Army	28/06/1918	France	Capture	Initiative	Attack	High	Wounded	Nominated
1016	Thomas AXFORD	NCO	Army	4/07/1918	France	Combat	Initiative	Attack	High	No	Nominated
1017	Henry DALZIEL	OR	Army	4/07/1914	France	Combat	Duty	Attack	High	Wounded	Nominated
1018	Walter BROWN	NCO	Army	6/07/1918	France	Capture	Initiative	Attack	High	No	Nominated

No.	Name	Rank	Service	Date	Place	Personal Action	Type of Personal Action	Military Task of Unit	Relevance of Action to Task	Casualty?	How Selected for Award
1019	Albert BORELLA	Junior Officer	Army	17/07/1918 - 18/07/1918	France	Lead	Duty	Attack	High	No	Nominated
1020	John MEIKLE	NCO	Army	20/07/1918	France	Lead	Initiative	Attack	High	Killed	Nominated
1021	Richard TRAVIS	NCO	Army	24/07/1918	France	Clear	Voluntary	Attack	High	No	Nominated
1022	Harold AUTEN	Junior Officer	Navy	30/07/1918	English Channel	Decoy	Duty	Destroy	High	No	Nominated
1023	Alfred GABY	Junior Officer	Army	8/08/1918	France	Lead	Duty	Attack	High	No	Nominated
1024	Herman GOOD	NCO	Army	8/08/1918	France	Lead	Duty	Attack	High	No	Nominated
1025	Herbert MINER	NCO	Army	8/08/1918	France	Combat	Duty	Attack	High	Killed	Nominated
1026	John CROAK	OR	Army	8/08/1918	France	Combat	Duty	Attack	High	Killed	Nominated
1027	Jean BRILLIANT	Junior Officer	Army	8/08/1918 - 9/08/1918	France	Lead	Initiative	Attack	High	Killed	Nominated
1028	James TAIT	Junior Officer	Army	8/08/1918 - 11/08/1918	France	Rally	Initiative	Attack	High	Killed	Nominated
1029	Andrew BEAUCHAMP-PROCTOR	Junior Officer	RAF	8/08/1918 - 8/10/1918	France	Combat	Duty	Sortie	High	No	Nominated
1030	Thomas HARRIS	NCO	Army	9/08/1918	France	Lead	Initiative	Attack	High	Killed	Nominated
1031	Raphael ZENGEL	NCO	Army	9/08/1918	France	Combat	Duty	Attack	High	No	Nominated
1032	Frederick COPPINS	NCO	Army	9/08/1918	France	Combat	Initiative	Attack	High	Wounded	Nominated
1033	Alexander BRERETON	NCO	Army	9/08/1918	France	Combat	Initiative	Attack	High	No	Nominated
1034	Robert BEATHAM	OR	Army	9/08/1918	France	Combat	Duty	Attack	High	Killed	Nominated
1035	Ferdinand WEST	Junior Officer	RAF	10/08/1918	France	Combat	Duty	Strafe	High	Wounded	Nominated
1036	Percy STATTON	NCO	Army	12/08/1918	France	Combat	Initiative	Attack	High	No	Nominated
1037	Thomas DINESEN	OR	Army	12/08/1918	France	Combat	Duty	Attack	High	No	Nominated
1038	Robert SPALL	NCO	Army	13/08/1918	France	Combat	Duty	Defend	High	Killed	Nominated
1039	Edward SMITH	NCO	Army	21/08/1918 - 23/08/1918	France	Lead	Initiative	Attack	High	No	Nominated

Number	Name	Rank	Service	Date	Country	Lead	Initiative	Attack	Rating	Killed	Nominated
1040	Richard WEST	Senior Officer	Army	21/08/1918 2/09/1918	France	Lead	Initiative	Attack	High		Nominated
1041	Daniel BEAK	Senior Officer	Navy	21/08/1918 - 25/08/1918 4/09/1918	France	Lead	Initiative	Attack	High	No	Nominated
1042	George ONIONS	NCO	Army	22/08/1918	France	Capture	Initiative	Contact	Low	Wounded	Nominated
1043	William JOYNT	Junior Officer	Army	23/08/1918	France	Lead	Duty	Attack	High	Wounded	Nominated
1044	Lawrence McCARTHY	Junior Officer	Army	23/08/1918	France	Lead	Initiative	Attack	High	No	Nominated
1045	Hugh McIVER	OR	Army	23/08/1918	France	Capture	Initiative	Attack	High	No	Nominated
1046	Samuel FORSYTH	NCO	Army	24/08/1918	France	Lead	Initiative	Attack	High	Killed	Nominated
1047	David MacINTYRE	Junior Officer	Army	24/08/1918 - 27/08/1918	France	Lead	Initiative	Attack	High	No	Nominated
1048	Harold COLLEY	NCO	Army	25/08/1918	France	Lead	Initiative	Hold	High	Killed	Nominated
1049	Charles RUTHERFORD	Junior Officer	Army	26/08/1918	France	Capture	Initiative	Attack	High	No	Nominated
1050	Reginald JUDSON	NCO	Army	26/08/1918	France	Capture	Duty	Attack	High	No	Nominated
1051	Henry WEALE	NCO	Army	26/08/1918	France	Capture	Initiative	Attack	High	No	Nominated
1052	Bernard GORDON	NCO	Army	26/08/1918 - 27/08/1918	France	Capture	Initiative	Attack	High	No	Nominated
1053	William CLARK-KENNEDY	Senior Officer	Army	27/08/1918 - 28/08/1918	France	Lead	Initiative	Attack	High	Wounded	Nominated
1054	Cecil SEWELL	Junior Officer	Army	29/08/1918	France	Rescue	Initiative	Attack	None	Killed	Nominated
1055	James HUFFAM	Junior Officer	Army	31/08/1918	France	Lead	Duty	Attack	High	No	Nominated
1056	George CARTWRIGHT	OR	Army	31/08/1918	France	Capture	Duty	Attack	High	No	Nominated
1057	Edgar TOWNER	Junior Officer	Army	1/09/1918	France	Capture	Initiative	Attack	High	Wounded	Nominated
1058	John GRANT	NCO	Army	1/09/1918	France	Lead	Duty	Attack	High	No	Nominated
1059	Albert LOWERSON	NCO	Army	1/09/1918	France	Capture	Duty	Attack	High	Wounded	Nominated
1060	William CURREY	OR	Army	1/09/1918	France	Capture	Duty	Attack	High	No	Nominated
1061	Robert MacTIER	OR	Army	1/09/1918	France	Rush	Initiative	Attack	High	Killed	Nominated
1062	Arthur HALL	NCO	Army	1/09/1918 - 2/09/1918	France	Capture	Duty	Attack	High	No	Nominated

229

No.	Name	Rank	Service	Date	Place	Personal Action	Type of Personal Action	Military Task of Unit	Relevance of Action to Task	Casualty?	How Selected for Award
1063	Alexander BUCKLEY	NCO	Army	1/09/1918 - 2/09/1918	France	Rush	Initiative	Attack	High	Killed	Nominated
1064	Claude NUNNEY	OR	Army	1/09/1918 - 2/09/1988	France	Lead	Initiative	Repulse	High	Killed	Nominated
1065	Cyrus PECK	Senior Officer	Army	2/09/1918	France	Lead	Duty	Attack	High	No	Nominated
1066	Bellenden HUTCHESON	Medical Officer	Army	2/09/1918	France	Rescue	Duty	Aid	High	No	Nominated
1067	George PROWSE	NCO	Navy	2/09/1918	France	Capture	Duty	Attack	High	No	Nominated
1068	Martin DOYLE	NCO	Army	2/09/1918	France	Lead	Duty	Attack	High	No	Nominated
1069	Arthur KNIGHT	NCO	Army	2/09/1918	France	Lead	Duty	Attack	High	Killed	Nominated
1070	Walter SIMPSON	NCO	Army	2/09/1918	France	Recon	Voluntary	Patrol	High	No	Nominated
1071	William METCALF	NCO	Army	2/09/1918	France	Guide	Initiative	Attack	High	Wounded	Nominated
1072	Lawrence WEATHERS	NCO	Army	2/09/1918	France	Bomb	Duty	Attack	High	No	Nominated
1073	Jack HARVEY	OR	Army	2/09/1918	France	Rush	Duty	Attack	High	No	Nominated
1074	John YOUNG	Medical OR	Army	2/09/1918	France	Rescue	Duty	Aid	High	No	Nominated
1075	Walter RAYFIELD	OR	Army	2/09/1918	France	Rush	Duty	Attack	High	No	Nominated
1076	John McNAMARA	NCO	Army	3/09/1918	France	Resist	Initiative	Defend	High	No	Nominated
1077	Samuel NEEDHAM	OR	Army	10/09/1918 - 11/09/1918	Palestine	Protect	Initiative	Patrol	Low	No	Nominated
1078	Laurence CALVERT	NCO	Army	12/09/1918	France	Capture	Initiative	Attack	High	No	Nominated
1079	Harry LAURENT	NCO	Army	12/09/1918	France	Charge	Duty	Attack	High	No	Nominated
1080	Alfred WILCOX	NCO	Army	12/09/1918	France	Capture	Initiative	Attack	High	No	Nominated
1081	David HUNTER	NCO	Army	16/09/1918 - 17/09/1918	France	Resist	Duty	Hold	High	No	Nominated
1082	Daniel BURGES	Senior Officer	Army	18/09/1918	Balkans	Lead	Duty	Attack	High	Wounded	Nominated
1083	Frank YOUNG	Junior Officer	Army	18/09/1918	France	Lead	Duty	Defend	High	Killed	Nominated
1084	William WHITE	Junior Officer	Army	18/09/1918	France	Capture	Initiative	Attack	High	No	Nominated
1085	Maurice BUCKLEY	NCO	Army	18/09/1918	France	Rush	Initiative	Attack	High	No	Nominated

230

1086	William WARING	NCO	Army	18/09/1918	France	Lead	Duty	Attack	High	Killed	Nominated
1087	James WOODS	OR	Army	18/09/1918	France	Capture	Initiative	Patrol	High	No	Nominated
1088	Allan LEWIS	NCO	Army	18/09/1918 21/09/1918	France	Combat	Duty	Attack	High	Killed	Nominated
1089	BADLU SINGH	Junior Officer	Army	23/09/1918	Palestine	Charge	Initiative	Attack	High	Killed	Nominated
1090	John BARRETT	Junior Officer	Army	24/09/1918	France	Charge	Duty	Attack	High	Wounded	Nominated
1091	Donald DEAN	Junior Officer	Army	24/09/1918 - 26/09/1918	France	Resist	Duty	Hold	High	No	Nominated
1092	John GORT	Senior Officer	Army	27/09/1918	France	Lead	Duty	Attack	High	Wounded	Nominated
1093	Cyril FRISBY	Junior Officer	Army	27/09/1918	France	Lead	Initiative	Attack	High	Wounded	Nominated
1094	Thomas JACKSON	NCO	Army	27/09/1918	France	Rush	Voluntary	Attack	High	Killed	Nominated
1095	Samuel HONEY	Junior Officer	Army	27/09/1918	France	Lead	Initiative	Attack	High	Killed	Nominated
1096	George KERR	Junior Officer	Army	27/09/1918	France	Capture	Duty	Attack	High	No	Nominated
1097	Thomas NEELY	NCO	Army	27/09/1918	France	Capture	Duty	Attack	High	No	Nominated
1098	Milton GREGG	Junior Officer	Army	27/09/1918 - 1/10/1918	France	Lead	Initiative	Attack	High	Wounded	Nominated
1099	Graham LYALL	Junior Officer	Army	27/09/1918 1/10/1918	France	Lead	Duty	Attack	High	No	Nominated
1100	Louis McGUFFIE	NCO	Army	28/09/1918	France	Lead	Duty	Attack	High	No	Nominated
1101	Henry TANDY	OR	Army	28/09/1918	France	Capture	Initiative	Attack	High	Wounded	Nominated
1102	Bernard VANN	Senior Officer	Army	29/09/1918	France	Lead	Duty	Attack	High	No	Nominated
1103	Ernest SEAMAN	NCO	Army	29/09/1918	Belgium	Capture	Duty	Attack	High	Killed	Nominated
1104	Blair WARK	Junior Officer	Army	29/09/1918 - 1/10/1918	France	Lead	Initiative	Attack	High	No	Nominated
1105	John McGREGOR	Junior Officer	Army	30/09/1918 - 3/10/1918	France	Lead	Duty	Attack	High	Wounded	Nominated
1106	James CRICHTON	OR	Army	30/09/1918	France	Deliver	Voluntary	Retire	High	Wounded	Nominated
1107	John RYAN	OR	Army	30/09/1918	France	Bomb	Initiative	Attack	High	Wounded	Nominated
1108	Robert GORLE	Junior Officer	Army	1/10/1918	Belgium	Rally	Initiative	Attack	High	No	Nominated
1109	William MERRIFIELD	NCO	Army	1/10/1918	France	Lead	Duty	Attack	High	Wounded	Nominated

No.	Name	Service	Rank	Date	Place	Personal Action	Type of Personal Action	Military Task of Unit	Relevance of Action to Task	Casualty?	How Selected for Award
1110	Frederick RIGGS	Army	NCO	1/10/1918	France	Lead	Duty	Attack	High	Killed	Nominated
1111	William JOHNSON	Army	NCO	3/10/1918	France	Lead	Duty	Attack	High	Wounded	Nominated
1112	Joseph MAXWELL	Army	Junior Officer	3/10/1918	France	Lead	Duty	Attack	High	No	Nominated
1113	William COLTMAN	Army	Medical NCO	3/10/1918 - 4/10/1918	France	Rescue	Initiative	Aid	High	No	Nominated
1114	George INGRAM	Army	Junior Officer	5/10/1918	France	Lead	Initiative	Attack	High	No	Nominated
1115	James TOWERS	Army	OR	6/10/1918	France	Deliver	Voluntary	Attack	High	No	Nominated
1116	John WILLIAMS	Army	NCO	7/10/1918 - 8/10/1917	France	Capture	Initiative	Attack	High	No	Nominated
1117	Coulson MITCHELL	Army	Junior Officer	8/10/1918 - 9/10/1918	France	Disarm	Duty	Attack	High	No	Nominated
1118	William HOLMES	Army	Medical OR	9/10/1918	France	Rescue	Duty	Aid	High	Killed	Nominated
1119	Wallace ALGIE	Army	Junior Officer	11/10/1918	France	Lead	Initiative	Attack	High	Killed	Nominated
1120	Frank LESTER	Army	NCO	12/10/1918	France	Protect	Voluntary	Clear	Low	Killed	Nominated
1121	Harry WOOD	Army	NCO	13/10/1918	France	Lead	Initiative	Attack	High	No	Nominated
1122	James JOHNSON	Army	Junior Officer	14/10/1918	France	Lead	Duty	Hold	High	No	Nominated
1123	James McPHIE	Army	NCO	14/10/1918	France	Repair	Duty	Bridge	High	Killed	Nominated
1124	Martin MOFFAT	Army	OR	14/10/1918	Belgium	Rush	Initiative	Attack	High	No	Nominated
1125	Thomas RICKETTS	Army	OR	14/10/1918	Belgium	Resupply	Voluntary	Outflank	High	No	Nominated
1126	John O'NEILL	Army	NCO	14/10/1918 20/10/1918	Belgium	Lead	Duty	Attack	High	No	Nominated
1127	Roland ELCOCK	Army	NCO	15/10/1918	France	Lead	Initiative	Attack	High	No	Nominated
1128	Horace CURTIS	Army	NCO	18/10/1918	France	Capture	Duty	Attack	High	No	Nominated
1129	John DAYKINS	Army	NCO	20/10/1918	France	Capture	Initiative	Attack	High	No	Nominated
1130	Alfred WILKINSON	Army	OR	20/10/1918	France	Deliver	Voluntary	Attack	High	No	Nominated
1131	David McGREGOR	Army	Junior Officer	22/10/1918	Belgium	Lead	Duty	Attack	High	Killed	Nominated
1132	Francis MILES	Army	OR	23/10/1918	France	Capture	Initiative	Attack	High	No	Nominated

No.	Name	Rank	Service	Date	Location	Action	Duty	Attack	Priority	Status	Nominated
1133	Harry GREENWOOD	Senior Officer	Army	23/10/1918 - 24/10/1918	France	Lead	Duty	Attack	High	No	Nominated
1134	Frederick HEDGES	Junior Officer	Army	24/10/1918	France	Lead	Initiative	Attack	High	No	Nominated
1135	William BISSETT	Junior Officer	Army	25/10/1918	France	Lead	Duty	Attack	High	No	Nominated
1136	Norman HARVEY	OR	Army	25/10/1918	Belgium	Rush	Initiative	Attack	High	No	Nominated
1137	William BARKER	Junior Officer	RAF	27/10/1918	France	Combat	Duty	Sortie	High	Wounded	Nominated
1138	William McNALLY	NCO	Army	27/10/1918 29/10/1918	Italy	Lead	Duty	Attack	High	No	Nominated
1139	Wilfred WOOD	OR	Army	28/10/1918	Italy	Capture	Initiative	Attack	High	No	Nominated
1140	Thomas CALDWELL	NCO	Army	31/10/1918	Belgium	Capture	Initiative	Attack	High	No	Nominated
1141	Hugh CAIRNS	NCO	Army	1/11/1918	France	Lead	Duty	Attack	High	Killed	Nominated
1142	James CLARKE	NCO	Army	2/11/1918	France	Lead	Initiative	Attack	High	No	Nominated
1143	Dudley JOHNSON	Senior Officer	Army	4/11/1918	France	Lead	Duty	Attack	High	No	Nominated
1144	James MARSHALL	Senior Officer	Army	4/11/1918	France	Lead	Duty	Attack	High	Killed	Nominated
1145	George FINDLAY	Junior Officer	Army	4/11/1918	France	Repair	Duty	Bridge	High	Wounded	Nominated
1146	Arnold WATERS	Junior Officer	Army	4/11/1918	France	Lead	Duty	Bridge	High	No	Nominated
1147	James KIRK	Junior Officer	Army	4/11/1918	France	Cover	Duty	Bridge	High	Killed	Nominated
1148	William AMEY	NCO	Army	4/11/1918	France	Capture	Initiative	Attack	High	No	Nominated
1149	Adam ARCHIBALD	OR	Army	4/11/1918	France	Construct	Duty	Bridge	High	Wounded	Nominated
1150	Brett CLOUTMAN	Junior Officer	Army	6/11/1918	France	Disarm	Duty	Bridge	High	No	Nominated
1151	Unknown US Warrior	Unkn.	Unkn.	1917-18	France	Unknown	Unknown	Unknown	Unknown	Killed	Random
1152	Augustus AGAR	Junior Officer	Navy	17/06/1919	Baltic	Torpedo	Duty	Attack	High	No	Nominated
1153	Arthur SULLIVAN	NCO	Army	10/08/1919	Russia	Rescue	Initiative	Cover	None	No	Nominated
1154	Claude DOBSON	Junior Officer	Navy	18/08/1919	Baltic	Torpedo	Duty	Attack	High	No	Nominated
1155	Gordon STEELE	Junior Officer	Navy	18/08/1919	Baltic	Torpedo	Duty	Attack	High	No	Nominated
1156	Samuel PEARSE	NCO	Army	29/08/1919	Russia	Charge	Duty	Attack	High	Killed	Nominated
1157	Henry ANDREWS	Medical Officer	Army	22/10/1919	Waziristan	Rescue	Duty	Aid	High	Killed	Nominated
1158	William KENNY	Junior Officer	Army	2/01/1920	Waziristan	Lead	Duty	Withdraw	High	Killed	Nominated

No.	Name	Rank	Service	Date	Place	Personal Action	Type of Personal Action	Military Task of Unit	Relevance of Action to Task	Casualty?	How Selected for Award
1159	George HENDERSON	Junior Officer	Army	24/07/1920	Iraq	Lead	Duty	Retire	High	Killed	Nominated
1160	ISHAR SINGH	OR	Army	10/04/1921	Waziristan	Charge	Duty	Recover	High	Wounded	Nominated
1161	Godfrey MEYNALL	Junior Officer	Army	29/09/1935	India	Lead	Duty	Hold	High	Killed	Nominated
1162	John LINTON	Senior Officer	Navy	09/1939 - 03/1943	Mediterranean	Lead	Duty	Patrol	High	Killed	Nominated
1163	Gerard ROOPE	Senior Officer	Navy	8/04/1940	Norway	Lead	Duty	Attack	High	Killed	Nominated
1164	Bernard WARBURTON-LEE	Senior Officer	Navy	10/04/1940	Norway	Lead	Duty	Attack	High	Killed	Nominated
1165	Richard STANNARD	Junior Officer	Navy	28/04/1940 - 2/05/1940	Norway	Lead	Duty	Defend	High	No	Nominated
1166	Donald GARLAND	Junior Officer	RAF	12/05/1940	Belgium	Bomb	Voluntary	Attack	High	Killed	Nominated
1167	Thomas GRAY	NCO	RAF	12/05/1940	Belgium	Bomb	Voluntary	Attack	High	Killed	Nominated
1168	Richard ANNAND	Junior Officer	Army	15/05/1940 - 16/05/1940	Belgium	Lead	Duty	Defend	High	Wounded	Nominated
1169	Christopher FURNESS	Junior Officer	Army	17/05/1940 - 24/05/1940	France	Cover	Duty	Withdraw	High	Killed	Nominated
1170	George GRISTOCK	NCO	Army	21/05/1940	Belgium	Cover	Duty	Hold	High	Killed	Nominated
1171	Harry NICHOLLS	NCO	Army	21/05/1940	Belgium	Lead	Duty	Counter-attack	High	Wounded	Nominated
1172	Harold ERVINE-ANDREWS	Junior Officer	Army	31/05/1940 1/06/1940	France	Lead	Duty	Defend	High	No	Nominated
1173	Geoffrey CHESHIRE	Junior Officer	RAF	06/1940-07/1944	Germany	Lead	Duty	Attack	High	No	Nominated
1174	Jack MANTLE	NCO	Navy	4/07/1940	England	Standfast	Duty	Defend	High	Killed	Nominated
1175	Eric WILSON	Junior Officer	Army	11/08/1940 - 15/08/1940	Somaliland	Lead	Duty	Defend	High	Wounded	Nominated
1176	Roderick LEAROYD	Junior Officer	RAF	12/08/1940	Germany	Bomb	Duty	Attack	High	No	Nominated
1177	James NICOLSON	Junior Officer	RAF	16/08/1940	England	Combat	Duty	Defend	High	Wounded	Nominated

1178	John HANNAH	NCO	RAF	15/08/1940	Belgium	Lead	Duty	Attack	Low	Wounded	Nominated
1179	Edward FEGAN	Senior Officer	Navy	5/11/1940	Atlantic	Lead	Duty	Defend	High	Killed	Nominated
1180	PREMINDRA SINGH BHAGAT	Junior Officer	Army	31/01/1941 - 4/02/1941	Abyssinia	Clearance	Duty	Pursuit	High	No	Nominated
1181	RICHHPAL RAM	Junior Officer	Army	7/02/1941 - 8/02/1941	Eritrea	Lead	Duty	Attack	High	Killed	Nominated
1182	Kenneth CAMPBELL	Junior Officer	RAF	6/04/1941	France	Torpedo	Duty	Attack	High	Killed	Nominated
1183	John EDMONDSON	NCO	Army	13/04/1941 - 14/04/1941	Libya	Charge	Duty	Counter-attack	High	Killed	Nominated
1184	John HINTON	NCO	Army	28/04/1941 - 29/04/1941	Greece	Charge	Initiative	Retreat	Contrary	Wounded	Nominated
1185	Alfred SEPHTON	NCO	Navy	18/05/1941	Crete	Standfast	Duty	Defend	High	Killed	Nominated
1186	Nigel LEAKEY	NCO	Army	19/05/1941	Abyssinia	Combat	Initiative	Defend	High	Killed	Nominated
1187	Alfred HULME	NCO	Army	20/05/1941 - 28/05/1941	Crete	Lead	Initiative	Hold	High	Wounded	Nominated
1188	Charles UPHAM	Junior Officer	Army	22/05/1941 - 30/05/1941	Crete	Lead	Duty	Defend	High	Wounded	Nominated
1189	Malcolm WANKLYN	Senior Officer	Navy	24/05/1941	Sicily	Torpedo	Duty	Patrol	High	No	Nominated
1190	Arthur CUTLER	Junior Officer	Army	19/06/1941 - 6/07/1941	Lebanon	Combat	Duty	Defend	High	Wounded	Nominated
1191	Hughie EDWARDS	Senior Officer	RAF	4/07/1941	Germany	Lead	Duty	Attack	High	No	Nominated
1192	James WARD	NCO	RNZAF	7/07/1941	Germany	Protect	Voluntary	Return	High	Wounded	Nominated
1193	James GORDON	OR	Army	10/07/1941 - 11/07/1941	Syria	Charge	Initiative	Attack	High	No	Nominated
1194	Geoffrey KEYES	Senior Officer	Army	17/11/1941 - 18/11/1941	Libya	Lead	Duty	Raid	High	Killed	Nominated
1195	George GUNN	Junior Officer	Army	21/11/1941	Libya	Lead	Duty	Defend	High	Killed	Nominated
1196	John BEELEY	OR	Army	21/11/1941	Libya	Charge	Initiative	Attack	High	Killed	Nominated
1197	John CAMPBELL	Senior Officer	Army	21/11/1941 - 22/11/1941	Libya	Lead	Duty	Defend	High	Wounded	Nominated

No.	Name	Rank	Service	Date	Place	Personal Action	Type of Personal Action	Military Task of Unit	Relevance of Action to Task	Casualty?	How Selected for Award
1198	Philip GARDNER	Junior Officer	Army	23/11/1941	Libya	Rescue	Initiative	Assist	Low	Wounded	Nominated
1199	James JACKMAN	Junior Officer	Army	25/11/1941	Libya	Lead	Duty	Support	High	No	Nominated
1200	Arthur SCARF	Junior Officer	RAF	9/12/1941	Malaya	Bomb	Duty	Attack	High	Killed	Nominated
1201	John OSBORN	NCO	Army	19/12/1941	Hong Kong	Protect	Initiative	Hold	High	Killed	Nominated
1202	Arthur CUMMING	Senior Officer	Army	3/01/1942	Malaya	Lead	Initiative	Withdraw	High	Wounded	Nominated
1203	Charles ANDERSON	Senior Officer	Army	18/01/1942 - 22/01/1942	Malaya	Lead	Duty	Withdraw	High	No	Nominated
1204	Eugene ESMONDE	Senior Officer	Fleet Air	12/02/1942	English Channel	Lead	Duty	Attack	High	Killed	Nominated
1205	Thomas WILKINSON	Junior Officer	Navy	14/02/1942	Java Sea	Lead	Duty	Attack	High	Killed	Represent-ative
1206	Peter ROBERTS	Junior Officer	Navy	16/02/1942	Mediterran-ean	Disarm	Voluntary	Protect	High	No	Nominated
1207	Thomas GOULD	NCO	Navy	16/02/1942	Mediterran-ean	Disarm	Voluntary	Protect	High	No	Nominated
1208	Anthony MIERS	Senior Officer	Navy	4/03/1942	Greece	Lead	Duty	Raid	High	No	Nominated
1209	Augustus NEWMAN	Senior Officer	Army	27/03/1942 - 28/03/1942	France	Lead	Initiative	Raid	High	No	Nominated
1210	Stephen BEATTIE	Senior Officer	Navy	27/03/1942 - 28/03/1942	France	Lead	Duty	Raid	High	No	Represent-ative
1211	Robert RYDER	Senior Officer	Navy	27/03/1942 - 28/03/1942	France	Lead	Duty	Raid	High	No	Nominated
1212	Thomas DURRANT	NCO	Army	27/03/1942 - 28/03/1942	France	Combat	Duty	Raid	High	Killed	Nominated
1213	William SAVAGE	OR	Navy	27/03/1942 - 28/03/1942	France	Combat	Duty	Raid	High	Killed	Represent-ative
1214	John NETTLETON	Senior Officer	RAF	17/04/1942	Germany	Lead	Duty	Attack	High	No	Nominated
1215	Henry FOOTE	Senior Officer	Army	27/05/1942 - 15/06/1942	Libya	Lead	Duty	Hold	High	Wounded	Nominated
1216	Leslie MANSER	Junior Officer	RAF	30/05/1942 - 31/05/1942	Germany	Protect	Initiative	Raid	Low	Killed	Nominated

236

No.	Name	Rank	Service	Date	Location	Lead	Duty	Type	Profile	Outcome	Status
1217	Quentin SMYTHE	NCO	Army	5/06/1942	Egypt	Lead	Duty	Attack	High	Wounded	Nominated
1218	Adam WAKENSHAW	OR	Army	27/06/1942	Egypt	Combat	Duty	Defend	High	Killed	Nominated
1219	Charles UPHAM	Junior Officer	Army	14/07/1942 - 15/07/1942	Egypt	Lead	Duty	Attack	High	Wounded	Nominated
1220	Keith ELLIOTT	NCO	Army	15/07/1942	Egypt	Lead	Duty	Attack	High	Wounded	Nominated
1221	Arthur GURNEY	OR	Army	22/07/1942	Egypt	Charge	Initiative	Attack	High	Killed	Nominated
1222	Charles MERRITT	Senior Officer	Army	19/08/1942	France	Lead	Duty	Raid	High	Wounded	Nominated
1223	John FOOTE	Chaplain	Army	19/08/1942	France	Rescue	Duty	Aid	High	POW	Nominated
1224	Patrick PORTEOUS	Junior Officer	Army	19/08/1942	France	Lead	Initiative	Raid	High	Wounded	Nominated
1225	Bruce KINGSBURY	OR	Army	29/08/1942	New Guinea	Charge	Initiative	Counter-attack	High	Killed	Nominated
1226	John FRENCH	NCO	Army	4/09/1942	New Guinea	Lead	Duty	Attack	High	Killed	Nominated
1227	William KIBBY	NCO	Army	23/10/1942 - 31/10/1942	Egypt	Lead	Duty	Attack	High	Killed	Nominated
1228	Percival GRATWICK	OR	Army	25/10/1942 - 26/10/1942	Egypt	Charge	Initiative	Attack	High	Killed	Nominated
1229	Victor TURNER	Senior Officer	Army	27/10/1942	Egypt	Lead	Duty	Defend	High	Wounded	Nominated
1230	Frederick PETERS	Senior Officer	Navy	8/11/1942	Algeria	Lead	Duty	Capture	High	Wounded	Nominated
1231	Hugh MALCOLM	Senior Officer	RAF	17/11/1942 - 4/12/1942	Tunisia	Lead	Duty	Raid	High	Killed	Nominated
1232	Rawdon MIDDLETON	NCO	RAF	28/11/1942 - 29/11/1942	Italy	Protect	Initiative	Raid	Low	Killed	Nominated
1233	Herbert LE PATOUREL	Junior Officer	Army	3/12/1942	Tunisia	Lead	Duty	Attack	High	Wounded	Nominated
1234	Robert SHERBROOKE	Senior Officer	Navy	31/12/1942	Norway	Lead	Duty	Convoy	High	Wounded	Nominated
1235	PARKASH SINGH	NCO	Army	6/01/1943 - 19/01/1943	Burma	Rescue	Initiative	Attack	Low	No	Nominated
1236	William NEWTON	Junior Officer	RAAF	16/03/1943 - 18/03/1943	New Guinea	Bomb	Duty	Attack	High	Killed	Nominated
1237	Derek SEAGRIM	Senior Officer	Army	20/03/1943 - 21/03/1943	Tunisia	Lead	Duty	Attack	High	Killed	Nominated

No.	Name	Rank	Service	Date	Place	Personal Action	Type of Personal Action	Military Task of Unit	Relevance of Action to Task	Casualty?	How Selected for Award
1238	MOANA-NU-A-KIWA NGARIMU	Junior Officer	Army	26/03/1943 - 27/03/1943	Tunisia	Lead	Duty	Attack	High	Killed	Nominated
1239	LALBAHADUR THARPA	Junior Officer	Army	5/04/1943 - 6/04/1943	Tunisia	Lead	Duty	Attack	High	No	Nominated
1240	Lorne CAMPBELL	Senior Officer	Army	6/04/1943	Tunisia	Lead	Duty	Attack	High	Wounded	Nominated
1241	Eric ANDERSON	Medical OR	Army	6/04/1943	Tunisia	Rescue	Duty	Aid	High	Killed	Nominated
1242	CHHELU RAM	NCO	Army	19/04/1943 - 20/04/1943	Tunisia	Lead	Duty	Attack	High	Killed	Nominated
1243	Charles LYELL	Junior Officer	Army	22/04/1943 - 27/04/1943	Tunisia	Lead	Duty	Attack	High	Killed	Nominated
1244	John ANDERSON	Junior Officer	Army	23/04/1943	Tunisia	Lead	Duty	Attack	High	Wounded	Nominated
1245	Wilward SANDYS-CLARKE	Junior Officer	Army	23/04/1943	Tunisia	Lead	Voluntary	Attack	High	Killed	Nominated
1246	John KENNEALLY	NCO	Army	28/04/1943 - 30/04/1943	Tunisia	Charge	Initiative	Hold	Contrary	Wounded	Nominated
1247	Leonard TRENT	Senior Officer	RNZAF	3/05/1943	Holland	Lead	Duty	Attack	High	POW	Nominated
1248	Guy GIBSON	Senior Officer	RAF	16/05/1943 - 17/05/1943	Germany	Lead	Duty	Attack	High	No	Nominated
1249	GAJE GHALE	NCO	Army	24/05/1943 - 27/05/1943	Burma	Lead	Duty	Attack	High	Wounded	Nominated
1250	Lloyd TRIGG	Junior Officer	RNZAF	11/08/1943	Atlantic	Bomb	Duty	Attack	High	Killed	Nominated
1251	Arthur AARON	NCO	RAF	12/08/1943 - 13/08/1943	Italy	Lead	Duty	Attack	High	Killed	Nominated
1252	Richard KELLIHER	OR	Army	13/09/1943	New Guinea	Charge	Initiative	Attack	High	No	Nominated
1253	Donald CAMERON	Junior Officer	Navy	22/09/1943	Norway	Lead	Duty	Attack	High	POW	Nominated
1254	Basil PLACE	Junior Officer	Navy	22/09/1943	Norway	Lead	Duty	Attack	High	POW	Nominated
1255	Peter WRIGHT	NCO	Army	25/09/1943	Italy	Lead	Duty	Attack	High	No	Nominated
1256	William REID	Junior Officer	RAF	3/11/1943	Germany	Lead	Duty	Attack	High	Wounded	Nominated

	Name	Rank	Service	Date	Location	Action	Motive	Type	Risk	Casualty	Status
1257	Thomas DERRICK	NCO	Army	24/11/1943	New Guinea	Lead	Voluntary	Attack	High	No	Nominated
1258	Paul TRIQUET	Junior Officer	Army	14/12/1943	Italy	Lead	Duty	Attack	High	No	Nominated
1259	Alec HORWOOD	Junior Officer	Army	18/01/1944 - 20/01/1944	Burma	Lead	Voluntary	Attack	High	Killed	Nominated
1260	George MITCHELL	OR	Army	23/01/1944 - 24/01/1944	Italy	Charge	Initiative	Attack	High	Killed	Nominated
1261	William SIDNEY	Junior Officer	Army	7/02/1944 - 8/02/1944	Italy	Lead	Duty	Counter-attack	High	Wounded	Nominated
1262	Charles HOEY	Junior Officer	Army	16/02/1944	Burma	Lead	Duty	Attack	High	Killed	Nominated
1263	NAND SINGH	NCO	Army	11/03/1944 - 12/03/1944	Burma	Charge	Duty	Recapture	High	Wounded	Nominated
1264	George CAIRNS	Junior Officer	Army	13/03/1944	Burma	Lead	Duty	Attack	High	Killed	Nominated
1265	Cyril BARTON	Junior Officer	RAF	30/03/1944 - 31/03/1944	Germany	Lead	Duty	Attack	High	Killed	Nominated
1266	ABDUL HAFIZ	Junior Officer	Army	6/04/1944	India	Lead	Duty	Attack	High	Killed	Nominated
1267	John HARMAN	NCO	Army	8/04/1944 - 9/04/1944	India	Charge	Duty	Recover	High	Killed	Nominated
1268	Norman JACKSON	NCO	RAF	26/04/1944 - 27/04/1944	Germany	Protect	Voluntary	Attack	Low	Wounded	Nominated
1269	John RANDLE	Junior Officer	Army	4/05/1944 - 6/05/1944	India	Charge	Initiative	Attack	High	Killed	Nominated
1270	KAMAL RAM	OR	Army	12/05/1944	Italy	Outflank	Voluntary	Attack	High	No	Nominated
1271	Richard WAKEFORD	Junior Officer	Army	13/05/1944 - 14/05/1944	Italy	Lead	Duty	Attack	High	Wounded	Nominated
1272	Francis JEFFERSON	OR	Army	16/05/1944	Italy	Resist	Initiative	Defend	High	No	Nominated
1273	John MAHONY	Junior Officer	Army	24/05/1944	Italy	Lead	Duty	Defend	High	Wounded	Nominated
1274	Maurice ROGERS	NCO	Army	3/06/1944	Italy	Charge	Duty	Attack	High	Killed	Nominated
1275	Stanley HOLLIS	NCO	Army	6/06/1944	France	Charge	Initiative	Attack	High	No	Nominated
1276	Hanson TURNER	NCO	Army	6/06/1944 - 7/06/1944	Burma	Lead	Initiative	Counter-attack	High	Killed	Nominated

No.	Name	Rank	Service	Date	Place	Personal Action	Type of Personal Action	Military Task of Unit	Relevance of Action to Task	Casualty?	How Selected for Award
1277	Michael ALLMAND	Junior Officer	Army	11/06/1944 13/06/1944 23/06/1944	Burma	Lead	Duty	Attack	High	Killed	Nominated
1278	GANJU LAMA	OR	Army	12/06/1944	Burma	Engage	Initiative	Counter-attack	High	Wounded	Nominated
1279	Andrew MYNARSKI	Junior Officer	RCAF	12/06/1944 - 13/06/1944	France	Rescue	Initiative	Abandon	None	Killed	Nominated
1280	SEFANAIA SUKANAIVALU	NCO	Army	23/06/1944	Solomon Is	Rescue	Voluntary	Withdraw	None	Killed	Nominated
1281	TULBAHADUR PUN	OR	Army	23/06/1944	Burma	Charge	Duty	Attack	High	No	Nominated
1282	David HORNELL	Junior Officer	RCAF	24/06/1944	Atlantic	Bomb	Duty	Attack	High	Killed	Nominated
1283	NETRABAHADUR THAPA	Junior Officer	Army	25/06/1944 - 26/06/1944	Burma	Lead	Duty	Defend	High	Killed	Nominated
1284	AGANSING RAI	NCO	Army	26/06/1944	Burma	Lead	Initiative	Attack	High	No	Nominated
1285	Frank BLAKER	Junior Officer	Army	9/07/1944	Burma	Lead	Duty	Attack	High	Killed	Nominated
1286	YESHWANT GHADGE	NCO	Army	10/07/1944	Italy	Charge	Duty	Attack	High	Killed	Nominated
1287	John CRUIKSHANK	Junior Officer	RAF	17/07/1944 - 18/07/1944	Atlantic	Bomb	Duty	Attack	High	Wounded	Nominated
1288	Ian BAZALGETTE	Junior Officer	RAF	4/08/1944	France	Lead	Duty	Bombard	High	Killed	Nominated
1289	Sidney BATES	NCO	Army	6/08/1944	France	Charge	Duty	Hold	High	Killed	Nominated
1290	David JAMIESON	Junior Officer	Army	7/08/1944 - 8/08/1944	France	Lead	Duty	Hold	High	Wounded	Nominated
1291	Tasker WATKINS	Junior Officer	Army	16/08/1944	France	Lead	Duty	Attack	High	No	Nominated
1292	David CURRIE	Junior Officer	Army	18/08/1944 - 20/08/1944	France	Lead	Duty	Attack	High	No	Nominated
1293	Gerald NORTON	Junior Officer	Army	31/08/1944	Italy	Lead	Initiative	Attack	High	Wounded	Nominated
1294	John GRAYBURN	Junior Officer	Army	17/09/1944 - 20/09/1944	Holland	Lead	Duty	Hold	High	Killed	Nominated

						Combat	Duty	Attack	High	Killed	Nominated
1295	SHERBAHADUR THAPA	OR	Army	18/09/1944 - 19/09/1944	Italy						Nominated
1296	Lionel QUERIPEL	Junior Officer	Army	19/08/1944	Holland	Lead	Duty	Attack	High	Killed	Nominated
1297	David LORD	Junior Officer	RAF	19/09/1944	Holland	Resupply	Duty	Attack	High	Killed	Nominated
1298	Robert CAIN	Junior Officer	Army	19/09/1944 - 25/09/1944	Holland	Lead	Duty	Defend	High	Wounded	Nominated
1299	John BASKEYFIELD	NCO	Army	20/09/1944	Holland	Engage	Duty	Defend	High	Killed	Nominated
1300	John HARPER	NCO	Army	29/09/1944	Belgium	Lead	Duty	Attack	High	Killed	Nominated
1301	Richard BURTON	OR	Army	8/10/1944	Italy	Charge	Initiative	Attack	High	No	Nominated
1302	George EARDLEY	NCO	Army	16/10/1944	Holland	Charge	Initiative	Attack	High	No	Nominated
1303	Ernest SMITH	OR	Army	21/10/1944 - 22/10/1944	Italy	Lead	Initiative	Hold	High	No	Nominated
1304	RAM SARUP SINGH	Junior Officer	Army	25/10/1944	Burma	Lead	Duty	Divert	High	Killed	Nominated
1305	THAMAN GURUNG	OR	Army	10/11/1944	Italy	Combat	Duty	Patrol	High	Killed	Nominated
1306	BHANDARI RAM	OR	Army	22/11/1944	Burma	Combat	Duty	Attack	High	Wounded	Nominated
1307	John BRUNT	Junior Officer	Army	9/12/1944	Italy	Lead	Duty	Hold	High	No	Nominated
1308	UMRAO SINGH	NCO	Army	15/12/1944 - 16/12/1944	Burma	Combat	Duty	Defend	High	Wounded	Nominated
1309	Robert PALMER	Senior Officer	RAF	23/12/1944	Germany	Lead	Duty	Bombard	High	Killed	Nominated
1310	George THOMPSON	NCO	RAF	1/01/1945	Germany	Rescue	Initiative	Bombard	None	Killed	Nominated
1311	Dennis DONNINI	OR	Army	18/01/1945	Germany	Charge	Duty	Attack	High	Killed	Nominated
1312	SHER SHAH	NCO	Army	19/01/1945 - 20/01/1945	Burma	Combat	Initiative	Defend	High	Killed	Nominated
1313	Henry HARDEN	Medical NCO	Army	23/01/1945	Holland	Rescue	Duty	Aid	High	Killed	Nominated
1314	George KNOWLAND	Junior Officer	Army	31/01/1945	Burma	Lead	Duty	Hold	High	Killed	Nominated
1315	PRAKASH SINGH	Junior Officer	Army	16/02/1945 - 17/02/1945	Burma	Lead	Duty	Defend	High	Killed	Nominated
1316	Edwin SWALES	Senior Officer	SAAF	23/02/1945	Germany	Lead	Duty	Bombard	High	Killed	Nominated
1317	Aubrey COUSENS	NCO	Army	25/02/1945 - 26/02/1945	Holland	Lead	Initiative	Attack	High	Killed	Nominated

241

No.	Name	Rank	Service	Date	Place	Personal Action	Type of Personal Action	Military Task of Unit	Relevance of Action to Task	Casualty?	How Selected for Award
1318	Frederick TILSTON	Junior Officer	Army	1/03/1945	Germany	Lead	Duty	Attack	High	Wounded	Nominated
1319	James STOKES	OR	Army	1/03/1945	Germany	Charge	Initiative	Attack	High	Killed	Nominated
1320	GIAN SINGH	NCO	Army	2/03/1945	Burma	Lead	Duty	Attack	High	Wounded	Nominated
1321	FAZAL DIN	NCO	Army	2/03/1945	Burma	Combat	Duty	Attack	High	Killed	Nominated
1322	William WESTON	Junior Officer	Army	3/03/1945	Burma	Combat	Duty	Attack	High	Killed	Nominated
1323	BHANBHAGTA GURUNG	OR	Army	5/03/1945	Burma	Combat	Duty	Attack	High	No	Nominated
1324	KARAMJEET SINGH JUDGE	Junior Officer	Army	18/03/1945	Burma	Lead	Duty	Attack	High	Killed	Nominated
1325	Claud RAYMOND	Junior Officer	Army	21/03/1945	Burma	Lead	Duty	Patrol	High	Killed	Nominated
1326	Reginald RATTEY	NCO	Army	22/03/1945	Solomon Is	Charge	Duty	Capture	High	No	Nominated
1327	Frederick TOPHAM	Medical NCO	Army	24/03/1945	Germany	Rescue	Initiative	Aid	High	Wounded	Nominated
1328	Albert CHOWNE	Junior Officer	Army	25/03/1945	New Guinea	Lead	Duty	Attack	High	Killed	Nominated
1329	Edward CHAPMAN	NCO	Army	2/04/1945	Germany	Combat	Duty	Defend	High	Wounded	Nominated
1330	Thomas HUNTER	NCO	Marines	2/04/1945	Italy	Lead	Duty	Attack	High	Killed	Nominated
1331	Ian LIDDELL	Junior Officer	Army	3/04/1945	Germany	Defuse	Duty	Capture	High	No	Nominated
1332	Anders LASSEN	Junior Officer	Army	8/04/1945 - 9/04/1945	Italy	Lead	Duty	Raid	High	Killed	Nominated
1333	ALI HAIDAR	OR	Army	9/04/1945	Italy	Charge	Initiative	Attack	High	Wounded	Nominated
1334	NAMDEO JADHAO	OR	Army	9/04/1945	Italy	Combat	Initiative	Attack	High	Wounded	Nominated
1335	Edward CHARLTON	OR	Army	21/04/1945	Germany	Counter-attack	Initiative	Hold	High	Killed	Nominated
1336	John MACKEY	NCO	Army	12/05/1946	Borneo	Lead	Duty	Attack	High	Killed	Nominated
1337	LACHHIMAN GURUNG	OR	Army	12/05/1945 - 13/05/1945	Burma	Repel	Duty	Hold	High	Wounded	Nominated
1338	Edward KENNA	OR	Army	15/05/1945	New Guinea	Engage	Initiative	Attack	High	No	Nominated
1339	Leslie STARCEVICH	OR	Army	25/05/1945	Borneo	Combat	Duty	Attack	High	No	Nominated

No.	Name	Rank	Service	Date	Location	Combat	Initiative	Action	Intensity	Wounded	Nominated
1340	Frank PARTRIDGE	OR	Army	24/07/1945	Solomon Is	Lead	Duty	Patrol	High	No	Nominated
1341	Ian FRASER	Junior Officer	Navy	31/07/1945	Singapore	Lead	Duty	Attack	High	No	Nominated
1342	James MAGENNIS	NCO	Navy	31/07/1945	Singapore	Mine	Duty	Attack	High	No	Nominated
1343	Robert GRAY	Junior Officer	Fleet Air	9/08/1945	Japan	Bomb	Duty	Attack	High	Killed	Nominated
1344	Kenneth MUIR	Junior Officer	Army	23/09/1950	Korea	Lead	Duty	Hold	High	Killed	Nominated
1345	James CARNE	Senior Officer	Army	22/04/1951 - 23/04/1951	Korea	Lead	Duty	Hold	High	POW	Nominated
1346	Philip CURTIS	Junior Officer	Army	22/04/1951 - 23/04/1952	Korea	Lead	Duty	Counter-attack	High	Killed	Nominated
1347	William SPEAKMAN	OR	Army	4/11/1951	Korea	Lead	Initiative	Counter-attack	High	Wounded	Nominated
1348	Kevin WHEATLEY	NCO	Army	13/11/1965	Vietnam	Rescue	Initiative	Search/Destroy	None	Killed	Nominated
1349	RAMBAHADUR LIMBU	NCO	Army	21/11/1965	Sarawak	Lead	Duty	Attack	High	No	Nominated
1350	Peter BADCOE	Junior Officer	Army	23/02/1967 7/03/1967 7/04/1967	Vietnam	Lead	Duty		High	Killed	Nominated
1351	Rayene SIMPSON	NCO	Army	6/05/1967 11/05/1967	Vietnam	Lead	Duty	Search/Clear	High	No	Nominated
1352	Keith PAYNE	NCO	Army	24/05/1969	Vietnam	Lead	Duty	Defend	High	Wounded	Nominated
1353	Herbert JONES	Senior Officer	Army	28/05/1982	Falkland Is	Lead	Duty	Attack	High	Killed	Nominated
1354	Ian McKAY	NCO	Army	12/06/1982	Falkland Is	Lead	Duty	Attack	High	Killed	Nominated
1355	Willie APIATA	NCO	Army	2004	Afghanistan	Lead	Duty	Counter-attack	High	No	Nominated
1356	Johnson BEHARRY	OR	Army	1/05/2004 11/06/2004	Iraq	Protect	Initiative	Replenish Interdict	Low	Wounded	Nominated
1357	Bryan BUDD	NCO	Army	27/07/2006 20/08/2006	Afghanistan	Lead	Duty	Patrol	High	Killed	Nominated
1358	Mark DONALDSON	OR	Army	2/09/2008	Afghanistan	Protect	Initiative	Patrol	Low	No	Nominated

No.	Name	Rank	Service	Date	Place	Personal Action	Type of Personal Action	Military Task of Unit	Relevance of Action to Task	Casualty?	How Selected for Award
1359	Benjamin ROBERTS-SMITH	NCO	Army	11/06/2010	Afghanistan	Storm	Initiative	Capture	High	No	Nominated
1360	Daniel KEIGHRAN	NCO	Army	24/08/2010	Afghanistan	Drew fire	Duty	Patrol	High	No	Nominated
1361	James ASHWORTH	NCO	Army	13/12/2012	Afghanistan	Lead	Duty	Neutralize	High	Killed	Nominated
1362	Cameron BAIRD	NCO	Army	22/06/2013	Afghanistan	Lead	Duty	Attack	High	Killed	Nominated
1363	Joshua LEAKEY	NCO	Army	22/08/2013	Afghanistan	Lead	Initiative	Disrupt	High	No	Nominated

Appendix 3

'How I Won the Victoria Cross'

(The sort of thing we must expect to hear after the war is ended)

YES, that's the red ribbon I'm wearing—
  Just a small strip of scarlet, you see,
But there's no one can tell how I prize it
  Nor the glow it occasions to me.
For it speaks of the broad fields of honour
  Which we wrung from the red jaws of hell—
And my eyes grow bedimmed for the cobbers *
  Who battled and conquered and fell.

Yes, that's the V.C. How I won it,
  It isn't for *me* to relate.
(We heroes are always so modest,
  And boasting's a thing that I hate.)
Well—seeing you write for the papers,
  I'll make an exception of you;
Don't mention *my* name if you write it,
  Tho' every partic'lar is true.

It was during a fight for an outpost—
  It was called the Green Knoll, I believe—
And the Turks on the top dealt out slaughter :
  They'd a week of defeat to retrieve.
It was five thousand feet to the summit,
  And almost as steep as a wall;
And they met every charge as we rushed it
  With bayonet, shrapnel, and ball.

  * Cobber is Australian for a tried and trusted friend.

UNCOMMON VALOUR

'Twas defended by nine tiers of trenches
  (That's strong for an outpost, you'll guess),
With twelve 42 centimetres,
  Which kicked up the deuce of a mess.
We'd been fighting five days without resting,
  When the eighth line of trenches we took;
For ev'ry man there was a hero—
  From me to the company's cook.

And there was the knoll just before us—
  Some two hundred paces or more;
With barb-wire and bayonets bristling,
  And the parapets sloppy with gore.
And the howitzers roared like perdition
  And vomited fire and death;
Till we saw it was madness to charge them,
  And halted a moment for breath.

Ah, stranger, imagine the picture,
  And then stand with horror aghast—
We had fought for a month without sleeping,
  And we stood facing failure at last!
We had squandered the best of our Army,
  We had " stuck " to our ultimate gasp;
And there, in the moment of triumph,
  The prize was to slip from our grasp.

Then suddenly out sprang the Major,
  His face lighted over with bliss—
" Pass the word there for Lance-Private Wilson;
  He'll find us a way out of this!"
(If there's one thing I hate, it is skiting,*
  When I hear it I always feel sore,
So you won't think I boast when I tell you
  He ought to have done it before!)

And a great cheer arose as I faced him
  And nodded (I never salute),
And said to him : " I'll see you thro', sir,
  And win you some glory to boot.
The chaps of the 16th Battalion
  Are not easy snoozers to beat;
I've a notion (I says) that will lick them—
  'Arf a dollar I line them a treat!

---

* Skiting—Australian for " swanking " in speech. " Skite "—blatherskite.

" I don't want no red-tapey orders,
  And I don't want no kudos nor pelf;
You get back to your own little dug-outs,
  And I'll tackle the knoll *by myself!*
I'll lay down my life for my country,
  For old England, the land of the free;
And you'll find that the bloke called Horatius
  Was only a trifle to me!"

Then I shook hands with all the battalion
  (There were only thirteen of us left),
And they cheered me again till the foemen
  Must have thought us of senses bereft.
And I gathered my arms and my rations,
  And girded myself for the fray—
If I live to be ninety or over,
  I will always remember that day!

I had five hundred rounds for my rifle,
  And of hand bombs I took forty-one;
A machine-gun was slung to my shoulders,
  And I carried a periscope gun.
As for rations—well, all I took with me
  Was a tin of Fray Bentos * or two,
And in my breast pocket I planted
  A nice Army biscuit to chew.

Then I waved a farewell to my cobbers—
  I was too much affected to speak;
There are times when the bravest of soldiers
  Have feelings that render them weak.
One tear—then I turned to the trenches,
  And charged like a lion at bay
As I caught the last words of our Colonel,
  Crying : " Bonzer † . . . Gorstrafem . . . **Hooray!"**

You talk of charmed lives—I'd a thousand;
  As I rushed up that hill like a goat
I got thirty-two shots thro' my trousers
  And nine shrapnel balls thro' my coat;
And a Japanese bomb burst beneath me
  —For a moment I gave up all hope,
But it proved the best thing that could happen,
  For it pushed me half-way up the slope.

* Fray Bentos is a brand of tinned meat.
† Bonzer—Australian for " excellent."

247

Then a fifteen-inch shell came straight at me
   —I hadn't a moment to shirk—
But it struck on that hard Army biscuit
   And rebounded—and blew up a Turk!
You doubt it? Well, if you want proof, sir,
   The truth of this tale to endorse,
Here's the biscuit—that dent in the middle
   Is where the shell struck it, of course!

Ah, yes, 'twas a terrible moment;
   I was then slightly wounded, 'tis true—
Just a bayonet stab in the gizzard
   And a crack from a bullet or two.
But I gathered new strength for the conflict,
   And, just as the darkness came down,
I was under their parapets, resting,
   And I knew I had beaten them brown!

For this was the scheme I had worked on,
   'Twas a little bit mean, you may say—
But I knew that the Turks were half-famished,
   And fought on one biscuit a day;
And the tins of Fray Bentos I carried,
   I chucked in the trench then and there;
And I heard the poor beggars pounce on it,
   And I knew they were caught in the snare!

    *   *   *   *   *   *

The morning broke, smiling and peaceful—
   Ah, shame that we soldiers must fight—
'Twas a piteous scene met my vision
   With the first rosy quivers of light.
When I peeped in the trench, not a Turk, sir,
   Was left of that legion accurst—
For they'd whacked the Fray Bentos among them,
   And each man had perished from thirst.

That's the yarn. If you know the 16th, sir,
   You'll know how our Colonel can smile.
He said to me: "*Corporal* Wilson,
   You've dished up the beggars in style."
Promotion! Some say I deserve it,
   But *that's* really nothing to me;
I don't want no honour or glory,
   But—that's how I won the V.C.

               "Crosscut," 16th Battalion, A.I.F.

Notes

1. What Price Glory?

1. *Telegraph* (London) 21 November 2009
2. P. de la Billière (*Supreme Courage*, Hachette Digital, London, 2004) 77-81
3. Crook (1975) 40
4. Brazier (2010) 343-4

2. Set in Bronze

1. 5 December 1854
2. Crook (1975) 6
3. *ibid* 13
4. The first two suggestions seem to contemplate fatal or potentially fatal deeds.
5. *ibid* 276-7
6. A later British government was similarly guilty. The Order of the British Empire was created in 1917 by a government already tainted by an honours-vending scandal. Instituted to reward non-military contributions to the war effort, after two years it had 22,000 members.
7. Crook (1975) 23
8. *ibid* 25
9. *London Gazette* No 21971 (Supplement) 24 February 1857
10. J. Greham and M. Mace, *British Battles of the Crimean War; Despatches from the Front*, Pen & Sword, Barnsley, 2014, p 208
11. English heraldic authorities have rejected cross paty and cross formy as possible descriptors because they are comparatively recent terms. See Crook (1975) Appendix XIX
12. G. Douglas and G. Dalhousie (eds.), *The Panmure Papers*, Hodder & Stoughton, London, 1908, vol 2, p 95. It became a tradition to tell recipients that their Crosses were only worth a copper (penny). Hancock's contract price was twenty shillings for 'a cross complete'.
13. *ibid* 138
14. The red ribbon is historically a reference to the army, not to sacrifice. Until 1920 Royal Navy and Royal Marine ribbons were dark blue. Rather than introduce light blue for the RAF, red became the ribbon colour for all VCs. In 1940 dark blue was reintroduced for the George Cross.

15. The provenance of the original metal remains a matter of debate. Since the First World War crosses have been cast from the cascabels of two nineteenth century cannon of Chinese manufacture.
16. *The Times* 27 June 1857
17. *Punch* 4 July 1857
18. Queen Victoria's journal 26 June 1857, quoted by Crook.
19. PBI was First World War Tommy slang. Data from Harvey (2008) Appendix: VCs by Mother Regiment
20. Victoria to Panmure, June 1857 in C. Hibbert, *Queen Victoria in Her Letters and Journals*, John Murray, London, 1984, p 135

3. The Virtue in Valour
1. T. Hobbes, (ed. B. Gert) *Man and Citizen*, Doubleday, New York, 1972, p 57
2. *London Gazette* No 31034 27 November 1918
3. Quoted in Moran (1945) 10
4. *ibid* 67
5. Thucydides (trans. R. Warner), *History of the Peloponnesian War*, Penguin, Harmondsworth, 1954, Book 2, chapter 40, p 119
6. Aristotle (trans. H. Rackham) *Nichomachean Ethics*, William Heinemann, London, 1926, Book 3, chapters 6-9
7. Aristotle (trans. G. A. Kennedy) *On Rhetoric*, Oxford University Press, New York, 1991, Book 1, chapter 9
8. Cicero (trans. W. Miller), *De Officiis*, William Heinemann, London, 1913, Book 1, pp 63-5. Effrontery, or shameless audacity, is akin to vainglory.
9. *ibid* p 84
10. Aristotle, *Ethics*, *op cit*, Book 3, chapter 8
11. Napoleon ranked endurance above courage as a desirable attribute in a soldier.
12. W. L. S. Churchill, *The Story of the Malakand Field Force*, Thomas Nelson, London, 1916, pp 235-6. The action also earned Churchill his first military distinction, mention in a dispatch for courage and resolution. Although there only as a newspaper correspondent, he had 'made himself useful at a critical moment'.
13. Bailey (2011) 354
14. Gort's evidence to the War Office Committee of Enquiry into 'Shell Shock' 1922. Colville (1972) 54
15. I. Hamilton, *The Soul and Body of an Army*, Edward Arnold, London 1921, p 105
16. W. J. Slim, *Courage and Other Broadcasts*, Cassell, London, 1957, pp 7-8
17. *London Gazette* No 36136 (Third Supplement) 13 August 1943
18. Quoted by Arthur (2005) 449-50
19. Quoted by Moran (1945) 108

4. The Vice of Distinction
1. St Gregory, *Morals on the Book of Job*, John Henry Parker, Oxford, 1845, vol 2, p 559
2. *London Gazette* No 22224 (Supplement) 31 January 1859

3. T. H. Kavanagh, *How I Won the Victoria Cross*, Ward & Lock, London, 1860, p 93
4. *ibid* p 94
5. *ibid* Preface
6. G. MacDonald Fraser, *Flashman in the Great Game*, Barrie & Jenkins, London, 1975, p 250. Flashman himself earns the VC during the Mutiny for 'luck, and survival through sheer funk, and suffering ignobly borne'.
7. The author was Private Thomas Wilson, 16th Battalion, AIF and his squib was published in C. E. W. Bean (ed.), *The Anzac Book*, Cassell, London, 1916. See Appendix 3.
8. Arthur (2005) 211-12
9. Creagh & Humphris (1921) 250
10. Cooksley & Batchelor, *The Air VCs* (2014) 135
11. The prohibition led off GHQ's *Instructions for Honours and Awards* but it was futile. Lieutenant Philip Neame, Royal Engineers, having repelled single-handed a German counter-attack with grenades at Neuve Chappelle in 1914, was told by his commanding officer that if he wasn't careful he might get a VC. At Christmas the divisional commander told the lieutenant that he had so recommended. Neame told no-one. He later discovered that his parents had learned of it from neighbours with a son in the same division who had written to them all about it. Bailey (2011) 13-14
12. Billière (2004) 347

5. Trophies of Honour

1. *London Gazette* No 21971 (Supplement) 24 February 1857
2. F.S. Roberts, *Forty-One Years in India*, Richard Bentley, London, 1897, vol 1, pp 385-6
3. P. Stanley, *White Mutiny*, New York University Press, New York, 1998, pp 94-5
4. *London Gazette* No 24717 2 May 1879
5. *London Gazette* No. 27160 2 February 1900
6. Crook (1975) 107
7. Crook (1975) 108

6. Duty and Disobdience

1. Crook (1975) 253
2. R. Kipling, *Land and Sea Tales for Scouts and Guides*, Macmillan, London, 1923, p. 22
3. Creagh & Humphris (1921) 44
4. Mayo (1897) vol 2 448. The italics are Mayo's.
5. Smyth (1959) 77-8
6. In World War II Japanese troops, indoctrinated with the values of bushido, sometimes preferred death by suicide to what was regarded as the dishonor of surrender. Devotion to the Emperor (duty) was the motivation for kamikaze pilots.
7. Bean (1933) 373
8. *London Gazette* No 31395 9 June 1919

9. *London Gazette* No 30667 3 May 1918
10. See Appendix 2
11. M. Walzer, Prisoners of War: Does the Fight Continue after the Battle? in Cody & Primoratz (2008). On the other hand, surrender does not deny a prisoner the right to escape unless he has given his parole.
12. *London Gazette* No 35729 (Supplement) 2 October 1942
13. Bailey (2011) 170

7. Highly Prized and Eagerly Sought After

1. L.J. Trotter, *The Bayard of India*, J M Dent, London, 1909, p.169
2. *ibid* 166. Campbell was even more critical. He told the Duke of Cambridge that Outram and Havelock had been very rash in going into Lucknow without knowing if they would be able to get out again. *Panmure Papers* 2 453
3. Quoted in F. J. Goldsmid, *James Outram*, Smith Elder, London, 1880, vol 2, pp 398-9
4. *The Victoria Cross; An Official Chronicle*, O'Byrne Brothers, London, 1865, p 63
5. J. C. Marshman, *Memoirs of Sir Henry Havelock*, Longman Green Longman & Roberts, London, 1860, p 365
6. Field Force Orders by Brigadier General Havelock CB Commanding, 9 October 1857
7. H. C. Maude, *Memories of the Mutiny*, 3rd edition, Remington, London, 1894, vol 2, p 330
8. Crook (1975) 95
9. The story comes from Maude (1894), who attributed it to a general of Campbell's relieving force. The protest successfully denied the 9th Lancers any Victoria Crosses for the second relief of Lucknow. Rudyard Kipling had friends in the regiment: their put-upon *bheestie* has much in common with *Gunga Din*.
10. Arthur (2005) 448-450

8. In the Absence of an Enemy

1. Crook (1975) 140-1
2. Kipling (1923) 161-72
3. O'Hea was reported to have perished in the Australian bush in 1874 but research by Elizabeth Read (*The Singular Journey of O'Hea's Cross*) suggests that he might have died in Ireland after discharge in 1868, and that his brother John then assumed his identity to retain the VC annuity.
4. Hansard 18 January 1944
5. Mead (2016) 149-83 discusses at length the institutional and personal biases that to date have excluded women from the Victoria Cross.

9. Stretching the Statutes

1. Crook (1975) 158-60
2. Crook (1975) 165

3. Creagh & Humphris (1921) 95
4. Crook (1975) 256
5. A letter published in *Soldier* in 1956 rejected the idea of representative awards on the grounds that in time the nature of the award would be forgotten and it would be seen as personal.
6. Major General G. C. Simonds, quoted in Halliday (2006) 212
7. It would differ from a unit citation in that only those members serving with the unit during the awarded action would be entitled to wear it. The unit itself might be as small as a patrol or a section.
8. A. Preston (ed.) *The South African Journal of Sir Garnet Wolseley*, Balkema, Capetown, 1973 pp 256-7. To Wolseley was delegated the duty of presenting the Cross to Private Alfred (Henry) Hook, one of the 'rats' of Rorke's Drift, who as rearguard had bayonetted numerous Zulus while covering the evacuation of patients from the hospital.
9. H.E. Wood, *Winnowed Memories*, Cassell, London, 1917, pp 288-91. Wood, whose career took him from midshipman to field marshal, was recommended for the Cross while serving in the Navy during the Crimean War. He had to wait until the Indian Mutiny, by which time he was in the Army, to be awarded one.
10. Remarkably, in the 25 years that a 'signal act of valour' had been a prime qualification for the Cross, only one citation had used the phrase. Captain John Cook's signal act had been to come to the assistance of a fellow officer who was about to be killed by an Afghan at Peiwar Kotal on 2 December 1878. He successfully parried the Afghan's bayonet with his sword until the adversary bit him on the arm. He would have been killed himself had not a Gurkha intervened. The phrase was reinstated in 1920 as 'some daring or pre-eminent act of valour'.
11. National Archives (NA) WO 32/7356, cited in Crook (1975) 159
12. NA WO 32/7470, cited in Crook (1975) 258

10. Brave by Choice

1. Quoted in Crook (1975) 263
2. *London Gazette* No 37349 (Supplement) 13 November 1945
3. *London Gazette* No 30726 (Supplement) 31 May 1918
4. Quoted by B. Nicholson, The Making of a VC, *Weekend Australian*, 23-24 April 2011
5. *ibid*
6. *Commonwealth of Australia Gazette* S12, 24 January 2011
7. *London Gazette* No 43959 (Second Supplement) 21 April 1966

11. England Expects

1. Creagh & Humphris (1921) 217-8
2. *London Gazette* No 30687 17 May 1918
3. Brazier (2010) 305-6

12. Tally Ho

1. J.B. McCudden, *Flying Fury*, John Hamilton, London, 1930, p 236
2. Civic groups, firms and individuals became quite creative in circumventing the restriction. War Bonds purchased in the recipient's name were popular.
3. I. Jones, *King of Air Fighters*, Ivor Nicholson & Watson, London, 1934, p 239
4. Cooksley & Batchelor (2014) 183
5. Boyle (1972) 237-8
6. Cheshire (1961) 11-12
7. *London Gazette* No 36693 (Fifth Supplement) 8 September 1944
8. Quoted by Halliday (2006) 29. NA Air 2/5686
9. Quoted by Jameson (1962) 163

13. The Politics of Empire

1. Crook (1975) 259
2. K.Q. Lockyer, *Keysor VC*, self-published, Ballarat, 2014, p 41
3. *Deeds that Thrill the Empire* p 12. In 1927 Keysor was wounded by a grenade while portraying himself in the film *For Valour*. His injuries were more serious than those he received at Lone Pine.
4. Crook (1975) 189-90
5. NA WO 98/10 *Examination of the Standards of Australian Citations for the Award of the Victoria Cross*. Mead (2015) 228

14. Soldiers of the Queen

1. *London Gazette* No 29070 (Fourth Supplement) 18 February 1915
2. G.B. Shaw, *Selected One Act Plays*, vol 1, Penguin, Harmondsworth, 1965
3. Crook (1975) 119-20
4. General Order, Bombay Army HQ, 18 September 1858, quoted by Creagh & Humphris (1921) 36
5. The word 'degree' in the General Order is subtly different to 'condition', which is used in the VC Warrant. Degree is a broader concept of social status, which then included considerations of race. The Warrant unequivocally placed 'all persons on a perfectly equal footing', irrespective of condition.
6. *London Gazette* No 26472 2 January 1894
7. Crook (1975) 121
8. Warrant of 21 October 1912
9. Creagh & Humphris (1921) 155
10. Quoted by the Gurkha Welfare Trust in Best of the Best www.gwt.org.uk
11. 'The Gurkhas are coming (to get you)'
12. *London Gazette* No 36190 (Supplement) 28 September 1943

15. Irrespective of Rank

1. Brevet promotion is elevation in rank without a corresponding rise in pay.
2. *London Gazette* No 21971 (Supplement) 24 February 1857

3. *London Gazette* No 35442 (Supplement) 30 January 1942
4. Brigadier in the army, commodore in the navy, air commodore in the air force.
5. E. E. Bradford, *Life of Admiral of the Fleet Sir Arthur Knyvet Wilson*, John Murray, London, 1923, p 90
6. The same of 'retire be damned!' fame in the Crimea.
7. Bradford (1923) 86
8. See Appendix 2
9. *London Gazette* No 22278 21 June 1859

16. Death or Victory

1. Quoted by General James Gavin (1958) (*War and Peace in the Space Age*, Harper & Brothers, New York, 1958, p 64), who recalled having heard it when Patton addressed troops in North Africa.
2. Crook (1975) 84
3. Crook (1975) 87-8
4. For the data from which the figures are derived see Appendix 2
5. Geddes in *Spearhead Assault*, quoted by Mead (2015) 237-8
6. Abols was later commissioned in the Parachute Regiment. For his action at Goose Green he was awarded the Distinguished Conduct Medal, one step down from a VC for a non-commissioned officer.
7. *Daily Telegraph*, 29 March 2005
8. *London Gazette* No 49134 (Supplement) 8 October 1982
9. *London Gazette* No 57587 (Supplement 1) 17 March 2005
10. *London Gazette* No 61154 (Supplement) 26 February 2015
11. Flying Officer John Cruikshank (Atlantic 1944) and Lance Corporal Rambahadur Limbu (Borneo 1965)

17. Fighting Mad

1. Probably not an insult but a seventeenth century British soldier's tribute to the potency of Dutch gin.
2. Brazier (2010) 248
3. *London Gazette* No 30400 (Supplement) 23 November 1917
4. *London Gazette* No 37091 (Supplement) 24 May 1945
5. *London Gazette* No 36627 (Supplement) 27 July 1944
6. *London Gazette* No 37033 (Supplement) 17 April 1945
7. Arthur (2005) 426
8. *London Gazette* No 30122 (Supplement) 8 June 1917
9. A. O. Pollard, *Fire Eater: The Memoirs of a VC*, Hutchinson, London, [1932], p 13.
10. Creagh & Humphris (1921) 181, Arthur (2005) 223
11. *Canberra Times* 19 November 1932
12. *Bathurst Times* 19 January 1925
13. *London Gazette* No 35306 (Second Supplement) 10 October 1941
14. For which he was Mentioned in Dispatches.

15. Quoted by K. Sandford in *The Mark of the Lion*, Penguin (NZ), Auckland, 2003, p 245
16. *ibid* p 190
17. *The Telegraph* (London) 23 November 1994
18. *Epistles* 1.2.62
19. Crook (1975) 97-99
20. The first list of awards (1857) included Captain Hugh Rowlands of the 41st Foot, who had rescued a wounded officer at Inkerman in November 1854. He had been recommended again for attacks on the Redan in September 1855 but was ruled ineligible for a second award because he had not (nor could before 1857) have received the first as required by rule 4. In 1900 Lance Corporal John MacKay was denied a bar on the same technicality.
21. Sandford (2003) 263
22. *London Gazette* No 37283 (Supplement) 25 September 1945

18. Happy Warriors

1. J. Blanch, *Gowrie VC*, Barbara Black, Hawthorn, 1998, p 35
2. *London Gazette* No 27057 28 February 1899
3. G. Slater, *My Warrior Sons*, Peter Davis, London, 1973, p 137
4. Maxwell (1932) 1
5. *London Gazette* No 29740 9 September 1916
6. Brazier (2010) 218
7. Bailey (2011) 87, 353

19. Shadows

1. J.A. Smith, K.L. Masuhara and B.C. Frueh, Documented Suicides Within the British Army during the Crimean War 1854-1856, *Military Medicine*, 179:721-3, July 2004. Comparable statistics are not available for the Indian Mutiny.
2. K. Thomas and D. Gunnell, Suicide in England and Wales 1861-2007: a time-trends analysis, *International Journal of Epidemiology*, 39:6:1464-75, December 2010
3. The VC figures are derived from the causes of death recorded in David Harvey's *Monuments to Courage*, Naval and Military Press, Uckfield, 2008.
4. Arthur (2005) 17-18
5. Thomas & Gunnell (2010) 6
6. Brazier (2010) 128-9
7. Crook (1975) 51

20. Instruments of War

1. *London Gazette* No 29740 9 September 1916
2. *London Gazette* No 22347 20 January 1860
3. *London Gazette*
4. Quoted in Arthur (2003) 149

NOTES

5. Creagh & Humphris (1921) 200
6. *London Gazette* No 30967 (Ninth Supplement) 22 October 1918
7. Creagh & Humphris (1921) 298
8. Crook (1975) 186-7

21. Comrades in Peril

1. Brazier (2010) 102
2. *London Gazette* No 29414 23 December 1915
3. J. Smyth, *The Story of the Victoria Cross*, Frederick Muller, London, 1963, pp 328-9
4. *The Young British Soldier*, Barrack Room Ballads, Methuen, London, 1892
5. *London Gazette* No 36744 (Supplement) 31 October 1944
6. *London Gazette* No 22268 27 May 1859
7. Presumably he would have endorsed such action if undertaken with offensive purpose, as in the case of Sergeant Robert Scott of the Cape Mounted Riflemen. He won his VC during the Basuto War in 1879, when he volunteered to throw time-fused shells as hand grenades and made his men take cover as a precaution against premature detonation. The second bomb went off in his hand, blowing it off and severely wounding him in the leg.
8. Creagh & Humphris (1921) 210
9. Military Secretary's Branch GHQ, *Instructions Regarding Recommendations for Honours and Awards*, [London], 1918, paragraph 47
10. [G. Roberts, R. Richards and S. Martin], *Thirteen Canadian VCs*, Skeffington, London, 1918

22. Writing It Up

1. For the record, it was at Sebastopol on 12 October 1854 that Francis Wheatley, having failed to disarm the fuse of a Russian shell using his rifle butt, heaved the shell over the parapet where it exploded without causing casualties. Brazier (2010) 85
2. *London Gazette* No 21971 (Supplement) 24 February 1857
3. Creagh & Humphris (1921) 13
4. Crook (1975) 47
5. *London Gazette* No 22986 22 September 1864
6. *London Gazette* No 29240 24 July 1915
7. *London Gazette* No 37465 (Supplement) 12 February 1946
8. Arthur (2005) 72
9. *London Gazette* No. 22154 18 June 1858
10. *London Gazette* No 30898 (Second Supplement) 13 September 1918
11. *London Gazette* No 31019 (Second Supplement) 19 November 1918
12. *London Gazette* No 31005 (Seventh Supplement) 12 November 1918
13. A serviceable alternative was available: Major William Trevor and Lieutenant James Dundas of the Royal Engineers had been awarded VCs for storming the 'blockhouse' at Dewan-Giri in Bhutan in 1865.

14. Crook (1975) 47-8
15. Grant (1989) 25
16. Laffin (1997) 11-12
17. Bailey (2011) 348-9
18. *ibid* 282-8
19. *The Victoria Cross*, [Ministry of Information], [London], 1943

23. Struck Off

1. WO 98/1 VC Warrant, rule 15. Crook (1975) 282
2. *London Gazette* No 21971 24 February 1857
3. Brazier (2010) 85, Crook (1975) 59
4. Arthur (2005) 87-8
5. *ibid* 118
6. Crook (1975) 62
7. Had he still been serving, sale of his medals would have been an offence under the Army Act.
8. Crook (1975) 63-4
9. *Soldier* (January 1956, p 13) sourced it to the Victoria Cross Register kept by the Ministry of Defence but in the 1970s Michael Crook was unable to find it there.
10. Crook (1975) 66
11. *ibid* 67

24. Under the Eye of the Commander

1. *London Gazette* No 21997 5 May 1857
2. Crook (1975) 43-4
3. *ibid* 207
4. *ibid* 226
5. Miller was referring to the VC awarded to Lieutenant Mark Walker of the 30th Foot, who at Inkerman discovered that rain had made his men's muskets inoperable. With two Russian battalions advancing towards the wall behind which the British were sheltering, Walker had ordered an over-the-wall bayonet charge that surprised and panicked the Russians into flight. *London Gazette* No 22149 4 June 1858
6. *London Gazette* No 22260 6 May 1859
7. Malleson (1898) 3:287-8
8. Crook (1975) 208

25. One for All

1. *London Gazette* No 31354 (Second Supplement) 24 May 1919
2. Creagh & Humphris (1921) 326
3. *London Gazette* No 34999 (Supplement) 22 November 1940
4. *London Gazette* No 30807 (Fourth Supplement) 23 July 1918

5. Crook (1975) 114
6. WO 32/3443 quoted in Crook (1975) 115
7. *London Gazette* No 35566 (Supplement) 19 May 1942
8. *ibid*
9. *London Gazette* No 37819 (Third Supplement) 13 December 1946
10. *Sydney Morning Herald* 26 December 2010
11. Crook (1975) 116
12. *ibid* 33

26. A Preference for Victory

1. *ibid* 255
2. Forlorn hope is commonly mistaken to mean a remote chance of success. Lugard was using the phrase in its original derivation from the Dutch *verloren hoop*, which literally means a lost heap or bunch, and refers to the heavy casualties expected when the foremost troops in an attack meet strong resistance. The French equivalent is *enfants perdus*.
3. Crook (1975) 174
4. Creagh & Humphris (1920) 51
5. *London Gazette* No 27596 11 September 1903
6. NA WO 373/19 f 229
7. *London Gazette* No 35600 (Second Supplement) 16 June 1942
8. E. Keyes, *Geoffrey Keyes*, George Newnes, London, 1956, p 257. The right of the line has been a post of honour since ancient times, when Greek hoplites fought with spear and shield. The best man was placed on the extreme right, where he lacked the protection of a comrade's shield.
9. Quoted by Boswell in his *Life of Johnson*, Everyman edition, London, 1960, vol 2, p 525

27. Rules and Exceptions

1. Maxwell (1932) 261-2
2. Quoted in Smyth (1963) 332
3. VC & GC Association website, accessed 9 May 2018
4. Defence Honours and Awards Appeals Tribunal, *The report of the inquiry into unresolved recognition for past acts of naval and military gallantry and valour*, Canberra, 2013, p 178

Bibliography

Abbott, P.E. & Tamplin, J.M.A., *British Gallantry Awards*, Nimrod Dix, London, 1981

Anon, *Deeds that Thrill the Empire*, Hutchinson, London, 1917-20

Anon, *The Victoria Cross*, [Ministry of Information], London, 1943

Aristotle (trans. H. Rackham), *Nichomachean Ethics*, William Heinemann, London, 1926

Aristotle (trans. G.A. Kennedy), *On Rhetoric*, Oxford University Press, New York, 1991

Arthur, M., *Symbol of Courage*, Pan Macmillan, London, 2005

Auten, H., *Q Boat Adventures*, Jenkins, London, 1919

Bailey, R., *Forgotten Voices: Victoria Cross*, Ebury Press, 2011

Bean, C.E.W. (ed.), *The Anzac Book*, Cassell, London, 1916

Bean, C.E.W., *The Australian Imperial Force in France 1917*, Angas & Robertson, Sydney, 1933

Beeton, S.O. (ed.), *Our Soldiers, and the Victoria Cross*, Ward, Lock & Tyler, London, [1867]

Billière, P. de la, *Supreme Courage*, Hachette Digital, London, 2004

Bishop, W.A., *Winged Warfare*, Hodder & Stoughton, London, 1918

Blanch, J., *Gowrie VC*, Barbara Black, Hawthorn, 1998

Boyle, A., *No Passing Glory*, Collins, London, 1972

Bradford, E.E., *Life of Admiral of the Fleet Sir Arthur Knyvet Wilson*, John Murray, London, 1923

Brazier, K., *The Complete Victoria Cross*, Pen & Sword Books, Barnsley, 2010

Carton de Wiart, A., *Happy Odyssey*, Jonathon Cape, London, 1950

Cheshire, L., *The Face of Victory*, Hutchinson, London, 1961

Churchill, W.L.S., *The Story of the Malakand Field Force*, Thomas Nelson, London, 1916

Cicero (trans. W. Miller), *De Officiis*, William Heinemann, London, 1913

Cody, C.A.J., & Primoratz, I. (eds.), *Military Ethics*, Ashgate, Farnham, 2008

Colville, J.R., *Man of Valour*, Collins, London, 1972

Cooksley, P.G. & Batchelor, P.F., *VCs of the First World War: The Air VCs*, History Press, Stroud, 2014

Creagh, O. & Humphris, E.M. (eds.), *The VC and DSO*, Standard Art Book Co., London, [1921], vol 1

BIBLIOGRAPHY

Crook, M.J., *The Evolution of the Victoria Cross*, Midas Books, Tunbridge Wells, 1975

Defence Honours and Awards Appeals Tribunal, *The report of the inquiry into unresolved recognition for past acts of naval and military gallantry and valour*, Canberra, 2013

Douglas, G. & Dalhousie, G. (eds.), *The Panmure Papers*, Hodder & Stoughton, London, 1908

Elliott, W.J. & Knollys, W.W., *The Victoria Cross: By Whom It Was Won*, Dean & Son, London, 3rd edition [1881]

Fraser, G.M., *Flashman in the Great Game*, Barrie & Jenkins, London, 1975

Gavin, J., *War and Peace in the Space Age*, Harper & Brothers, New York, 1958

Gliddon, G., *VCs of the First World War: Cambrai 1917*, Sutton Publishing, Stroud, 2004

Goldsmid, F.J., *James Outram*, Smith Elder, London, 1880

Grant, I., *Jacka VC*, McMillan, South Melbourne, 1989

Greham, J. and Mace, M., *British Battles of the Crimean War; Despatches from the Front*, Pen & Sword Books, Barnsley 2014

Halliday, H.A., *Valour Reconsidered*, Robin Brass Studio, Quebec, 2006

Hamilton, I., *The Soul and Body of an Army*, Edward Arnold, London, 1921

Hamilton, R., *Victoria Cross Heroes of World War One*, Atlantic Publishing, Croxley Green, 2015

Harvey, D., *Monuments to Courage*, Naval and Military Press, Uckfield, 2008.

Haydon, A.L., *The Book of the VC*, E.P. Dutton, New York, 1907

Hibbert, C., *Queen Victoria in Her Letters and Journals*, John Murray, London, 1984

Hieronymussen, P., *Orders, Medals and Decorations of Britain and Europe*, Blandford, London, 1967

Hobbes, T (ed. B. Gert), *Man and Citizen,* Doubleday, New York, 1972

Hodder, E., *Heroes of Britain in Peace and War*, Cassell, London, [c.1880]

Illustrated War News, Illustrated London News & Sketch, London, vols 3-4, 1915

Jameson, W.S., *Submariners VC*, Peter Davies, London, 1962

Jones, I., *King of Air Fighters*, Ivor Nicholson & Watson, London, 1934

Kavanagh, T.H., *How I Won the Victoria Cross*, Ward & Lock, London, 1860

Keyes, E., *Geoffrey Keyes*, George Newnes, London, 1956

Kipling, R., *Land and Sea Tales for Scouts and Guides*, Macmillan, London, 1923

Kipling, R., *Barrack Room Ballads*, Methuen, London, 1892

Laffin, J., *British VCs of World War 2*, Sutton, Stroud, 1997

Lockyer, K.Q., *Keysor VC*, self-published, Ballarat, 2014

Malleson, G.B. (ed.), *Kaye and Malleson's History of the Indian Mutiny*, Longmans Green, London, 1898

Marshman, J.C., *Memoirs of Sir Henry Havelock*, Longman Green Longman & Roberts, London, 1860

Maude, H.C., *Memories of the Mutiny*, 3rd edition, Remington, London, 1894

Maxwell, J., *Hell's Bells and Mademoiselles*, Angus & Robertson, Sydney, 1932

Mayo, J.H., *Medals and Decorations of the British Army and Navy*, Archibald Constable, Westminster, 1897

McCudden, J.B., *Flying Fury*, John Hamilton, London, 1930

Mead, G., *Victoria's Cross*, Atlantic Books, London, 2015

Military Secretary's Office GHQ, *Instructions for Honours and Awards* [War Office, London], 1918

Moran, Lord, *The Anatomy of Courage*, Constable, London, 1945

Mullholland, J. & Jordan, A., *Victoria Cross Bibliography*, Spink & Son, London, 1999

Nicholson, B., 'The Making of a VC', *Weekend Australian*, 23-24 April 2011

O'Byrne, R.W. (ed.), *The Victoria Cross; An Official Chronicle*, O'Byrne Brothers, London, 1865

Parry, D.H., *Britain's Roll of Glory*, Cassell, London, 1906

Pollard, A.O., *Fire Eater: The Memoirs of a VC*, Hutchinson, London, [1932]

Preston, A. (ed.), *The South African Journal of Sir Garnet Wolseley*, Balkema, Capetown, 1973

Roberts, F.S., *Forty-One Years in India*, Richard Bentley, London, 1897

[Roberts, G., Richards, R. & Martin, S.], *Thirteen Canadian VCs*, Skeffington, London, 1918

St Gregory the Great (trans. J. Bliss), *Morals on the Book of Job*, John Henry Parker, Oxford, 1845

Sandford, K., *The Mark of the Lion*, Penguin (NZ), Auckland, 2003

Slater, G., *My Warrior Sons*, Peter Davis, London, 1973

Slim, W.J., *Courage and Other Broadcasts,* Cassell, London, 1957

Smith, J.A., Masuhara, K.L., & Frueh, B.C., Documented Suicides Within the British Army during the Crimean War 1854-1856, *Military Medicine*, 179, July 2004.

Smyth, J.G., *The Only Enemy*, Hutchinson, London, 1959

Smyth, J., *The Story of the Victoria Cross*, Frederick Muller, London, 1963

Snelling, S., *VCs of the First Word War: Gallipoli*, History Press, Stroud, 2010

Stewart, R., *The Victoria Cross: The Empire's Roll of Valour*, Hutchinson, London [1928]

Thomas, K. & Gunnell, D., Suicide in England and Wales 1861-2007: a time-trends analysis, *International Journal of Epidemiology*, 39, December 2010

Thucydides (trans. R. Warner), *History of the Peloponnesian War*, Penguin, Harmondsworth, 1954

Trotter, L.J., *The Bayard of India*, J M Dent, London, 1909

Tyquin, M.B., *Neville Howse*, OUP, Oxford, 1999

Wilkins, P.A., *The History of the Victoria Cross*, Archibald Constable, London, 1904

Wilkinson, S., *Illustrated London News Record of the Transvaal War 1899-1900*, ILN, London, [1900]

Wilson, A. & McEwen, J.A.F., *Gallantry*, Oxford University Press, London, 1939

Wood, H.E., *From Midshipman to Field Marshal*, Cassell, London, 1917

Wood, H.E., *Winnowed Memories*, Cassell, London, 1917

Index

INDEX

INDEX

INDEX